William Riley (1798–1873) of Connecticut and Montgomery County, Pennsylvania

His Descendants in Southeastern Pennsylvania and Atlantic City, New Jersey

MONTGOMERY COUNTY

1784

BY

DAVID JOSEPH RILEY

Heritage Books
2022

HERITAGE BOOKS

AN IMPRINT OF HERITAGE BOOKS, INC.

Books, CDs, and more—Worldwide

For our listing of thousands of titles see our website
at
www.HeritageBooks.com

Published 2022 by
HERITAGE BOOKS, INC.
Publishing Division
5810 Ruatan Street
Berwyn Heights, MD 20740

Library of Congress Control Number: 2022913449

Heritage Books by the author:

*Nathan Terriberry (1815–86) of Hunterdon County, New Jersey:
His Descendants, and Allied and Associated Families*

*William Riley (1798–1873) of Connecticut and Montgomery County, Pennsylvania:
His Descendants in Southeastern Pennsylvania and Atlantic City, New Jersey*

The illustration on the cover and title page is the official seal of Montgomery County, Pennsylvania.

International Standard Book Number
Paperbound: 978-0-7884-2651-3

TABLE OF CONTENTS

Genealogical Summary

Numbers refer to family members using the *National Genealogical Society Quarterly* system.

Individuals listed only with their parents had no children or died young.

William Riley and His Children

Children and Grandchildren of William Riley

Grandchildren and Great Grandchildren of William Riley

PREFACE

"In the end, we'll all become stories." ~Margaret Atwood

I sought in this endeavor to find my family's origins. That story was not to be, as explained herein. What I wrote instead was a story about my ancestors from 1830 to the late twentieth century. They mostly did physical labor, worked in cities, and had a modest degree of material comfort. Remember those ancestors as we write our own stories.

ABBREVIATIONS

a.k.a., also known as

bur., buried

ca., circa

Co., County

col., column

da., days

dwell., dwelling

ED, enumeration district

ed., editor

fam., family

FHL, Family History Library

ibid., ibidem

mo., months

n.d., no date of publication

n.p., no page, no publication place, no publisher

NA, National Archives

NARA, National Archives and Records Administration

no., number

p., page

PDF, portable document format

pop. sch., population schedule

RG, record group

Twp., township

yr., years

William Riley (1798–1873) of Connecticut and Montgomery County, Pennsylvania: His Descendants in Southeastern Pennsylvania and Atlantic City, New Jersey

by

David Joseph Riley

Most stories start at the beginning. William Riley's story necessarily starts in the middle. The first record about him was in 1829, when he was taxed in Montgomery County, Pennsylvania.[1] By then, he was married with two children.[2] He told the 1850 census taker that he was born in Connecticut, was a shoemaker, and that his age was fifty-two,[3] thus born about 1798. No record of his birth or baptism has been found in Connecticut,[4] and family lore provides no important clues about his earlier life.[5]

William Riley settled in lands that William Penn purchased in 1684 from Monghongsin, an Indigenous person, of "…all his land lying on the Pahkehoma."[6] Located just northwest of Philadelphia (Figure 1, Appendix), Montgomery County has rich soil, rolling hills, and wide

The author thanks A. Landis Riley for his contributions[7] and Gavin Douglas Riley for photographic editing.

[1] Joel D. Alderfer, Mennonite Historians of Eastern Pennsylvania, Harleysville, Pa., to A. Landis Riley, Pasadena, Calif., letter, 26 Sep. 1991, transmitting tax records of William Riley; copy in author's file. Abstracted tax records from the Montgomery County Historical Society, Norristown, Pa., arranged by year and surname. "Collections returned for 1829…Riley, William"; 1831, "Reily [sic] W^m"; tax notice dated 8 Jun. 1844, Riley William Shoe Maker." Mr. Alderfer wrote: "…William Riley first appears in Upper Providence Twp. in 1829 with no land and remains there (with no land) until 1831. He then appears in Lower Providence [Township] in 1834 and remains there until 1844. In 1835, he appears with one cow; in 1838 he shows up with '1 acre & Dwelling.' This remains the same until 1841, when the real estate disapears [sic] again. In 1843, one cow shows up again; in 1844 (and only then) his occupation is shoemaker. In 1845, he is back in Upper Providence Twp. with one cow, and remains there until 1850 (when he appears in the census)."

[2] 1830 U.S. census, Montgomery Co., Pa., population schedule, Upper Providence, p. 241, line 17, William Riley; National Archives and Records Administration (NARA), microfilm no. M19, roll 154.

[3] 1850 U.S. census, Montgomery Co., Pa., pop. sch., Upper Providence, p. 308A, dwelling 334, family 336, William Riley; NARA M432, roll 799.

[4] Negative searches, *Ancestry.com* (https://www.ancestry.com/) > Card Catalogue > Title=Connecticut, Keyword(s)=Births > Connecticut, U.S., Town Birth Records, pre-1870 (Barbour Collection) > First & Middle Names(s)=William, Last Name=Riley, Birth year=1798. *FamilySearch.org* (https://familysearch.org/) > Search > Catalogue > Place > United States, Connecticut > Vital Records > Connecticut, Charles R. Hale Collection, Vital Records, 1640-1955 > First Names=William, Last Names=Riley, Year=1798. *AmericanAncestors.org*. (https://americanancestors.org) > Search > A to Z list of all databases > Connecticut: Vital Records (The Barbour Collection), 1630-1870 (Soundex) > First Name=William, Last Name=Riley, Years=1795-1800, Record Type=Baptism, Location=Connecticut.

[5] Henrietta Kesler (Riley) Camp [NORTHFIELD, N.J.] to A. Landis Riley [ADDRESS FOR PRIVATE USE], Pasadena, Calif., notes, undated. Mrs. Camp, a great-granddaughter of William Riley, wrote "Tinker" Riley married a Cherokee woman in Connecticut. (Tinker implies an itinerant who repairs kitchen pots and pans). He had two [sic] sons and two daughters, and one of the daughters married a Brown who ran tugboats on the Hudson River.

[6] Charles S. Keyser, *Penn's Treaty* (Philadelphia: David McKay, 1882), 24. "How Penn Divided his Vast Holdings of Land," *Reading (Pa.) Eagle*, 21 Jul. 1932, p. 6, cols. 5-7.

[7] A. Landis Riley, "Descendants of William Riley," PDF, 6 Sep. 2020, in author's file.

valleys carved by rivers and streams (Figure 2). Penn's "First Purchasers" were mostly English;[8] German-speaking settlers from the southern Rhine River Valley came during the eighteenth century.[9] They became prosperous farmers, and the area was well-settled. Land was expensive when William Riley arrived.[10] Within fifty years, turnpikes, canals, and railroads were built, crisscrossing the area and connecting Philadelphia to the interior.[11] William resided near the center of the county in Upper Providence and Lower Providence Townships,[12] which are bound by the Schuylkill River and are separated by the Perkiomen Creek (Figure 3).

William was a shoemaker, and his shop was situated near a stone-surfaced road leading to Philadelphia.[13] Before railways, "...people were addicted to going either by horseback or by foot... to Philadelphia..., a distance of thirty-seven miles,...and return[ing] the following day."[14] The nearby Schuylkill Canal, running along the Schuylkill River, became the country's greatest coal carrying canal.[15] In the 1850s, a railway depot was constructed near the village of Oaks where William lived.[16] Directly across the street from the shop was a tannery,[17] a convenient source of leather. Travelers going by road, canal, or rail needed boots and shoes, and William's shop was well-situated (Figure 4). The location probably brought in a steady flow of customers, which sustained his shoemaking trade for many years.

William was poor and probably led a simple life. He owned little that was taxed – one cow and a dwelling, the latter taxed for only three years.[18] He sought relief to pay for the education of his oldest son, who was on the County's poor children's roll for two years.[19] The only recorded land transaction by William – a quarter-acre lot for a consideration of $30 – was made when he

---

[8] *The Encyclopedia of Greater Philadelphia* (https://philadelphiaencyclopedia.org/) > Search the Encyclopedia > First Purchasers of Pennsylvania.

[9] Historical Society of Pennsylvania, "German Settlement in Pennsylvania: An Overview," PDF, (https://hsp.org/).

[10] James T. Lemon, *The Best Poor Man's Country: A Geographical Study of Early Southeastern Pennsylvania* (Baltimore: The Johns Hopkins University Press, 1972), 180.

[11] Theodore W. Bean, ed., *History of Montgomery County, Pennsylvania* (Philadelphia: Evarts & Peck, 1884), 1044.

[12] Alderfer to Riley, 26 Sep. 1991.

[13] Frederick C. Sweinhart, "The Turnpikes of Pennsylvania," *Bulletin of the Historical Society of Montgomery County, Pennsylvania* 9 (April 1955): 254-62. Bean, *History of Montgomery County*, 456, 1045.

[14] Bean, *History of Montgomery County*, 457.

[15] Chester Lloyd Jones, "The Economic History of the Anthracite-Tidewater Canals," *Series in Political Economy and the Public Law*, no. 22 (Philadelphia: John C. Winston, 1908), 129-31.

[16] Bean, *History of Montgomery County*, 1058.

[17] William E. Morris, *Map of Montgomery County, Pennsylvania: From Original Surveys* (Philadelphia: Smith & Wistar, 1849). Online at https://www.loc.gov/resource/g3823m.la000777/?r=0.281,0.423,0.05,0.02,0. The tannery was near the home of David Rittenhouse, grantor to William Riley. Montgomery County, Pennsylvania, Deeds 97: 55-56, David Rittenhouse and Mary, his wife, to William Riley, 27 March 1854; Recorder of Deeds, Norristown.

[18] Alderfer to Riley, 26 Sep. 1991.

[19] Judith A. Meier, The Historical Society of Montgomery County, Norristown, Pa., to A. Landis Riley, Pasadena, Calif., letter, 9 Feb. 1993, transmitting tax assessor's records and Poor Children's Lists; in author's file. Imaged copies from Judith A. H. Meier, ed. "Poor Children to be Educated at County Expense: Montgomery County, Pennsylvania, 1810-1846" (Norristown, Pa.: The Historical Society of Montgomery County, n.d.), 81-83. Listed by year are: 1836, "Wm Riley Samuel [age] 8"; 1837, "Wm Riley Samuel"; and 1838, "Wm Riley Samuel--."

was fifty-six-years old.[20] He had strong ties to the Dunkard church,[21] a fundamentalist denomination formally known as the German Baptist Brethren.[22] Brethren dressed plainly and believed in peace, simplicity, and equality. If William adopted these manners and beliefs, he likely lived simply.

The Civil War and the post-war period radically changed living arrangements of the family. William's three sons and two sons-in-law served in the Union Army.[23] After the War, these children moved to Philadelphia, where they worked as a carpenter, butcher, blacksmith, and laborer.[24] Philadelphia grew rapidly after the War,[25] and they likely prospered in these trades. Near the end of the nineteenth century, three sons moved to the coastal resort of Atlantic City, New Jersey[26] (Figure 5).

Later Riley descendants made their livings mainly doing physical work in factories or mills. Some of the jobs were plainly disagreeable, like supervising grinding in a glue factory,[27] a place where the bones of old horses were ground down and used for glue products. A few rose to be managers or professionals.[28] In an era when almost all women were homemakers, several women worked outside the home: a postmistress,[29] a gas station owner,[30] an Olympiad in swimming who

---

[20] Alderfer to Riley, 26 Sep. 1991.

[21] Green Tree Church of the Brethren (Oaks, Pennsylvania), Baptisms, p. 9, 29, 33, 61; "Pennsylvania and New Jersey, U.S., Church and Town Records, 1669-2013," digital images, *Ancestry.com* (https://www.ancestry.com/).

[22] *Wikipedia* (https://en.wikipedia.org/), "Dunkard Brethren," rev. 22:53, 18 Aug. 2021.

[23] "United States Civil War Soldiers Index, 1861-1865," database, *FamilySearch.org* (https://www.familysearch.org/). Samuel W. Reilly [sic], Band, 2nd Regiment, Pennsylvania Reserve Inf. (31st Volunteers); Christian F. Riley, Band, 2nd Regiment, Pennsylvania Reserve Inf. (31st Volunteers); Thomas M. Riley, Pvt., Co. B, 73rd Regiment, Pennsylvania Inf.; Robert S. Getty, Pvt., Independent Battery H, Pennsylvania Light Artillery; Renwick W. Brown, Pvt., Co. D, 213th Regiment, Pennsylvania Inf.

[24] *Philadelphia City Directory for 1867-8* (Philadelphia: James Gopsill, 1867-68), 1074, "Riley Thomas M., carpenter, h 2105 Oxford"; ibid., 290, "Brown Renwick W., butcher, h 1918 N 20th"; By the same title: (1875), 1266, "Riley Samuel W., carpenter, h 2421 Jefferson"; ibid., 1265, "Riley Christian F., blacksmith, 2244 & h 2216 N Broad"; (1882), 590, "Getty Robert, laborer, h 4635 Hedge, Fkd [Frankford]."

[25] Dorothy Gondos Beers, "The Centennial City, 1865-1876," in Russell F. Weigley, ed., *Philadelphia: A 300-Year History* (New York: W.W. Norton, 1982), 419-22.

[26] *Atlantic City Directory for 1894* (Philadelphia: James Gopsill's Sons, 1894), 169, "Riley Samuel W., carpenter, h 214 N North Carolina av"; By the same title: (1898), 222, "Riley Christian F., blacksmith, h r 121 S New York av." 1900 U.S. census, Atlantic Co., N.J., pop. sch., Atlantic City, ED 9, p. 10, dwell. 151, fam. 213, Thomas M. Riley in the household of Christian Riley, Sr.; NARA T623, roll 953.

[27] "U.S., World War II Draft Cards Young Men, 1940-1947," digital images, *Ancestry.com* (https://www.ancestry.com/), Walter Irvin Bowker. Supervisor of grinding and shipping, F.W. Tunnelle [sic] Co. [F.W. Tunnel Co.]. The company made glue and fertilizer. "Typical Fires and Their Lessons," *Insurance Engineering* 18 (Jul. – Dec. 1909): 136.

[28] "Deaths [obituary of Walter B. Riley]," *The Philadelphia Inquirer*, 24 Apr. 1962, p. 8, col. 5. A vice president at an engineering and supply company. "Dr. Edwin G. Riley, Public Health Physician [obituary]," *The Baltimore Sun*, 21 Jul. 1989, p. 45, col. 2.

[29] *Official Register of the United States Containing a List of Officers and Employes* [sic] *in the Civil, Military, and Naval Service on the First of July, 1881*, Vol. 2 (Washington, D.C.: Government Printing Office, 1881), 554. Entry for Anna Maria Hallman, Skippack, Montgomery Co., Pa.

[30] *Atlantic City Directory for 1941* (Philadelphia: R. L. Polk & Co., 1941), 418, "Riley Lillie C (wid Abr L Riley; Riley's Esso Station) h Absecon Blvd nw cor N Indiana av."

later was a hotel convention manager,[31] and a matron for an old age home.[32] A thirteen-year-old girl was employed in a carpet factory.[33] Her children, too, worked as child laborers: a fifteen-year-old as a weaver of gingham and a thirteen-year-old as a winder in a cotton mill.[34] At that time, little girls in silk mills worked for the "miserable pittance" of $1.80 to $2.10 per week.[35]

Atlantic City descendants were employed in typical resort occupations: hotel clerk,[36] theatrical agent,[37] entertainer,[38] and golf caddy.[39] Several worked in theaters (Figures 6-7). In that era, very few students finished high school, and even fewer graduated from college.[40] Among the college graduates were a civil engineer,[41] a bacteriologist,[42] and a teacher.[43] One was a public health official who had four advanced degrees.[44] Another, the future wife of a descendant, graduated from college in the 1850s.[45] Others were committed to the care of public institutions for mental or physical incapacities[46] or were imprisoned.[47] Many men served in the military, one of whom died in combat in World War II.[48] Later generations of William Riley's descendants were mostly urban blue-collar workers. It is likely they had a modest degree of wealth and material comfort since, in that era, blue-collar jobs afforded solidly middle-class incomes and lifestyles.[49]

---

[31] "New Yorker Marries Shore Swimming Star," *The Philadelphia Inquirer*, 23 Jul. 1924, p. 2, col. 1. *Atlantic County Women's Hall of Fame* (https://acwhf.org/) > Menu > Honorees > 2003 > Ada Taylor Sackett.

[32] 1920 U.S. census, Bucks Co., Pa., pop. sch., New Britain Twp., ED 17, p. 2A, dwell. 29, fam. 33, William R. Riley; NARA T625, roll 1542.

[33] 1880 U.S. census, Philadelphia Co., Pa., pop. sch., Philadelphia, ED 481, p. 286B, dwell. 227, fam. 230, Mary A. Getty; NARA T9, roll 1182.

[34] 1900 U.S. census, Philadelphia Co., Pa., pop. sch., Philadelphia, ED 518, p. 12, dwell. 295, fam. 238, William Emmitt; NARA T623, roll 1465.

[35] William S. Waudby, "The Industrial Crime: Child Labor," *American Federationist* 10 (May 1903): 357-58.

[36] 1930 U.S. census, Atlantic Co., N.J., pop. sch., Atlantic City, ED 2, p. 6A, dwell. 117, fam. 126, Edward H. Brown, hotel clerk, in the household of Robert Brown; NARA T626, roll 1308.

[37] *Atlantic City Directory for 1918-19* (Philadelphia: James Gopsill's Sons, 1919), 661, "Riley Brad theatrical agt h The Regent."

[38] "Russell F. Sackett, Shore Musician, Dies," *The Morning Post (Camden, N.J.)*, 21 Mar. 1936, p. 3, col. 7.

[39] New Jersey death certificate no. 21118, George F. Albrecht (1967); Vital Statistics and Registrar, Trenton.

[40] "The Life of American Workers in 1915," *Monthly Labor Review* (Summer 2016), e-journal, (https://www.bls.gov/opub/mlr/2016/article/the-life-of-american-workers-in-1915.htm).

[41] 1940 U.S. census, Camden Co., N.J., pop. sch., Haddon, ED 4-69, p. 18B, dwell. 463, Charles Albrecht; NARA T627, roll m-t0627-02321.

[42] 1940 U.S. census, Cambria Co., Pa., pop. sch., Southmont, ED 11-144A, p. 9B, dwell. 194, Courtney M. Ogborn; NARA T627, roll m-t0627-03457.

[43] "Mary Barbara Alice (Stuck) Albrecht; teacher, volunteer," *St. Louis (Mo.) Post-Dispatch*, 21 Mar. 2002, p. 138, cols. 1-4.

[44] "Dr. Edwin G. Riley, Public Health Physician [obituary]," *The Baltimore Sun*, 21 Jul. 1989, p. 45, col. 2.

[45] "Quintennial Catalogue of the Students, from 1851 to 1856," in *Quadrennial Catalogue of the Pennsylvania Female College, at Perkiomen Bridge, Montgomery County, Penn,...* (Philadelphia: Oliver P. Gelssner, 1857), 7, Anna Maria Hallman; "U.S., School Catalogues, 1765-1935," digital images, *Ancestry.com* (https://www.ancestry.com/).

[46] Pennsylvania death certificate no. 019870-68, Susie F. Bowker (1968); Vital Statistics, Harrisburg.

[47] "Pennsylvania, U.S., Prison, Reformatory, and Workhouse Records, 1829-1971," database and images, *Ancestry.com* (https://www.ancestry.com/), Western State Penitentiary, Harold Seeds Braidwood.

[48] "Pennsylvania, U.S., Veteran Compensation Application Files, WWII, 1950-1966," digital images, *Ancestry.com* (https://www.ancestry.com/), Robert Fullmer Riley, deceased, Army Air, 5 Jan. 1945, "Central Pacific."

[49] Gene Smiley, "The U.S. Economy in the 1920s," PDF, *EH.net* (https://eh.net/encyclopedia/the-u-s-economy-in-the-1920s/).

GENEALOGICAL SUMMARY

Generation One

1. WILLIAM[1] RILEY, was born in Connecticut ca. 1798,[50] 1799,[51] 1800,[52] or on 20 January 1798,[53] and was baptized as an adult ca. 1840 at the Green Tree Church of the Brethren, Oaks, Upper Providence Township, Montgomery County, Pennsylvania.[54] William died "after a long and serious illness," age 75, in Oaks on 1 April 1873[55] and was buried there in the Green Tree Church of the Brethren Cemetery.[56] He married ca. 1828 (first-known child),[57] HARRIET/HENRIETTA (−?−).[58] She was born in Westchester [sic, probably West Chester], Chester County, Pennsylvania, in August 1805,[59] 28 August 1806,[60] or 1807, and was baptized with her husband.[61] Harriet/Henrietta died of typhoid fever at the home of her son, Thomas, in Philadelphia, Philadelphia County, Pennsylvania, on 31 March 1885, age 79 years, 7 months,[62] and was buried with her husband.[63]

William lived in Upper Providence Township by 1829, in Lower Providence Township from 1834 to 1844,[64] and returned to Upper Providence Township where he died in 1873.[65] He purchased a small lot of land in 1854 which was sold by his widow Harriet in 1874[66] (Figure 8). The original house stood in 1996 (Figure 9). Two sons left home at young ages and lived nearby: Samuel with a neighbor who ran a tannery, perhaps as part of William's shoemaking business; Mark in the household of a farmer.[67] After the Civil War, William and Harriet lived alone in

---

[50] 1850 U.S. census, Montgomery Co., Pa., p. 308A, dwell. 334, fam. 336. Green Tree Church of the Brethren (Oaks, Pa.), Baptisms, p. 9; "Pennsylvania and New Jersey, U.S., Church and Town Records, 1669-2013," digital images, *Ancestry.com* (https://www.ancestry.com/). Birth year calculated from age when baptized.

[51] 1870 U.S. census, Montgomery Co., Pa., p. 363A, dwell. 313, fam. 330.

[52] 1860 U.S. census, Montgomery Co., Pa., p. 571, dwell. 936, fam. 1040.

[53] *Find A Grave*, database and images (http://findagrave.com), William Riley, memorial no. 94,756,187.

[54] Green Tree Church of the Brethren (Oaks, Pa.), Baptisms, p. 9, William Riley baptism; "Pennsylvania and New Jersey, U.S., Church and Town Records, 1669-2013," digital images, *Ancestry.com* (https://www.ancestry.com/).

[55] "Died [death notice of William Riley]," *Public Ledger,* 4 April 1875.

[56] *Find A Grave*, William Riley, memorial no. 94,756,187.

[57] 1900 U.S. census, Atlantic Co., N.J., Atlantic City, ED 9, p. 10, dwell. 151, fam. 213, Thomas M. Riley, in the household of Christian Riley, Sr.

[58] *Philadelphia City Directory for 1877* (Philadelphia: James Gopsill, 1877), 1221, "Riley, Harriet, wid William, h 2222 Tulip."

[59] City of Philadelphia, Return of Death, Harriet Riley, 31 Mar. 1885; City Archives, Philadelphia.

[60] *Find A Grave*, database and images (http://findagrave.com), Harriet Riley, memorial no. 94,756,158.

[61] Green Tree Church of the Brethren (Oaks, Pa.), Baptisms, p. 9, William Riley baptism.

[62] "Harriet Riley [death notice]," *The Philadelphia Inquirer,* 4 Apr. 1885, p. 5, col. 2.

[63] *Find A Grave*, Harriet Riley, memorial no. 94,756,158.

[64] Alderfer to Riley, 26 Sep. 1991.

[65] *Find A Grave*, William Riley, memorial no. 94,756,187. "Died," *Public Ledger,* 4 April 1875.

[66] Montgomery Co., Pa. Deed Book 97: 55; ibid., Deeds 221: 134, Harriet Riley to William Snyder, 28 May 1874.

[67] 1850 U.S. census, Montgomery Co., Pa., pop. sch., Upper Providence, p. 308A, dwell. 331, fam. 332, Samuel Reily [sic], laborer, in the household of Joseph C. Brower; NARA M432, roll 799. Ibid., p. 306A, dwell. 305, fam. 307. Ibid., p. 306A, dwell. 305, fam. 307, Mark Rily [sic] in the household of John Halloway; NARA M432, roll 799.

Upper Providence Township.[68] A record of William's estate was filed in Montgomery County; no estate record for Harriet has been located.[69]

Children of William and Harriet/Henrietta (–?–) Riley, children i., ii., iii., and vii. probably born in Upper Providence Township, and children iv., v., and vi. probably born in Lower Providence Township, both in Montgomery County, Pennsylvania, were:[70]

2.   i.   SAMUEL WARNER RILEY, b. Dec. 1827;[71] m. (1) ANN/ANNA REBECCA HALLMAN/HOLLMAN,[72] and (2) LAURA ELIZABETH COOK;[73] d. Atlantic City, Atlantic Co., N.J. 20 Feb. 1905.[74]

3.   ii.   UNNAMED RILEY CHILD, b. bef. 1830;[75] d. unknown.[76]

4.   iii.   CHRISTIAN FULMER RILEY, b. 10 Feb. 1833[77]; m. ANNA T. or F. LANDIS;[78] d. Atlantic City 12 Mar. 1906.[79]

---

[68] 1870 U.S. census, Montgomery Co., Pa., p. 363A, dwell. 313, fam. 330.

[69] "Pennsylvania, U.S., Wills and Probate Records, 1683-1993," database with images, *Ancestry.com* (https://www.ancestry.com/), Browse this Collection=Montgomery > Estate Index, Surname R > image 459 of 584. William Riley, vol. 23: 191. Ibid., Estate Index, Surname R > image 115 of 584. No entry for Harriet Riley.

[70] Montgomery County Will Book 23: 191, no. 5692, will of William Riley, made 28 Feb. 1872, proved 10 Apr. 1873; Register of Wills, Norristown. Alderfer to Riley, 26 Sep. 1991.

[71] 1900 U.S. census, Atlantic Co., N.J., pop. sch., Atlantic City, ED 10, p. 2, dwell. 20, fam. 20, household of Saml Riley; NARA T623, roll 953.

[72] Evidence for this marriage is indirect and is based the association of Ann Rebecca (Hallman) Riley with her sister, Anna Maria (Hallman) Riley, and the burial of two of Ann Rebecca's children with their Hallman grandmother. Anna Maria married Ann Rebecca's brother-in-law, Thomas M. Riley. Cohocksink M.E. Church (Philadelphia, Pa.), Marriages, Thomas M. Riley-Anna M. Hallman, 20 Apr. 1865; "Pennsylvania and New Jersey, U.S., Church and Town Records, 1669-2013," digital images, *Ancestry.com* (https://www.ancestry.com/). The brother-sister couples lived in the same household. 1870 U.S. census, Philadelphia Co., Pa., pop. sch., Philadelphia, p. 493A, dwell. 912, fam. 971; NARA M593, roll 1407. Sam¹ W. Riley and Rebecca Riley. Ibid., dwell. 912, fam. 972. Thomas Riley and Maria Riley. Two young children of Samuel W. and Ann Rebecca Riley were buried in the same cemetery as their maternal grandparents. *Find A Grave*, database and images (http://findagrave.com), Catharine Hallman, memorial no. 112,805,126. Inscription, "Wife of Jacob Hallman"; ibid., John Howard Riley, memorial no.112,805,936, inscription, "Son of Samuel H. [sic] and A. Rebecca Riley"; ibid., Annie Kate Riley, memorial no. 112,805,904, inscription, "Daughter of Samuel H. [sic] and Ann R. Riley." For the relationship of Anna Marie (Hallman) Riley to her parents, 1860 U.S. census, Montgomery Co., Pa., pop. sch., Lower Providence, p. 348, dwell. 504 [sic], fam. 500 [sic], Ann M. Hallman in the household of Jacob and Catharine Hallman; NARA M653, roll 1145.

[73] "U.S., Civil War Pension Index: General Index to Pension Files, 1861-1934," digital images, *Ancestry.com* (https://www.ancestry.com/); index card for Samuel W. Riley (Musician, 31 Pa. Inf.) and widow Laura E. Riley.

[74] New Jersey death certificate no. [blank], Samuel Riley (1905); Vital Statistics, Trenton. "Died [death notice of Samuel W. Riley])," *The Philadelphia Inquirer*, 20 Feb. 1905, p. 7, col. 4.

[75] 1830 U.S. census, Montgomery Co., Pa., p. 241, line 17, female under 5, household of Wm. Reily [sic].

[76] Negative searches: "Death, Burial, Cemetery & Obituaries," *Ancestry.com* (https://www.ancestry.com/), First and Middle Names=blank, Last Name=Riley (exact, sounds like, and similar), Birth year=1830±10, Lived in=Montgomery County, Pennsylvania, USA (exact). "1840 United States Federal Census," database, *Ancestry.com* First & Middle Name(s)=William, Last Name=Riley, Location=Montgomery County, Pennsylvania, USA.

[77] Circular to verify veteran's identity, 11 Jun. 1904, Christian F. Riley, Sr., veteran's pension application no. S.C. 1,069,104, certificate no. 778,349; service of Christian F. Riley (Musician, 31st Pa. Vols., Civil War); "Case Files of Approved Pension Applications . . ., 1861–1934"; Record Group (RG) 15: Civil War and Later Pension Files; Department Veterans Affairs; National Archives (NA)-Washington, D.C. New Jersey death certificate no. [blank], Christian F. Riley (1906); Vital Statistics, Trenton. 1900 U.S. census, Atlantic Co., N.J., pop. sch., Atlantic City, ED 9, p. 10A, dwell. 152, fam. 214, Christian Riley, Sr.; NARA T623, roll 953.

[78] German Reformed Church (Norristown, Pa.), marriage certificate, Christian F. Riley-Annie Landis, 16 Oct. 1856; photocopy supplied 1991 by A. Landis Riley, Pasadena, Calif.

[79] New Jersey death certificate [blank] (1906), Christian F. Riley.

5. iv. MARK MORRIS RILEY, b. 4 Sep. 1835;[80] m. SARAH ANN BILLEW;[81] d. Oaks 6 Sep. 1866.[82]

6. v. THOMAS MURRAY RILEY, b. Dec. 1838;[83] m. ANNA/ANN MARIA HALLMAN;[84] d. probably Atlantic City ca. 1903.[85]

7. vi. LYDIA ANN RILEY, b. 24 Nov. 1842;[86] m. RENWICK WILLIAM/WILSON BROWN;[87] d. Elizabeth, Union Co., N.J. 3 Jul. 1917.[88]

8. vii. MARY REBECCA RILEY a.k.a. MARY CAREY,[89] b. 1847[90] or July 1848;[91] m. ROBERT S. GETTY, SR.;[92] d. Philadelphia, Philadelphia Co., Pa. 30 Oct. 1901.[93]

Generation Two

2. SAMUEL WARNER[2] RILEY (*William[1] Riley*), was born probably in Upper Providence Township, Montgomery County, Pennsylvania,[94] in December 1827[95] and died of pulmonary emphysema in Atlantic City, Atlantic County, New Jersey, on 17 February 1905, age 77.[96] Samuel was buried in Saint Peter Evangelical Lutheran Church Cemetery, Lafayette Hill, Whitemarsh Twp., Pennsylvania.[97] He married (1) ca. 1858 (first-known child)[98] ANN/ANNA REBECCA

---

[80] Green Tree Church of the Brethren (Oaks, Pa.), p. 33, Mark Morris Riley baptism.

[81] Ibid., p. 15, Mark Morris Riley-Sarah Ann Billew marriage.

[82] *Find A Grave*, database and images (http://findagrave.com), Mark Morris Riley, memorial no. 96,477,610.

[83] 1900 U.S. census, Atlantic Co., N.J., Atlantic City, ED 9, p. 10, dwell. 151, fam. 213, Thomas M. Riley, in the household of Christian Riley, Sr.

[84] Cohocksink M.E. Church, Marriages, Thomas M. Riley-Anna M. Hallman, 20 Apr. 1865; *Ancestry.com* (https://www.ancestry.com/).

[85] *Atlantic City Directory for 1903* (Philadelphia: James Gopsill, 1903), 337, "Riley Thomas M., h 118 St. James pl"; By the same title: (1904), 347, no listing for Thomas Riley.

[86] Widow's petition for increase in pension allotment, Lydia A. Brown, 9 Dec. 1916, widow's pension file, certificate no. 778,956; service of Renwick W. Brown (Pvt., Co. D, 213 Pa. Vol. Inf. Regt.); "Case Files of Approved Pension Applications…1861-1934"; Civil War and Later Pension Files; Department of Veterans Affairs, Record Group 15; NA-Washington.

[87] City of Philadelphia, Return of Marriages, January 1 to April 1, 1869, Renwick W. Brown-Lydia R. Riley, 7 Mar. 1869; City Archives, Philadelphia.

[88] New Jersey death certificate, no. [blank], Lydia A. Brown (1917); Vital Statistics, Trenton. "Obituary Notes [Mrs. Renwick W. Brown]," *Elizabeth (N.J.) Daily Journal,* evening edition, 5 Jul. 1917, p. 4, col. 8.

[89] For mother's name, Mary Carey [sic], birth record of child. St. Stephen′s Episcopal Church (Philadelphia, Pa.), Baptisms, p. 52, Mary Anne Getty; "Pennsylvania and New Jersey, U.S., Church and Town Records, 1669-2013," database and digital images, *Ancestry.com* (https://www.ancestry.com/).

[90] "Mary Getty [official list of deaths]," *The Philadelphia Inquirer*, 2 Nov. 1901, p. 14, col. 5. Age, 54. Died, "30th ult. [30 Oct. 1901]." Birth year calculated from age at death.

[91] 1900 U.S. census, Philadelphia Co., Pa., pop. sch., Philadelphia, ED 527, p. 7, dwell. 145, fam. 149, Mary Getty; NARA T623, roll 1465.

[92] Ibid. Married, 35 years.

[93] City of Philadelphia, Return of Death, no. 6939, Mary Getty; "Pennsylvania, Philadelphia City Death Certificates, 1803-1915," digital images, *FamilySearch.org* (https://www.familysearch.org/).

[94] Alderfer-Riley, 26 Sep. 1991.

[95] 1900 U.S. census, Atlantic Co., N.J., Atlantic City, ED 10, p. 2, dwell. 20, fam. 20.

[96] New Jersey death certificate no. [blank] (1905), Samuel Riley. "Died," *The Philadelphia Inquirer*, 20 Feb. 1905.

[97] *Find A Grave*, database and images (http://findagrave.com), Pvt. Samuel W. Riley, memorial no. 15,159,114.

[98] 1900 U.S. census, Northampton Co., Pa., pop. sch., Lower Saucon Twp., ED 117, p. 25, dwell. 485, fam. 509, Mark Reilly [sic]; NARA T623, roll 1447.

HOLLMAN/HALLMAN,[99] daughter of Jacob and Catharine (Weber) Hallman.[100] She was born probably in Lower Providence Township, Montgomery County, Pennsylvania, on 22 July 1839 and died of consumption in Philadelphia, Philadelphia County, Pennsylvania, on 4 February 1878, age 38 years, 6 months, and 13 days, and was buried in Freeland Cemetery, Collegeville, Pennsylvania.[101] Samuel married (2) ca. 1883[102] LAURA ELIZABETH COOK,[103] daughter of George and Elizabeth (Galinger/Gilinger) Cook.[104] Laura was born in Norristown, Montgomery County, Pennsylvania, on 11 December 1856[105] or in December 1857[106] and died in St. Petersburg, Pinellas County, Florida, on 7 April 1941, age 84,[107] and was buried with her husband.[108]

Samuel left the family home in his early twenties, worked as a laborer, and lived with a neighbor, Joseph C. Brower, a tanner.[109] The tannery was across the road from William Riley's house (Figure 4). He married and fathered two children, and by 1860, lived in a neighbor's household which was adjacent to that of his parents.[110] Joining the Union Army in May 1862, he was as a musician in the same regimental band as his brother, Christian Fulmer Riley.[111] The brothers may have been present when President Abraham Lincoln visited the unit in July 1862 in

[99] Cohocksink M.E. Church, Marriages, Thomas M. Riley-Anna M. Hallman, 20 Apr. 1865; *Ancestry.com* (https://www.ancestry.com/). 1870 U.S. census, Philadelphia Co., Pa., pop. sch., Philadelphia, p. 493A, dwell. 912, fam. 971. Ibid., dwell. 912, fam. 972. *Find A Grave*, memorial no. 112,805,126.

[100] 1850 U.S. census, Montgomery Co., Pa., pop. sch., Lower Providence, p. 120A, dwell. 232, fam. 238, Rebecca Hallman in the household of Jacob Hallman; NARA M432, roll 800. Lower Skippack Mennonite Cemetery, Gravestone Inscriptions, Skippack Twp., Montgomery Co., Pa., p. 53 (penned), Jacob Hallman-Catharine Weber marriage; "Pennsylvania and New Jersey, U.S., Church and Town Records, 1669-2013," digital images, *Ancestry.com* (https://www.ancestry.com/).

[101] Registration of Deaths in the City of Philadelphia, Ann R. Riley, 4 Feb. 1878; "Pennsylvania, Philadelphia, Death Certificates, 1803-1915," digital images, *FamilySearch.org* (https://www.familysearch.org/). Trinity Christian Church, Collegeville, Pa., Register of Deaths, p. 204. "Wife of Sam¹ W. Riley." Birth calculated from age at death.

[102] 1900 U.S. census, Atlantic Co., N.J., Atlantic City, ED 10, p. 2, dwell. 20, fam. 20. Marriage year estimated from number of years married.

[103] New Jersey marriage certificate no. 12159, Charles William Albrecht-Emma Riley, 15 Oct. 1902; State Archives, Trenton. Bride's parents, Samuel W. Riley and Laura E. Cook.

[104] Florida death certificate no. 9151, Laura Elizabeth Riley (1941); Vital Statistics, Jacksonville. Name of father, Gilinger [sic]. For alternate spelling of mother's birth surname as Galinger, Pennsylvania death certificate no. 46755, Mrs. Elizabeth Cook (1919); Vital Statistics, Harrisburg.

[105] Florida death certificate no. 9151 (1941), Laura Elizabeth Riley.

[106] 1915 New Jersey state census, Warren Co., pop. sch., Phillipsburg, ED Fifth Ward, p. 14A, dwell. 332, fam. 342, Laura Riley, widow, in the household of William Cook.

[107] Florida death certificate no. 9151 (1941), Laura Elizabeth Riley. "Mrs. Laura E. Riley [obituary]," *Tampa Bay Times (St. Petersburg, Fla.)*, 8 Apr. 1941, p. 3, col. 5.

[108] *Find A Grave*, database and images (http://findagrave.com), Laura E. Riley, memorial no. 205,823,775.

[109] 1850 U.S. census, Montgomery Co., Pa., Upper Providence, p. 308A, dwell. 331, fam. 332.

[110] 1860 U.S. census, Montgomery Co., Pa., pop. sch., Upper Providence, p. 571, dwell. 939, fam. 1043, Samuel W. Riley in the household of Benjamin Casselbery; NARA M653, roll 1145.

[111] Christian F. Riley, Sr., pension application no. S.C. 1,069,104, Civil War, RG 15, NA-Washington.

Harrison's Landing, Virginia.[112] He and Christian were probably discharged there in August 1862 "…under provisions of Act of Congress abolishing Regimental Bands."[113]

In March 1863, after his military service terminated, Samuel moved to Philadelphia.[114] Samuel had a close relationship with his brother Thomas: their wives were sisters, the families lived in the same dwelling at one time,[115] and both were carpenters.[116] In 1880, Samuel was declared an invalid in a military pension,[117] and that year he lived alone as a lodger.[118] He moved to Atlantic City by 1894[119] and lived near his son Jacob.[120]

In June 1906, widow Laura received allotments of her widow's pension.[121] From 1908 to 1920, she lived in Phillipsburg, Warren County, New Jersey, with her bachelor brother and her mother.[122] After her mother died in 1919,[123] Laura returned to Atlantic City and boarded in a

---

[112] E. M. Woodward, *Our Campaigns; or, the Marches, Bivouacs, Battles, Incidents of Camp Life and History of Our Regiment During Its Three Years Term of Service* (Philadelphia: John E. Potter and Co., 1865), 162.

[113] Muster rolls, Band, 2nd Regiment, Pennsylvania Reserve Regiment, 1 Aug. 1861 to 5 Nov. 1862, card of Christian F. Reilly [sic], 5 Nov. 1862; "Records of the Adjutant General's Office, 1790s-1917"; Record Group 94, NA-Washington.

[114] Gopsill's *Philadelphia City Directory,* for 1875, 1266.

[115] 1870 U.S. census, Philadelphia Co., Pa., Philadelphia, p. 493A, dwell. 912, fam. 971. Ibid., dwell. 912, fam. 972.

[116] *Philadelphia City Directory for 1868-9* (Philadelphia: James Gopsill, 1868-69), 1340, "Riley Thomas M. (*Hoovan, Riley & Bro.*), h 2105 Oxford"; ibid., 1340, "Riley Samuel W. (*Hoovan, Riley & Bro.*), h 2105 Oxford."

[117] "U.S., Civil War Pension Index: General Index to Pension Files, 1861-1934," digital images, *Ancestry.com*, index card for Samuel W. Riley and widow Laura E. Riley.

[118] 1880 U.S. census, Philadelphia Co., Pa., pop. sch., Philadelphia, ED 222, p. 319B, dwell. 146, fam. 163, Samuel W. Riley in the hotel of Charles Roberts; NARA T9, roll 1173.

[119] *Atlantic City Directory for 1894* (Philadelphia: James Gospill's Sons, 1894), 169; By the same title: (1895), 266, "Riley Samuel W., carpenter, h 124 N Vermont av"; (1897), 228, "Riley Samuel W., carpenter, h 139 Mt. Vernon av"; (1898), 222; (1899), 249; (1901), 303; (1902), 348; (1903), 337, "Riley Samuel W. (Laura E.), carpenter, h 114 Ocean av"; (1904), 347, "Riley Samuel W. (Laura E.), carpenter, h 210 N Rhode Island av."

[120] New Jersey death certificate no. [blank] (1905), Samuel Riley. Resided 210 N. Rhode Island Ave. *Atlantic City Directory for 1903* (Philadelphia: James Gopsill's Sons, 1903), 336, "Riley Jacob D. (Mary), plumber, h 113 N Rhode Island av."

[121] *Atlantic City Directory for 1906* (Philadelphia: James Gospill's Sons, 1906), 408, "Riley Harry N., (Laura), clerk, P.O., h 2 Reed apartments." "United States Veterans Administration Payment Cards, 1907-1933," database and digital images, *FamilySearch.org* (https://www.familysearch.org/), card for Laura E. Riley.

[122] *City Directory for Easton Including…Phillipsburg, N.J. for 1908* (Easton, Pa.: George W. West, 1908), 544, "Riley Laura E. Mrs. widow res. 222 Fillmore"; By the same title: (1910), 786, "Riley Laura E. Mrs. res. 222 Fillmore"; (1912), 818; (1914), 814; (1916), 815; (1918), 830; (1920), 835; (1923), 844, no listing for Laura E. Riley. By the same title: (1910), 688, "Cook William, engr. res. 222 Fillmore"; (1912), 668; (1914) 732; (1916), 730; (1918), 734; (1920), 746; By the same title: (1910), 668, "Cook Elizabeth Mrs. res. 222 Fillmore"; (1912), 668;"; (1914), 732; (1916), 730; (1918), 734. 1910 U.S census, Warren Co., N.J., pop. sch., Phillipsburg, ED 146, p. 4A, dwell. 72, fam. 73, Laura Riley in the household of William Cook; NARA T624, roll 912. 1920 U.S census, Warren Co., N.J., pop. sch., Phillipsburg, ED 175, p. 5A, dwell. 95, fam. 98, Laura Riley in the household of William Cook; NARA T625, roll 1073.

[123] *Find A Grave*, database and images (http://findagrave.com), Elizabeth Cook, memorial no. 114,993,089.

rooming house with her stepson, Harry N. Riley.[124] By 1937, Laura began visiting St. Petersburg, Pinellas County, Florida,[125] and she was enumerated there in the 1940 census, employed as a seamstress in a shirt factory, age 82.[126]

Children of Samuel Warner Riley and Ann/Anna Rebecca Hollman were:[127]

9. i.   MARK M. RILEY, b. Upper Providence Twp., Montgomery Co., Pa.[128] Feb. 1859;[129] m. CATHARINE "KATE" SIMON;[130] d. South Bethlehem, Northampton Co., Pa. 7 Aug. 1906,[131] bur. Saint Michael's Cemetery, Bethlehem, Northampton Co., Pa.[132]

10. ii. JOHN HOWARD RILEY, b. Upper Providence Twp.[133] 14 Oct.1859;[134] d. of pericarditis in Philadelphia 6 Jan. 1869[135] or 6 Feb. 1869, age 9 yr., 3 mo., 22 da., bur. Trinity Reformed Church Cemetery, Collegeville, Pa.[136]

11. iii. ANNIE KATE RILEY, b. possibly Upper Providence Twp. 18 Apr. 1862; d. 8 Mar. 1863, age 10 mo. 18 da., bur. Trinity Reformed Church Cemetery, Collegeville.[137]

12. iv. JACOB H. RILEY, b. Philadelphia 5 Feb. 1864;[138] m. ADDA/ADA MAY SMITH;[139] d. Zanesville, Muskingum Co., Ohio, 1 Aug. 1931, age 67.[140]

---

[124] 1930 U.S. census, Atlantic Co., N.J., pop. sch., Atlantic City, ED 14, p. 6B, dwell. 61, fam. 120, Laura E. Riley and Harry N. Riley in lodging house of John B. Betlew; NARA T626, roll 1308.

[125] "Winter Visitor Registrations Jump to 3,400," *Tampa Bay Times (St. Petersburg, Fla.)*, 21 Oct. 1937, p. 10, col. 3. Among registrants was "…Mrs. Laura E. Riley, Atlantic City…."

[126] 1940 U.S. census, Pinellas Co., Florida, pop. sch., St. Petersburg, ED 52-27, p. 5B, dwell. 148, Laura Riley; NARA T627, roll m-t0627-00609.

[127] 1860 U.S. census, Montgomery Co., Pa., pop. sch., Upper Providence, p. 571, dwell. 939, fam. 1044, Samuel W. Riley in the household of Benjamin Casslebery; NARA 653, roll 1145. 1870 U.S. census, Philadelphia Co., Pa., Philadelphia, p. 493A, dwell. 912, fam. 972. The date of the 1870 enumeration was 30 Jun. 1870. If son Harry N. Riley was b. Feb. 1870, he should have been listed.

[128] 1860 U.S. census, Montgomery Co., Pa., Upper Providence, p. 571, dwell. 939, fam. 1044, Mark Riley, age 2, and Samuel W. Riley in the household of Benjamin Casslebery.

[129] 1900 U.S. census, Northampton Co., Pa., Lower Saucon Twp., ED 117, p. 25, dwell. 485, fam. 509.

[130] "Mrs. Catharine Riley," *The Morning Call (Allentown, Pa.)*, 16 Oct. 1947, p. 8, col. 4. "Mrs. Catharine C. (Simon) Riley, widow of Mark Riley…." Philadelphia, Pa., City Archives, 10 Apr. 2022, email reporting negative marriage-record search for Mark M. Riley and Catherine Simon, Jan. to Dec. 1881-1883.

[131] "Death of Mark Riley," *The Allentown (Pa.) Leader*, 8 Aug. 1906, p. 6, col. 7.

[132] *Find A Grave*, database and images (http://findagrave.com), Mark Riley, memorial no. 131,643,396.

[133] 1860 U.S. census, Montgomery Co., Pa., Upper Providence, p. 571, dwell. 939, fam. 1044, John H. Riley, age 1, and Samuel W. Riley in the household of Benjamin Casslebery.

[134] Wilmer Reinford, "Burials in the Trinity Reformed Church Cemetery [Collegeville, Pa.]," typescript, 1962, entry for John Howard Riley: "Pennsylvania and New Jersey, U.S., Church and Town Records, 1669-2013," digital images, *Ancestry.com* (https://www.ancestry.com/).

[135] "Pennsylvania, Philadelphia City Death Certificates, 1803-1915," database and digital images, *FamilySearch.org* (https://www.familysearch.org/), John Riley, d. 9 Jan. 1869, age, 9 yr. and [illegible] mo., b. Montgomery Co. Pa., parents, Samuel and Rebecca Riley, bur. Freeland [Cemetery], Montgomery Co., Pa.

[136] Reinford, "Trinity Reformed Church Cemetery," John Howard Riley.

[137] Ibid. Annie Kate Riley. Birth date based on age at death.

[138] Ohio death certificate no. 50497, Jacob H. Riley (1931); Vital Statistics, Columbus.

[139] Belmont County Marriage Records, 1890-1899, p. 241, Riley-Smith, 3 Mar. 1892; "Ohio, U.S., County Marriage Records, 1774-1993," digital images, *Ancestry.com* (https://www.ancestry.com/). "Licensed to Marry," *Belmont Chronicle (St. Clairsville, Ohio)*, 10 Mar. 1892, p. [blank], Riley-Adda M. Smith.

[140] Ohio death certificate no. 50497 (1931), Jacob H. Riley. "Jacob H. Riley Dies Suddenly at Home Sunday," *The Times-Recorder (Zanesville, Ohio)*, 3 Aug. 1931, p. 3, col. 1.

13. v. HARRY NEWCOURT RILEY, b. Philadelphia 15 Feb. 1871;[141] d. Atlantic City, Atlantic Co., N.J. 10 Jul. 1955, age 85, bur. Saint Peter Evangelical Lutheran Church Cemetery, Lafayette Hill, Whitemarsh Twp., Montgomery Co., Pa.[142]

14. vi. LIZZIE RILEY, b. Philadelphia ca. 1874; d. there of "anginae [angina]" 28 Apr. 1875, age 1 yr., bur. Montgomery Co., Pa.[143]

15. vii. EMMA RILEY, b. Pa. Jun. 1879[144] or Jun. 1880;[145] m. CHARLES WILLIAM ALBRECHT;[146] d. aft. Apr. 1941.[147]

4. CHRISTIAN FULMER[2] RILEY (*William[1] Riley*), was born probably in Lower Providence Township, Montgomery County, Pennsylvania,[148] on 10 February 1833,[149] and was baptized as an adult at the Green Tree German Baptist Brethren Church, Oaks, Montgomery County, Pennsylvania, in 1857.[150] Christian died at his home in Atlantic City, Atlantic County, New Jersey, of "oedema of the lungs complicating chronic heart disease" on 12 March 1906, age 73 years, 1 month, and 2 days.[151] Christian was buried at the Atlantic City Cemetery, Pleasantville, New Jersey.[152] In his will, he named wife Anna F. Riley and sons Christian F. Riley, Jr., Thomas M. Riley, and Abraham L. Riley.[153] He was married by the Rev. John S. Emantvout in the German Reformed Church in Norristown, Montgomery County, Pennsylvania, on 16 October

---

[141] City of Philadelphia, Return of Births From the 1st Day of Jan to the 1st Day of March 1871, Harry Newcourt Riley; City Archives, Philadelphia.

[142] *Find A Grave*, database and images (http://findagrave.com), Harry N. Riley, memorial no. 205,823,345.

[143] City of Philadelphia, Return of Deaths, Lizzie Riley; City Archives, Philadelphia. Calculated from age at death.

[144] 1900 U.S. census, Atlantic Co., N.J., Atlantic City, ED 10, p. 2, dwell. 20, fam. 20. Emma Riley, Family Tree ID LVMJ-NTN, *FamilySearch.org*. Gives birth as 6 Jun. 1879.

[145] 1905 New Jersey state census, Atlantic Co., pop. sch., Atlantic City, p. 6B, dwell. 43, fam. 45, Emma Albrecht in the household of Charles Albrecht.

[146] New Jersey marriage certificate no. 12159, Charles William Albrecht-Emma Riley, 15 Oct. 1902; State Archives, Trenton.

[147] "Mrs. Laura E. Riley," *Tampa Bay Times*, 8 Apr. 1941. Survivors included a "daughter," Mrs. Emma Albrecht.

[148] Alderfer to Riley, 26 Sep. 1991.

[149] Circular to verify veteran's identity, Christian F. Riley, Sr., pension application no. S.C. 1,069,104, Civil War, RG 15, NA-Washington, Christian F. Riley.

[150] Green Tree Church of the Brethren (Oaks, Pa.), p. 33, Christian Riley baptism (1859).

[151] New Jersey death certificate [blank] (1906), Christian F. Riley.

[152] *Find A Grave*, database and images (http://findagrave.com), Christian Fulmer Riley, memorial no. 232,348,846.

[153] Will of Christian F. Riley, Sr., made 27 Jan. 1902, Christian F. Riley, Sr., in pension application no. S.C. 1,069,104, Civil War, RG 15, NA-Washington. Bequeathed to wife all personal and private property. Estate divided in equal portions among his children with monies to be distributed first to Christian F. Riley, Jr., Thomas J. Riley, and Abraham L. Riley for "...money furnished by my sons to wit ; for building house &c."

1856[154] to ANNA T.[155] or F.[156] LANDIS,[157] daughter of Henry George and Magdalena Showalter (Alderfer) Landis.[158] She was born probably in Lower Providence Township,[159] on 16 October 1833,[160] and was baptized with her husband.[161] She applied for a Civil War widow's pension.[162] Anna died at the home of her son, William R. Riley, in Chalfont, Bucks County, Pennsylvania, on 28 August 1910, age 76 years, 10 months, and 12 days,[163] and was buried with her husband.[164]

According to family lore,[165] Christian Riley was a schoolteacher in "Perkasie" (perhaps Perkiomen Township, Montgomery County, Pennsylvania), married Anna Landis, and "played horn [in a band] in the Civil War." He fathered two girls and ten boys, seven of whom lived. A blacksmith, he owned a "very large" shop at 18th and Broad Streets in Philadelphia. In 1881, Christian moved to Atlantic City and ran a hotel at Connecticut and Atlantic Avenues. With few exceptions, these facts roughly correspond to the documented evidence below.[166]

Christian served in the early years of the Civil War.[167] He was a musician in the Regimental Band, Thirty-First Regiment–Second Reserve, Pennsylvania Volunteers, and was discharged on 10 August 1862 at "Harrison Station [Harrison's Landing]," Virginia.[168] By 1863

---

[154] German Reformed Church (Norristown, Pa.), marriage certificate, Riley-Landis.

[155] Middle initial "T." Christian F. Riley, Sr., et ux. and Horace F. Nixon, mortgage deed, Christian F. Riley, Sr., pension application no. S.C. 1,069,104, Civil War, RG 15, NA-Washington. *Atlantic City Directory for 1905* (Philadelphia: James Gospill's Sons, 1905), 378, "Riley Christian F. (Anna T.)…"; By the same title: (1909), 531, "Riley Anna T, widow, h 118 St. James pl. "U.S., Civil War Pension Index: General Index to Pension Files, 1861-1934," digital images, *Ancestry.com* (https://www.ancestry.com/), entry for Anna T. Riley, 2 Oct. 1906, widow's application no. 856,796, certificate no. 647,275. Pennsylvania death certificate no. 77377, Anna Tyson Riley (1910); Vital Statistics, Harrisburg. Informant was her son, William R. Riley.

[156] Middle initial "F." Circular to verify veteran's identity, Christian F. Riley, Sr., pension application no. S.C. 1,069,104, Civil War, RG 15, NA-Washington. Ibid. will of Christian F. Riley. "…my wife Anne F. Riley…." New Jersey death certificate [blank] (1906), Christian F. Riley, middle name "Fulmer." Index of death records, *Pennsylvania Historical and Museum Commission* (https://www.phmc.pa.gov/Archives/Research-Online/Pages/Death-Indices.aspx) > D-10 P-Q-R.pdf > image 206 of 283, "Anna F. Riley."

[157] German Reformed Church (Norristown, Pa.), marriage certificate, Riley-Landis.

[158] Helen Alderfer Stanley, *The Alderfers of America: History and Genealogy* (Allentown, Pa.: Schlechters, 1972), 191. Henry S. Landes, *Descendants of Jacob Landes of Salford Township, Montgomery Co. Pennsylvania* (Souderton, Pa.: H. S. Landes, 1943). The probable immigrant was Jacob Landes who came in 1727.

[159] 1840 U.S. census, Montgomery Co., Pa., pop. sch., Lower Providence, p. 216, female, age 5-10, in the household of Henry Landis; NARA M704, roll 478. 1850 U.S. census, Montgomery Co., Pa., pop. sch., Lower Providence, p. 119B, dwell. 231, fam. 237, Ann Landis in the household of Henry Landis; NARA M432, roll 800.

[160] Pennsylvania death certificate no. 77377 (1910), Anna Tyson Riley.

[161] Green Tree Church of the Brethren (Oaks, Pa.), p. 33, Ann Riley baptism (1859).

[162] "U.S., Civil War Pension Index: General Index to Pension Files, 1861-1934," digital images, *Ancestry.com* (https://www.ancestry.com/), Anna T. Riley, 2 Oct. 1906, widow's application no. 856,796, certificate no. 647,275.

[163] Pennsylvania death certificate no. 77377 (1910), Anna Tyson Riley.

[164] *Find A Grave*, database and images (http://findagrave.com), Anna Tyson Riley, memorial no. 232,349,058.

[165] Camp to Riley, notes, undated. Mrs. Camp was the granddaughter of Christian Fulmer Riley.

[166] Evidence is lacking that Christian had been a teacher or owned a hotel in Atlantic City.

[167] 1890 U.S. census, Atlantic Co., N.J., "Special Schedule: Surviving Soldiers, Sailors, and Marines, and Widows, Etc.," Atlantic City, ED 1, p. 5, Christian F. Riley; NARA M123, roll [blank]. Served 15 Jul. 1861 to 10 Aug. 1862.

[168] Samuel P. Bates, *History of Pennsylvania Volunteers, 1861-5*, (Harrisburg, Pa.: B. Singerly, 1869), 1: 575-98. Major battles of the Regiment to 15 Aug. 1862 were Mechanicsville, Gaines' Mill, and Malvern Hill. Ibid., 1: 591. Christian, who enlisted for a three-year term, served 1 yr., 1 mo., and 24 da.

he had settled in Philadelphia.[169] From 1866-74, he worked there as a machinist,[170] employed at one time by a railway company.[171] From 1875-83, he was a blacksmith on North Broad Street near Twenty-second Street.[172] People with surnames other than Riley owned these properties.[173] Two of Christian's sons, William R.[174] and Henry/Harry,[175] probably worked with him, since both were blacksmiths and lived within a few blocks of Christian's shop[176] (Figure 10). Late in life, Christian received a military pension.[177] In 1883, Christian removed to Atlantic City[178] and worked there for a few years as a blacksmith.[179] His home was at 118 St. James Place[180] (Figures 11-13). Anna remained in Atlantic City for several years,[181] received a widow's pension,[182] and removed to her son's home where she died.[183]

Children of Christian Fulmer Riley, Sr. and Anna T. or F. Landis, children i. to iv. born in Upper Providence Township, Montgomery County, Pennsylvania, and v. to xii. in Philadelphia, were:[184]

---

[169] *Philadelphia City Directory for 1863* (Philadelphia: A. McElroy & Co., 1863), 686, "Riley Christian, blacksmith, 2136 Thouron."

[170] *Philadelphia City and Business Directory for 1867-68* (Philadelphia: James Gopsill, 1867), 1073, "Riley Christian F., machinist, 2136 Thompson [sic]"; By the same title: (1868), 1339, "Riley Christian F., machinist, 2136 Thouron"; (1870), 1285; (1871), 1197; (1872), 1121; (1873), 1101; (1874), 1115.

[171] "City Intelligence," *The Philadelphia Inquirer*, 4 Dec. 1866, p. 6, col. 1. Witnessed a fire at the railway's stables.

[172] *Philadelphia City Directory for 1875* (Philadelphia: James Gospel, 1875), 1265; By the same title: (1876), 1268; (1877), 1221; (1878), 1319; (1879), 1361; (1880), 1423; (1881), 1381; (1882), 1809; (1883), 1352; (1884), 1346, not listed.

[173] Joshua K. Blay [Registrar and Collections Manager, Philadelphia City Archives], to author, email, 31 May 2022. No records were found of Riley (or spelling variations) ownership on any of these properties: 2216 North Broad St., 2244 North Broad St., and 2136 Thouron St.

[174] 1880 U.S. census, Philadelphia Co., Pa., Philadelphia, ED 595, p. 4D, dwell. 29, fam. 42. *Philadelphia City Directory for 1883* (Philadelphia: James Gopsill, 1883), 1354, "Riley William R., horseshoer, h 2424 N 15th"; By the same title: (1884), 1347; (1885), 1483; (1886), 1453; (1887), 1432; (1888), 1470; (1889), 1512.

[175] *Philadelphia City Directory for 1877* (Philadelphia: James Gopsill, 1877), 78, "Riley Henry L, blacksmith, h 2216 N Broad"; By the same title: (1881), 1382.

[176] For Christian's residence, Philadelphia City Death Certificates, 1803-1915," database and digital images, *FamilySearch.org* (https://www.familysearch.org/), Anna Elizabeth Riley, b. 1877, d. 9 Sep. 1877. Parents, Christian F. and Anna Riley. Father's address, 2216 N. Broad St.

[177] Christian F. Riley, Sr., pension application no. S.C. 1,069,104, Civil War, RG 15, NA-Washington.

[178] Circular to verify veteran's identity, Christian F. Riley, Sr., pension application no. S.C. 1,069,104, Civil War, RG 15, NA-Washington. 1885 New Jersey state census, Atlantic Co., pop. sch., Atlantic City, p. 191, dwell. 1256, fam. 1286, Christian Rieley [sic].

[179] *Atlantic City Directory for 1897* (Philadelphia: James Gospill's Sons, 1897), 227, "Riley Christian F., h r 121 S New York av"; By the same title: (1898), 222; (1899) 249, "Riley Christian F., blacksmith, h 2121 [sic] S New York av"; (1901), 303, "Riley Christian F., h 118 St. James pl"; (1902), 348; (1903), 336; (1904), 346; (1905), 378; (1906), 408, "Riley Anna, wid Christian, h Madeira Villa"; ibid., "Riley Christian, foreman, h Madeira Villa"; (1909), 531, "Riley Anna T, widow, h 118 St. James pl."

[180] Gospill's *Atlantic City Directory*, for 1905, 378.

[181] 1910 U.S. census, Atlantic Co., N.J., pop. sch., Atlantic City, ED 13, p. 5A, dwell. 68, fam., 82, Annie Riley; NARA T624, roll 867. The date of the enumeration was Apr. 1910.

[182] "US Veterans Administration Pension Payment Cards," digital images, *Fold3.com* (https://www.fold3.com/), Anna T. Riley, widow's certificate no. 641275, service of Christian F. Riley (Musician, Band, 31st Pa.).

[183] Pennsylvania death certificate no. 77377 (1910), Anna Tyson Riley.

[184] Circular to verify veteran's identity, Christian F. Riley, Sr., pension application no. S.C. 1,069,104, Civil War, RG 15, NA-Washington.

16.   i.   WILLIAM R. RILEY, SR., b. 7 Jun. 1857;[185] m. (1) ELIZABETH/LIZZIE/ELIZA H. HOUCK/HAUCK[186] and (2) LOUISA/LOUISE (PRAHL) BRUNNER;[187] d. Chalfont, Bucks Co., Pa. 6 Aug. 1933, age 76,[188] bur. there in Saint James Church Cemetery.[189]

17.   ii.   HENRY/HARRY LANDIS RILEY, b. 6 Sep. 1858;[190] m. EDWARDENE/EDITH/EDA MAGILL COPE;[191] d. Atlantic City 29 Dec. 1936, age 81, bur. Laurel Memorial Park, Egg Harbor Twp., N.J.[192]

18.   iii.   THOMAS J. RILEY, b. Dec. 1859;[193] d. Atlantic City 1903 or 1904.[194]

19.   iv.   ALBERT MAGILTON RILEY, b. Oct. 1861; d. Philadelphia of "dropsy of brain" (hydrocephalus), 20 May 1865, age 3 yr., 7 mo., bur. Montgomery Co., Pa.[195]

20.   v.   MAGDALINE RILEY, b. Nov. 1863; d. of convulsions (epilepsy), Philadelphia 31 Mar. 1864, age 5 mo., bur. Upper Providence, Pa.[196]

---

[185] Ibid.

[186] Pennsylvania death certificate no. 70089, Elizabeth H. Riley (1916); Vital Statistics, Harrisburg. Mother's birth surname, Houck. Ibid., death certificate no. 4, Mary B. Worthington (1921). Mother's birth surname, Houck. Social Security Administration, "U.S., Social Security Applications and Claims Index, 1936-2007," database, *Ancestry.com* (https://www.ancestry.com/), Kathryn H. Maurer, SS no. 197-14-2019. Mother's birth surname, Hauck [sic]. Philadelphia, Pa., City Archives, 7 Apr. 2022, email, negative marriage-record search for William R. Riley and Elizabeth Houck.

[187] Bucks County, Pennsylvania, Index to Marriage Applications, 1885–1946, p. 2105, William R. Riley-Louise Brunner, 1 Mar. 1918; "Pennsylvania County Marriages, 1885-1950," database and digital images, *FamilySearch.org* (https://www.familysearch.org/).

[188] Pennsylvania death certificate no. 69925, William R. Riley (1933); Vital Statistics, Harrisburg.

[189] *Find A Grave*, database and images (http://findagrave.com), William R. Riley, memorial no. 99,593,969.

[190] Circular to verify veteran's identity, Christian F. Riley, Sr., pension application no. S.C. 1,069,104, Civil War, RG 15, NA-Washington.

[191] City of Philadelphia, Marriage Returns, 1 Oct. to 31 Dec. 1881, Harry L. Riley-Eda Cope, 14 Nov. 1881; City Archives, Philadelphia.

[192] First Presbyterian Church (Atlantic City, N.J.), Register of Deaths, Henry Landis Riley, 30 Dec. 1937; "U.S., Presbyterian Church Records, 1701-1970," database and digital images, *Ancestry.com* (https://search.ancestry.com/). Place of burial now called Laurel Memorial Park Cemetery & Crematory, Egg Harbor Twp., N.J. No record of burial in this cemetery. Negative search on Find A Grave.com > Search Memorials in Laurel Memorial Park and Crematory, First Name=Henry/Harry, Middle Name=Landis, Last Name=Riley, Year Died=1937.

[193] 1900 U.S. census, Atlantic Co., N.J., Atlantic City, ED 9, p. 10, dwell. 151, fam. 214, Thomas J. Riley, son, in the household of Christian Riley, Sr.

[194] Gopsill's *Atlantic City Directory*, for (1903), 337, (1904), 347, no listing. Thomas Riley (1859-1904), Family Tree ID L8Q6-42F, "Family Tree," database, *FamilySearch.org* (https://www.familysearch.org/tree/person/sources/L8Q6-42F).

[195] Return of Death in the City of Philadelphia, Albert Magilton Riley, 20 May 1865; "Pennsylvania, Philadelphia City Death Certificates, 1803-1915," database and digital images, *FamilySearch.org* (https://www.familysearch.org/). Birth based on age at death.

[196] Registration of Deaths in the City of Philadelphia, 1864, p. 110-11, Magdaline Riley, 31 Mar. 1864; "Pennsylvania, Philadelphia City Death Certificates, 1803-1915," database and digital images, *FamilySearch.org* (https://www.familysearch.org/). Birth based on age at death.

21. vi. CHARLES BRADFORD "BRAD" RILEY, b. 2 Jun. 1865[197] or 22 Jun. 1865[198]; m. (1) MARGARET "MAGGIE" T. PETERS[199] and (2) ORA LOUISE MAY (TYSON) KELLEY BACON CONRAD;[200] d. probably in Atlantic City aft. 13 Apr. 1940[201] and bef. 31 Dec. 1940.[202]

22. vii. VIRGINIA "JENNIE" GERTRUDE RILEY, b. 3 Feb. 1867;[203] m. HARRY GRANT FREEMAN, SR.;[204] d. of acute pulmonary edema in Atlantic City 7 Jul. 1920, age 53 yr., 5 mo., 4 da., bur. Pleasantville Cemetery, Pleasantville, N.J.[205]

23. viii. JACOB DAVID RILEY, b. 17 Nov. 1868;[206] m. MAMIE/MAMYE/MAME CARTER SHOWELL;[207] d. Northfield, Atlantic Co., N.J. 22 Apr. 1949, age 80.[208]

---

[197] Circular to verify veteran's identity, Christian F. Riley, Sr., pension application no. S.C. 1,069,104, Civil War, RG 15, NA-Washington.

[198] Social Security Administration, "U.S, Social Security Applications and Claims Index, 1936-2007," database, *Ancestry.com* (https://search.ancestry.com/), Charles Bradford Riley, SS no. 155-01-7384.

[199] "New Jersey, U.S., Marriage Records, 1670-1965," database, *Ancestry.com* (https://search.ancestry.com/), Chas. B. Riley-Margaret T. Peters, 7 Mar. 1885, Atlantic City. New Jersey State Archives, 17 Dec. 2021, letter reporting negative marriage-record search for Charles B. Riley and Margaret T. Peters.

[200] Delaware death certificate no. 160, Ora May Riley (1935); Vital Statistics, Dover. For correct spelling of mother's birth surname and likely place of birth, 1880 U.S. census, Lancaster Co., Pa., pop. sch., Bart, ED 175, p. 516A, dwell. 133, fam. 133, Ora Tyson, granddaughter, in the household of Eavens Benn; NARA T9, roll 1143.

[201] 1940 U.S. census, Atlantic Co., N.J., pop. sch., Atlantic City, ED 1-27, p. 8A, dwell. 204, Charles B. Riley in the household of Lillian Knauer; NARA T627, roll m-t0627-02300.

[202] *Find A Grave*, database and images (http://findagrave.com), Charles B. Riley, memorial no. 184,888,841.

[203] Circular to verify veteran's identity, Christian F. Riley, Sr., pension application no. S.C. 1,069,104, Civil War, RG 15, NA-Washington.

[204] New Jersey marriage return, F20, Harry Grant Freeman-Virginia Gertrude Riley, 28 Oct. 1894; New Jersey State Archives, Trenton.

[205] New Jersey death certificate no. [blank], Virginia G. Freeman (1920); Vital Statistics and Registrar, Trenton.

[206] Circular to verify veteran's identity, Christian F. Riley, Sr., pension application no. S.C. 1,069,104, Civil War, RG 15, NA-Washington. Jacob D. Riley.

[207] New Jersey marriage return, R63, Jacob D. Riley-Mamie E. Showell, 21 Jun. 1886; State Archives, Trenton. "MARRIED RILEY-SHOWELL," *The Philadelphia Inquirer*, 1 Nov. 1894, p. 9, col. 5. For middle name, Mayme Carter Showell (1872-1952), Family Tree ID 9N89-P1R, "Family Tree," database, *FamilySearch.org*, (https://www.familysearch.org/tree/person/sources/9N89-P1R).

[208] New Jersey death certificate no. 12030, Jacob D. Riley (1949); Vital Statistics and Registry, Trenton.

24. ix. ELMIRA/ELLA/ADA BREESE/BRACE RILEY, b. 14 Mar. 1871;[209] m. (1). THOMAS RUTHERFORD
          SACKETT,[210] (2) WILLIAM T. BRAIDWOOD,[211] and possibly (3) J. JAMES ROGERS a.k.a. JAMES J.
          ROGERS a.k.a. JEROME J. ROGERS; [212] d. 22 Sep. 1943.[213]

25. x.   CHRISTIAN FULMER RILEY, JR., b. 24 Dec. 1872;[214] d. Atlantic City, 17 Nov. 1931, age 58,[215] bur
          Pleasantville, N.J.[216]

26. xi. ABRAHAM "ABE" LANDIS RILEY, SR., b. 15 Dec. 1874;[217] m. LILLIE CAROLINIA/CAROLINE
          KESLER;[218] d. Atlantic City, 9 Sep. 1939, age 64,[219] bur. Atlantic City Cemetery, Pleasantville,
          N.J.[220]

27. xii. ANNA ELIZABETH RILEY, b. Mar. 1877; d. of diarrhea in Philadelphia 9 Sep. 1877, age 6 mo.,
          bur. Upper Providence Twp., Pa.[221]

5. MARK MORRIS[2] RILEY (*William*[1] *Riley*), was born probably in Upper Providence Township,
Montgomery County, Pennsylvania,[222] on 4 September 1835[223] and died there "…suddenly…"

---

[209] Circular to verify veteran's identity, Christian F. Riley, Sr., pension application no. S.C. 1,069,104, Civil War,
RG 15, NA-Washington. Elmira B. Riley. Philadelphia, Pa., City Archives, 31 May 2022, email reporting negative
birth-record search for Elmira Breese Riley.

[210] "New Jersey, Marriage Records, 1670-1965," database, *Ancestry.com* (https://www.ancestry.com/), Thomas R.
Sackett-Elmira B. Riley, 20 Jul. 1888. First Methodist Episcopal Church (Atlantic City, N.J.), Marriage Record,
Thomas Rutherford Sackett-Emma Brace Riley; "New Jersey, United Methodist Church Records, 1800-1970,"
database and digital images, *Ancestry.com* (https://search.ancestry.com/).

[211] St. Paul's Methodist Church (Atlantic City, N.J.), Register of Marriages, William Braidwood-Ella Sackett [no
date]; "New Jersey, United Methodist Church Records, 1800-1970," database and digital images, *Ancestry.com*
(https://search.ancestry.com/).

[212] 1915 New Jersey state census, Atlantic Co., pop. sch., Atlantic City, p. 4A, dwell. 76, fam. 79, Ella Rogers [sic]
in the household of Sophia Weaver; "New Jersey, U.S., State Census, 1915," digital images, *Ancestry.com*
(https://www.ancestry.com/). Ibid., p. 4A, dwell. 77, fam. 80, J. James Rogers, Dahlgren A. Braidwood, Horace Mc.
Braidwood, and Harold S. Braidwood. Ella's marital status was "M [married]." "U.S., World War I Draft
Registration Cards, 1917-1918," digital images, *Ancestry.com* (https://www.ancestry.com/), card for Dahlgren
Albertson Braidwood. Closest relative, "Mrs. J.J. Rogers." *Atlantic City Directory for 1916* (Philadelphia: C.E.
Howe Co., 1916), 758, "Rogers Jerome J (Ella) superintendent, h 3 Turner pl"; By the same title: (1918), 1109,
"Rogers Jerome J (Ella) supt h 46 E Washington [Pleasantville, N.J.]"; Ibid., (1109), "Rogers Dahlgren A candymkr
h 46 E Washington." 1920 U.S. census, Cape May Co., N.J., pop. sch., Middle Twp., ED 123, p. 1B, dwell. 16, fam.
16, Ella B. [sic] Rogers, in the household of Cornealore E. Fort; NARA T625, roll 1025.

[213] "Public Member Trees," database, *Ancestry.com* (http://www.ancestry.com/), "Smith/Schoepfin Tree2 Family
Tree" family tree by BSmith817, profile for Elmira Breese Riley (1872-1943).

[214] "U.S., World War I Draft Registration Cards, 1917-1918," database and digital images, *Ancestry.com*
(https://www.ancestry.com/), Christian Fullmer [sic] Riley.

[215] First Presbyterian Church (Atlantic City), Register of Deaths, Christian F. Riley, 17 Nov. 1931; "U.S.,
Presbyterian Church Records, 1701-1970," digital images, *Ancestry.com* (https://www.ancestry.com/). *Atlantic City
Directory for 1931* (Philadelphia: R.L. Polk, 1931), 627, "Riley Christian F clk PO h3 S Iowa av."

[216] *Find A Grave*, database and images (http://findagrave.com), Christian Fuler [sic] Riley, Jr., memorial no.
232,425,332.

[217] "United States World War I Draft Registration Cards, 1917-1918," database and digital images,
FamilySearch.org (https://www.familysearch.org/), Abraham Landis Riley.

[218] New Jersey marriage certificate no. 12107 (1902), Riley-Kesler; State Archives, Trenton.

[219] New Jersey death certificate, no. [blank] (1939), Abraham Landis Riley; Vital Records and Registrar, Trenton.

[220] *Find A Grave*, database and images (http://findagrave.com), Abraham Landis Riley, memorial no. 232,425,171.

[221] "Pennsylvania, Philadelphia City Death Certificates, 1803-1915," database and digital images, *FamilySearch.org*
(https://www.familysearch.org/), Anna Elizabeth Riley.

[222] Alderfer to Riley, 26 Sep. 1991.

[223] Green Tree Church of the Brethren (Oaks, Pa.), p. 33, Mark Morris Riley baptism (1835).

on 6 September 1866, age 31 years.[224] Mark was buried there in Green Tree Church of the Brethren Cemetery.[225] He married in the Green Tree Church of the Brethren on 17 January 1861 SARAH ANN BILLEW, daughter of Elijah and Catharine (Dettra) Billew.[226] She was born probably in Upper Providence Township[227] on 11 August 1837 and died on 7 February 1908.[228] Sarah was buried with her husbands.[229] She married (2) Abraham H. Hallman.[230]

In 1850, Mark, age 14 or 15, resided with a farmer's family near his parents' home.[231] A decade later, as a carpenter, he resided with his parents.[232] Widow Sarah resided with her parents; she was a farm laborer and seamstress and later married a widower.[233] Sarah may have worked as a postmistress.[234]

Children of Mark Morris Riley and Sarah Ann Billew, all born probably in Upper Providence Township,[235] were:[236]

---

[224] "Died [death notice of Mark M. Riley]," *The Independent Phoenix (Phoenixville, Pa.)*, 13 Oct. 1866. Newspaper clipping; Riley Family History, privately held by Deborah (Le Van) Swift [ADDRESS FOR PRIVATE USE] Las Vegas, Nev., 2022. Inherited from her mother, Barbara (Martin) Le Van, who inherited it from her mother, Helen Bechtel (Riley) Martin. Provenance of the newspaper clipping is unknown.

[225] *Find A Grave*, Mark Morris Riley, memorial no. 96,477,610.

[226] Green Tree German Baptist Brethren Church (Oaks, Pa.), p. 15, Riley-Billew marriage, 1861; "Pennsylvania and New Jersey, U.S., Church and Town Records, 1669-2013," digital images, *Ancestry.com* (https://www.ancestry.com/). For Sarah's father, Montgomery County, Pennsylvania, Wills, Vol. 17: 397, will of Elijah Billew, made 1 Jan. 1879, proved 21 May 1885; "Pennsylvania, U.S., Wills and Probate Records, 1683-1993," database and digital images, *Ancestry.com* (https://www.ancestry.com/). "I appoint - my six Children to settle my affairs. Namely … Sarah Ann…." 1850 U.S. census, Montgomery Co., Pa., pop. sch., Upper Providence, p. 399 (stamped), dwell. 395, fam. 398, Sarah Ann Billew in the household of Elijah Billew; NARA M432, roll 799. For Sarah's mother's surname, "Pennsylvania Marriages, 1709-1940," database, *FamilySearch.org* (https://www.familysearch.org/), Elija [sic] Billew-Catharine Deterer [sic], 29 Jun. 1834, citing Vincent Reformed Church, East Vincent Twp., Chester Co., Pa.

[227] 1840 U.S. census, Montgomery Co., Pa., pop. sch., Upper Providence Twp., p. 182, line 27, household of Elija Bileau [sic], which includes three females under five; NARA M704, roll 476.

[228] *Find A Grave*, database and images (http://findagrave.com), Sarah Hallman, memorial no. 29,224,836.

[229] Ibid., A.H. Hallman, memorial no. 221,109,278.

[230] The evidence for this marriage is indirect. In 1880, Sarah, a widow, resided in the household of her parents. 1880 U.S. census, Montgomery Co., Pa., pop. sch., Upper Providence Twp., ED 33, p. 182D, dwell. 59, fam. 71, Sarah Riley, widow, in the household of Elijah Billew; NARA T9, roll 1159. Sarah was enumerated as the wife of Abraham H. Hallman in 1900. 1900 U.S. census, Montgomery Co., Pa., pop. sch., Upper Providence Twp., ED 266, p. 3, dwell. 39, fam. 44, Sarah A. Hallman, wife, in the household of Abraham H. Hallman; NARA T623, roll 1444. Also enumerated were Charles M. Riley, boarder; Martha A. Riley, lodger; and Blanche Riley, b. Oct. 1885, lodger.

[231] 1850 U.S. census, Montgomery Co., Pa., Upper Providence Twp., p. 306A, dwell. 305, fam. 307. Mark Rily [sic] in the household of John Halloway.

[232] 1860 U.S. census, Montgomery Co., Pa., Upper Providence Twp., p. 571, dwell. 936, fam. 1040.

[233] 1880 U.S. census, Montgomery Co., Pa., Upper Providence Twp., ED 33, p. 182D, dwell. 59, fam. 71. 1900 U.S. census, Montgomery Co., Pa., Upper Providence Twp., ED 266, p. 3, dwell. 39, fam. 44.

[234] *Official Register of the United States…on the First of July, 1881*, 554.

[235] 1860 U.S. census, Montgomery Co., Pa., Upper Providence Twp., p. 571, dwell. 936, fam. 1040.

[236] Green Tree Church of the Brethren (Oaks, Pa.), Baptisms, 33; "Pennsylvania and New Jersey, U.S., Church and Town Records, 1669-2013," digital images, *Ancestry.com* (https://www.ancestry.com/).

28.   i.   CHARLES MORRIS RILEY, SR., b. 19 Dec. 1861,[237] bapt. 14 Apr. 1909 at St. Peter's Episcopal Church, Phoenixville, Pa.;[238] m. MARY "MINNIE" (MCADAM) HARRIS;[239] d. Salisbury, Lancaster Co., Pa. 3 Sep. 1927.[240]

29.   ii.   MARTHA ALICE RILEY, b. 16 July 1863; d. of pneumonia complicating arthritis deformans, Philadelphia Home for the Incurables 1 Nov. 1930, age 67,[241] and bur. Green Tree Church of the Brethren Cemetery, Oaks, Upper Providence Twp., Pa.[242]

30.   iii.   JESSE MARK RILEY, b. 15 Aug. 1866;[243] m. SALLIE/SARAH/SARA S. BECHTEL;[244] d. Linden, Union Co. N.J. 16 May 1943.[245]

6. THOMAS MURRAY[2] RILEY (*William*[1] *Riley*), was born probably in Upper Providence Township, Montgomery County, Pennsylvania,[246] in December 1838,[247] and was baptized with his sister, Lydia Riley, at the Green Tree Church of the Brethren, Oaks, Upper Providence Township, on 4 March 1858.[248] Thomas died probably in Atlantic City in 1903.[249] He married in Philadelphia on 20 April 1865 ANNA/ANN MARIA HALLMAN,[250] daughter of Jacob and Catharine (Weber) Hallman.[251] She was probably born in Lower Providence Township, Montgomery County, Pennsylvania,[252] on 10 February 1836, and died of consumption in Philadelphia on 27 February 1875, age 38 years, 2 months, and 17 days.[253] Anna/Ann was buried in Freeland Cemetery, Freeland (now Collegeville), Montgomery County, Pennsylvania.[254]

---

[237] Pennsylvania death certificate no. 42, Charles Morris Riley (1927); Vital Statistics, Harrisburg.

[238] St. Peter's Episcopal Church (Phoenixville, Pa.), Parish Register, 1843-1943, baptisms, Charles Morris Riley, bapt. 14 Apr. 1909: "Pennsylvania and New Jersey, U.S., Church and Town Records, 1669-2013," digital images, *Ancestry.com* (https://www.ancestry.com/).

[239] Pennsylvania death certificate no. 27771, Mary Riley (1910); Vital Statistics, Harrisburg. Informant, Charles Riley, Mont Clare, Pa.

[240] Pennsylvania death certificate no. 42 (1927), Charles Morris Riley.

[241] Pennsylvania death certificate no. 21784, Martha A. Riley (1930); Vital Statistics, Harrisburg. Informant, Jesse Riley, Mont Clare, Pa.

[242] *Find A Grave*, database and images (http://findagrave.com), Martha A. Riley, memorial no. 96,477,415.

[243] Social Security Administration, "U.S., Social Security Applications and Claims Index, 1936-2007," database, *Ancestry.com* (https://www.ancestry.com/), Jesse Mark Riley, SS no. 204-05-6643.

[244] Montgomery County Register of Wills, Marriage License Docket, 1885-1901, 22: 4190, Jesse M. Riley-Sallie S. Bechtel, m. 21 May 1892; "Pennsylvania, U.S., County Marriage Records, 1845-1963," digital images, *Ancestry.com* (https://www.ancestry.com/).

[245] *Find A Grave*, database and images (http://findagrave.com), Jesse M. Riley, memorial no. 192,065,352.

[246] Alderfer to Riley, 26 Sep. 1991.

[247] 1900 U.S. census, Atlantic County, N.J., Atlantic City, ED 9, p. 10, dwell. 151, fam. 214, Thomas M. Riley, brother, in the household of Christian Riley, Sr.

[248] Green Tree Church of the Brethren (Oaks, Pa.), p. 29, Thomas Riley baptism (1858).

[249] Gopsill's *Atlantic City Directory*, for (1903), 337, (1904), 347, and (1905), 378.

[250] Cohocksink M.E. Church, Marriages, Thomas M. Riley-Anna M. Hallman, 20 Apr. 1865; *Ancestry.com* (https://www.ancestry.com/).

[251] Lower Skippack Mennonite Cemetery, Gravestone Inscriptions, Hallman-Weber; *Ancestry.com* (https://www.ancestry.com/). 1860 U.S. census, Montgomery Co., Pa., Lower Providence Twp., p. 348, dwell. 504 [sic], fam. 500 [sic], Ann M. Hallman in the household of Jacob Hallman.

[252] 1840 U.S. census, Montgomery Co., Pa., pop. sch., Lower Providence, p. 217, line 24, two white females, under age 5 in the household of Jacob Hallman; NARA M740, rolls 477-78. 1850 U.S. census, Montgomery Co., Pa., Lower Providence Twp., p. 120A, dwell. 232, fam. 238, Ann Hallman.

[253] City of Philadelphia, Return of Deaths, Ann Marie Riley, 27 Feb. 1875; City Archives, Philadelphia.

[254] *Ordnung der Mennonitischen Gemeinschaft* (Regulations of the Mennonite Community), Register of Deaths, Trinity Christian Church (Collegeville, Pa.), no. 268, p. 92, Maria Riley; "Pennsylvania and New Jersey, U.S., Church and Town Records, 1669-2013," database and digital images, *Ancestry.com* (https://www.ancestry.com/).

After enlisting in the Union Army in 1863, Thomas served two years before sustaining wounds which left him totally disabled by 1890.[255] Deaths of his wife and child within a few years[256] probably left Thomas depended on his siblings; he resided with Samuel in Philadelphia,[257] briefly with Lydia,[258] and later with Christian in Atlantic City.[259] His wife, Anna, attended the Pennsylvania Female College, Collegeville, Pennsylvania, in the 1850s.[260]

Child of Thomas Murray Riley and Anna/Ann Maria Hallman was:[261]

31.   i.   LEWIS W. RILEY, b. Philadelphia 25 Aug. 1868; d. there of "paralysis of the lungs," possibly poliomyelitis, 8 Jan. 1881.[262]

7. LYDIA ANN[2] RILEY (*William[1] Riley*), was born in Lower Providence Township, Montgomery County, Pennsylvania,[263] on 24 November 1842.[264] She was baptized with her brother, Thomas Riley, at the Green Tree German Baptist Brethren Church, Oaks, Upper Providence Township,

---

[255] "CONSOLIDATED LIST of all persons…subject to do military duty in the Fourth Congressional District…of Philadelphia…enumerated during the month of May and June 1863…," no. 20, p. 528 (penned), Thomas Riley; "U.S., Civil War Draft Registration Records, 1863-1865," digital images, *Ancestry.com* (https://www.ancestry.com/). 1890 U.S. census, "Surviving Soldiers, Sailors, and Marines, and Widows, etc.," Philadelphia, Pa., ED 103, p. 1, Thomas M. Riley; "1890 Veterans Schedules of the U.S. Federal Census," digital images, *Ancestry.com* (https://www.ancestry.com/). "Wounded in hip and leg…[and]…Totally disabled." "Index to Veterans Pension Applications," Thomas M. Riley (Pvt., Co. B. 73rd Pa. Vol. Inf., Civil War), digital images, *Fold3.com* (https://www.fold3.com/). Invalid certificate no. 417,931.

[256] City of Philadelphia, Return of Deaths, Lewis W. Riley, 8 Jan. 1881; City Archives, Philadelphia. "Ann Maria Riley [death notice]," *The Philadelphia Inquirer*, 3 Mar. 1875, p. 4, col. 5.

[257] *Philadelphia City Directory for 1867-8* (Philadelphia: James Gopsill, 1867-68), 1074; By the same title: (1868-69), 1340; (1870), 1286, "Riley Thomas M., carpenter, h 2007 Jefferson"; (1871), 1198; (1872), 1122; (1873), 1102; (1874), 1116; (1875), 1266; (1876), 1269; (1877), 1222, "Riley Thomas M., carpenter, h 2222 Tulip"; (1878), 1319; (1879), 1362, "Riley, Thomas M., carpenter, 2243 Memphis"; (1880), 1424; (1882), 1311; (1883), 1354; (1884). 1346; (1885), 1483; (1889), 1512, "Riley, Thomas M., supt., h 256 S Front"; (1890), 1561, "Riley, Thomas, carpenter, h 256 S Front"; (1891), 1578, "Riley, Thomas M., carpenter, h 101 Dock"; (1892), 1627, no listing. By the same title: (1868-69), 1340, "Riley Samuel W. (*Hoovan* [sic], *Riley & Bro.*), h 2105 Oxford"; (1870), 1286; (1871), 1198; (1872), 1122; (1873), 1102; (1874), 1116; (1875), 1266; (1876), 1269; (1878), 1319. By the same title: (1877), 1221, "Riley Harriet, wid William, 2222 Tulip"; (1879), 1361; (1880), 1424; (1882), 1310; (1883), 1353; (1884), 1347.

[258] *Philadelphia City Directory for 1886* (Philadelphia: James Gopsill, 1886), 1453, "Riley, Thomas M., carpenter, h 2404 Serrill"; ibid., 255, "Brown Renwick W., foreman, h 2404 Serrill"; (1888), 1432, "Riley, Thomas M., carpenter, h 2404 Sergeant"; ibid., 261, "Brown Renwick W., foreman, h 2404 Sergeant."

[259] *Atlantic City Directory for 1898* (Philadelphia: James Gopsill, 1898), 223, "Riley, Thomas M., carpenter, h r S 121 New York av; (1899), 247; (1901), 303, "Riley, Thomas M., carpenter, h 115 St. James Pl"; (1902), 348; (1903), 337; (1904), 347, no listing. By the same title: (1898), 222, "Riley Christian F., blacksmith, h r 121 S New York av"; (1899), 247; (1901), 336, "Riley Christian F., (Anna), h 115 St. James Pl"; (1902), 336; (1903), 336. 1900 U.S. census, Atlantic County, N.J., Atlantic City, ED 9, p. 10, dwell. 151, fam. 213, Thomas M. Riley, in the household of Christian Riley, Sr.

[260] *Quadrennial Catalogue of the Pennsylvania Female College…*, 7.

[261] 1870 U.S. census (2nd enumeration), Philadelphia Co., Pa., pop. sch., Philadelphia, p. 271B, dwell. [blank], fam. [blank], Thomas M. Riley, Lewis W. Riley, in the household of Saml W. Riley; NARA M593, roll 1434. 1880 U.S. census, Philadelphia Co., Pa., pop. sch., Philadelphia, ED 679, p. 519B, dwell. 190, fam. 202, Lewis Riley in the household of Thomas L. [sic] Riley; NARA T9, roll 1190.

[262] Philadelphia, Pa., City Archives, death return, Lewis W. Riley, 8 Jan. 1881.

[263] Alderfer to Riley, 26 Sep. 1991.

[264] Widow's petition for increase in pension allotment, Lydia A. Brown, widow's pension file, certificate no. 778,956, Civil War, RG 15, NA-Washington.

Montgomery County, Pennsylvania, on 4 March 1858.[265] Lydia died in Elizabeth, Union County, New Jersey, on 3 July 1917, age 70,[266] and was buried in Evergreen Cemetery, Hillside, Union County, New Jersey.[267] She married in Philadelphia, Philadelphia County, Pennsylvania, on 7 March 1869 RENWICK WILLIAM/WILSON BROWN,[268] son of Irish-born William and Scottish-born Agnes (Robertson) Brown.[269] Renwick was born in Philadelphia on 22 May 1845,[270] died of endocarditis in Elizabeth on 14 May 1914,[271] and was buried with his wife.[272]

Renwick served as a private in the Union Army for about eight months.[273] Moving to Philadelphia at end of the Civil War, he worked as a butcher, confectioner, and foreman.[274] In 1892, he relocated to Tottenville, Richmond County, New York, and, in 1899, moved to nearby Perth Amboy, Middlesex County, New Jersey.[275] In Perth Amboy, Renwick was a yardmaster for the "LV RR (Lehigh Valley Railroad)."[276] By 1907, the Browns resided in Elizabeth, Union

[265] Green Tree Church of the Brethren (Oaks, Pa.), Baptisms, p. 29; "Pennsylvania and New Jersey, U.S., Church and Town Records, 1669-2013," digital images, *Ancestry.com* (https://www.ancestry.com/).

[266] New Jersey death certificate no. [blank] (1917), Lydia A. Brown. *Elizabeth (N.J.) Daily Journal*, 5 Jul. 1917, p. 4, col. 8.

[267] *Find A Grave*, database and images (http://findagrave.com), Lydia A. Brown, memorial no. 203,730,647.

[268] Philadelphia, Pa., Marriage Return, Brown-Riley, 7 Mar. 1869.

[269] 1850 U.S. census, Philadelphia Co., Pa., pop. sch., Frankford, p. 131B, dwell. 106, fam. 111, Renwick Brown in the household of William Brown; NARA M423, roll 824. 1860 U.S. census, Philadelphia Co., Pa., pop. sch., Philadelphia, p. 442, dwell. 2099, fam. 2243, Renwick W. Brown in the household of William Brown; NARA M653, roll 1157. For Renwick's mother's surname, "Public Member Trees," database, *Ancestry.com* (http://ancestry.com/), "Cooper Family Tree," family tree by Barbara and Dan Gleason, profile for Agnes Robertson (1812/1813-?).

[270] Record of death, Renwick W. Brown (1914); City Clerk's Office, Elizabeth, N.J. Invalid's pension file, certificate no. 1027938; service of Renwick W. Brown (Pvt., Co. D, 213 Pa. Vol. Inf. Regt.); "Case Files of Approved Pension Applications…1861-1934"; Civil War and Later Pension Files; Department of Veterans Affairs, Record Group 15; NA-Washington. Recorded age at death of 68 yr., 11 mo., and 22 da. (calculated birth, 22 May 1845). New Jersey death certificate no. [blank], Renwick Wilson Brown (1914); Vital Statistics and Registry, Trenton. Born, 22 May 1845. Informant, Wm. Brown.

[271] New Jersey death certificate, no. [blank] (1914), Renwick Wilson Brown. "Funeral of Renwick W. Brown [funeral notice]," *Elizabeth Daily Journal*, 19 May 1914, p. 11, col. 5.

[272] *Find A Grave*, database and images (http://findagrave.com), Pvt. Renwick W. Brown, memorial no. 177,799,430.

[273] Declaration for widow's pension, Lydia A. Brown, widow's pension file, certificate no. 778,956, Civil War, RG 15, NA-Washington.

[274] *Philadelphia City Directory for 1868* (Philadelphia: James Gopsill, 1868), 290, "Brown Renwick W., butcher, h 1918 N 20th"; By the same title: (1870), 282, "Brown Renwick W., butcher, h 1341 Cabot"; (1871), 271; (1872), 266; (1873), 261; (1874), 238; (1875), 244; (1876), 242; (1877), 235, "Brown Renwick W., forem, h 1110 E Huntingdon"; (1878), 242; (1882), 242, "Brown Renwick W., foreman, h 903 Sergeant"; (1883), 246, "Brown Renwick W., foreman, h 903 Serrill"; (1884), 244; (1885), 264; (1886), 255, "Brown Renwick W., foreman, h 2404 Serrill"; (1888), 261, "Brown Renwick W., foreman, h 2404 Sergeant"; (1889), 266, "Brown Renwick W., confectioner, 2576 Cedar"; (1890), 273; (1891), 248, "Brown Renwick W., foreman, h2158 E Huntingdon"; (1892), 254; (1893), 255, no listing for Renwick Brown.

[275] Circular giving personal information, Renwick W. Brown, 10 May 1901, invalid's pension file, certificate no. 1027938; Civil War, RG 15, NA-Washington.

[276] 1900 U.S. census, Middlesex Co., N.J., pop. sch., Perth Amboy, ED 48, p. 3, dwell. 45, fam. 56, household of Reincke [sic] W. Brown; NARA T623, roll 984.

County, New Jersey.[277] Renwick's death certificate gave his occupation as "Foreman on Coal Docks."[278] Lydia lived in Elizabeth in her widowhood.[279]

Children of Renwick William/Wilson Brown and Lydia Ann Riley, all born in Philadelphia, were:[280]

32.   i.   ROBERT WILEY BROWN, b. 27 Dec. 1869,[281] bapt. Port Richmond Methodist Episcopal Church, Philadelphia, 26 May 1872;[282] m. MARGARET CHRISTIAN;[283] d. 14 Apr. 1941 and bur. Laurel Memorial Park, Egg Harbor Twp., N.J., age 71.[284]

33.   ii.   EDWARD HENRY "HARRY" BROWN, b. 24 Feb. 1872, bapt. Port Richmond Methodist Episcopal Church, Philadelphia, 26 May 1872;[285] d. probably Atlantic City, Atlantic Co., N.J. aft. 1938 and bef. 1941.[286]

34.   iii.   WILLIAM BROWN, b. 4 April 1876;[287] m. EUPHEMIA WILLIAMS;[288] d. St. Petersburg, Pinellas Co., Fla. 25 Dec. 1943, age 67 yr., 8 mo., and 21 da., bur. there in a vault at Greenwood Cemetery.[289]

35.   iv.   HARRIET "HATTIE" RILEY BROWN, b. 14 Feb. 1878[290]; m. WILLIAM BUCHANAN MCKITTRICK;[291] d. of a fall in Richmond Hill, Queens Co., N.Y. 17 Oct. 1944, age 62.[292]

---

[277] *Elizabeth City Directory for 1907* (Newark, N.J.: Price & Lee Co., 1907), 122, "Brown Renwick W., clerk, h 14 Delaware." By the same title: (1909), 125; (1911), 130; (1913), 146." "Society," *Perth Amboy (N.J.) Evening News*, 2 May 1911, p. 3, col. 2. "Mrs. Renwick W. Brown, of Elizabeth, a former resident here…"

[278] New Jersey death certificate [blank] (1914), Renwick Wilson Brown.

[279] *Elizabeth City Directory for 1915* (Newark, N.J.; Price & Lee Co., 1915), 144, "Brown Lydia Mrs h 14 Delaware"; By the same title: (1917), 158. 1915 New Jersey state census, Union Co., pop. sch., Elizabeth, ED 3, p. 17A, dwell. 257, fam. 346, household of Lydia A. Brown.

[280] Circular giving personal information, Renwick W. Brown; Civil War, RG 15, NA-Washington. 1900 U.S. census, Middlesex Co., N.J., Perth Amboy, ED 48, p. 3, dwell. 45, fam. 56.

[281] City of Philadelphia, Return of Births, Robt. W [Brown]; City Archives, Philadelphia.

[282] Port Richmond Methodist Episcopal Church, (Philadelphia, Pa.), Record of Baptisms, 1863-1887, Robert Wiley Brown, bapt. 26 May 1872; "Pennsylvania and New Jersey, U.S., Church and Town Records, 1669-2013," digital images, *Ancestry.com* (https://www.ancestry.com/).

[283] "Pennsylvania, U.S., Marriages, 1852-1968," database, *Ancestry.com* (https://www.ancestry.com/), Robt W. Brown-Margt Christian, Philadelphia, 7 Jun. 1899. Social Security Administration, "U.S., Social Security Applications and Claims Index, 1936-2007," database, *Ancestry.com* (https://www.ancestry.com/), Robert William Brown, SS no. 150-07-4639, parents, Robert W. Brown and Margaret Christian. 1915 New Jersey state census, Atlantic Co., pop. sch., Atlantic City, p. 8A, dwell. 86, fam. 183, Robert Brown, Jr. in the household of Robt. W. Brown.

[284] *Find A Grave*, database and images (http://findagrave.com), Robert W. Brown, memorial no. 138,488,529.

[285] Port Richmond Methodist Episcopal Church (Philadelphia, Pa.), Record of Baptisms, 1863-1887, Edward Henry Brown, b. 24 Feb. 1872, bapt. 26 May 1872; "Pennsylvania and New Jersey, U.S., Church and Town Records, 1669-2013," digital images, *Ancestry.com* (https://www.ancestry.com/).

[286] *Atlantic City Directory for 1938-39* (Philadelphia: R.L. Polk, 1938), 141, "Brown Edw H (Scott & Brown) r126 Adriatic av"; By the same title: (1941), 90. No listing for Edward. By the same title; (1938), 144, "Brown Robt W (Margt) carpet contr 126 Adriatic av h do"; (1941), 90.

[287] Florida death certificate no. 23007, William Brown (1943); Vital Statistics, Jacksonville. Informant, Euphemia Brown.

[288] Ibid., certificate no. 60-017819, Euphemia Brown (1960). "Mrs. Euphemia Brown [obituary]," *Tampa Bay Times (St. Petersburg, Fla.)*, 10 Apr. 1960, p. 33, col. 1.

[289] Florida death certificate no. 23007, (1943), William Brown. "William Brown…[obituary]," *Tampa Bay Times*, 26 Dec. 1943, p. 2, col. 6.

[290] New York City death certificate no. 7987, Harriet McKittrick (1944); Municipal Archives, New York City.

[291] New Jersey certificate and record of marriage no. 404, William Buchanan McKittrick-Harriet Riley Brown, 29 Jul. 1909; State Archives, Trenton.

[292] New York City death certificate no. 7987 (1944), Harriet McKittrick.

36.   v.   AGNES ROBERTSON BROWN, b. 6 Nov. 1882;[293] m. HARLAN HOUGH COVENTRY;[294] d. Roselle
      Park, Union Co., N.J. 21 Jul. 1944, age 61.[295]

8. MARY REBECCA[2] RILEY a.k.a. MARY CAREY[296] (*William[1] Riley*), was born probably in Lower
Providence Township, Montgomery County, Pennsylvania,[297] in 1847[298] or July 1848[299] and died
of "Organic Heart disease [heart failure]" in Philadelphia, Philadelphia County, Pennsylvania, on
30 October 1901, age 54.[300] Mary was buried there in North Cedar Hill Cemetery.[301] She married
ca. 1865 ROBERT S. GETTY, SR.,[302] son of Irish-born Joseph and Ann (Selfridge) Getty.[303] He
was born in Philadelphia on 7 June 1845 and died there of pneumonia related to endocarditis on
5 February 1911, age 65,[304] and was buried with his wife.[305]

Robert served in the Civil War as a private in a Pennsylvania light artillery battery.[306] He and
Mary probably settled in Philadelphia in 1865 after their marriage.[307] He was a laborer who lived

---

[293] City of Philadelphia, Return of Births…for the month of November 1882, Agnes Robertson Brown, 2 Nov. 1882;
City Archives, Philadelphia.

[294] New Jersey certificate and record of marriage, no. 6-176, Harlan Hough Coventry-Agnes Robertson Brown
(1905); State Archives, Trenton.

[295] "Mrs. Harlan H. [sic] Coventry [obituary]," *Elizabeth Daily Journal*, 22 Jul. 1944, p. 2, col. 4.

[296] The name Mary Carey appeared on her death certificate. Philadelphia, Pa., Return of Death no. 6939, Mary
Getty. Also, that named appeared in records of her children. St. Stephen's Episcopal Church (Philadelphia, Pa.),
baptism, Mary Anne Getty. Pennsylvania death certificate no. 24715, Mary Ann Emmitt (1936); Vital Statistics,
Harrisburg. Ibid., no. 3962, Ellen J. Bowker (1914). Ibid., no. 23730, Emma Haines (1935).

[297] Alderfer to Riley, 26 Sep. 1991.

[298] "Mary Getty," *The Philadelphia Inquirer*, 2 Nov. 1901. Birth calculated from age at death, 54 yrs.

[299] 1900 U.S. census, Philadelphia Co., Pa., Philadelphia, ED 527, p. 7, dwell. 145, fam. 149.

[300] Philadelphia, Pa., return of death no. 6939, Mary Getty.

[301] *Find A Grave*, database and images (http://findagrave.com), Mary Rebecca Getty, memorial no. 223,847,338.

[302] 1900 U.S. census, Philadelphia Co., Pa., Philadelphia, ED 527, p. 7, dwell. 145, fam. 149, Robert Getty. Stated
married 35 years (year of marriage, 1865). However, Robert was recorded as father of a child in 1863. City of
Philadelphia, Return of Births…from the first day of January to the 30th day of March 1867, name of child, [blank]
23 Feb. 1867, parents [sic], Robert Getty, soldier, U.S. Arsenal; City Archives, Philadelphia.

[303] Pennsylvania death certificate no. 3340, Robert Getty (1911); Vital Statistics, Harrisburg. Identity of parents
based on records of sister, Mary A. Shaw. Physician's Certificate of Record of Death in Philadelphia, Mary A. Shaw
[indexed as Shan], no. 18877, b. 1837, d. 23 Jul. 1906; "Pennsylvania, U.S., Death Certificates, 1906-1968," digital
images, *Ancestry.com* (https://www.ancestry.com/). This record names her parents, Joseph Getty and Ann Selfridge,
and gives their places of birth. For evidence that Mary A. Shaw and Robert Getty were siblings, 1850 U.S. census,
Philadelphia County, Pa., pop. sch., Richmond, p. 191A, dwell. 154, fam. 156, Mary Ann Getty, age 14, and Robert
Getty in the household of Joseph and Ann Getty; NARA M432, roll 820. Mary Ann Getty's birth from age.

[304] Pennsylvania death certificate no. 3340, Robert Getty (1911); Vital Statistics, Harrisburg. "Robert Getty [death
notice]," *The Philadelphia Inquirer*, 7 Feb. 1911, p. 7, col. 2.

[305] *Find A Grave*, database and images (http://findagrave.com), Robert Getty, memorial no. 223,902,746.

[306] "U.S., Civil War Pension Index: General Index to Pension Files, 1861-1934," database and digital images,
Ancestry.com (https://www.ancestry.com/); Robert S. Getty (Indpt. Batt. H, Pa. L A. [light artillery]), index card;
imaged from *General Index to Pension Files, 1861-1934*, T288 (Washington, D.C.), roll 173. Invalid application no.
594,142, filed 18 Jan. 1887, certificate no. 370,039. Widow, Mary Getty, application no. 679,213, filed 8 Jul. 1898,
certificate no. 490,757.

[307] 1900 U.S. census, Philadelphia Co., Pa., Philadelphia, ED 527, p. 7, dwell. 145, fam. 149.

in the Frankford neighborhood of Philadelphia.[308] After his wife Mary died, Robert resided in the household of his son-in-law, Samuel J. Bowker.[309]

Children of Robert S. Getty, Sr. and Mary Rebecca Riley, all born in Philadelphia, were:[310]

37.   i.   MARY ANNE GETTY, b. 23 Feb. 1867,[311] bapt. Philadelphia in St. Stephen's Episcopal Church 26 Nov. 1871;[312] m. WILLIAM HENRY EMMITT;[313] d. there 12 Dec. 1936, age 69,[314] bur. there in East Cedar Hill Cemetery.[315]

38.   ii.   SAMUEL GETTY, b. 26 Dec. 1869,[316] bapt. Philadelphia in St. Mark's Episcopal Church 26 Sep. 1870;[317] d. there of "congestion [edema] of the brain," 30 Sep. 1870, age 8 mo., bur. there in Greenwood Cemetery.[318]

---

[308] *Philadelphia City Directory for 1882* (Philadelphia: James Gopsill, 1882), 590, "Getty Robert, laborer, h 4635 Hedge, Fkd"; By the same title: (1883), 608; (1884), 607; (1885), 667, "Getty Robert, laborer, h 3301 Fkd av"; (1886), 642, "Getty Robert, tollkeeper, h Fkd ave Harrowgate la"; (1887), 638, "Getty Robert, gatekeeper, h 3509 Fkd av"; (1888), 665; (1890), 697, "Getty Robert, laborer, h 4539 Hedge Fkd"; (1891), 684; (1892), 704; (1893), 708; (1894), 727; (1895), 682; (1897), 725; (1898), 794; (1899), 828; (1900), 827; (1901), 920; (1902), 887. *Philadelphia City Directory for 1907* (Philadelphia: James Gopsill, 1907), 680, "Getty Robt, h 1661 Haworth Fkd"; (1908), 722; *Philadelphia City Directory for 1909* (Philadelphia: C.E. Howe, 1909), 759, "Getty Robt lab h 1661 Haworth Fkd"; By the same title: (1910), 748.

[309] 1910 U.S. census, Philadelphia Co., Pa., pop. sch., Philadelphia, ED 476, p. 8A, dwell. 188, fam. 188, Robert Getty in the household of Samuel J. Bowker; NARA T624, roll 1397.

[310] 1870 U.S. census, Philadelphia Co., Pa., pop. sch., Philadelphia, p. 214A, dwell. 592, fam. 568, household of Robert Getty; NARA M593, roll 1410. 1880 U.S. census, Philadelphia Co., Pa., pop. sch., Philadelphia, ED 481, p. 286B, dwell. 297, fam. 230, household of Robert Getty; NARA T9, roll 1182.

[311] City of Philadelphia, Return of Births, name of child [blank], 23 Feb. 1867, parents [sic], Robert Getty.

[312] St. Stephen's Episcopal Church (Philadelphia, Pa.), Baptisms, p. 52, no. 62, Mary Anne Getty; "Pennsylvania and New Jersey, U.S., Church and Town Records, 1669-2013," database and digital images, *Ancestry.com* (https://www.ancestry.com/).

[313] St. Mark's Episcopal Church (Philadelphia, Pa.), Marriages 1884-85, no. 649, William Emmitt-Mary Ann Getty, 7 Feb. 1885; "Pennsylvania and New Jersey, U.S., Church and Town Records, 1669-2013," database and digital images, *Ancestry.com* (https://www.ancestry.com/). City of Philadelphia, Return of Marriages, 1 Jan. to 1 Apr. 1885, William Emmitt-Mary Ann Getty, 7 Feb. 1885; City Archives, Philadelphia.

[314] Pennsylvania death certificate no. 24715, Mary Ann Emmitt (1936); Vital Statistics, Harrisburg. "Mary A. Emmitt [death notice]," *The Philadelphia Inquirer*, 15 Dec. 1936, p. 35, col. 2.

[315] *Find A Grave*, database and images (http://findagrave.com), Mary Ann Emmitt, memorial no. 183,355,048.

[316] City of Philadelphia, Register of Births, 1869, Samuel Getty, 26 Dec. 1869; City Archives, Philadelphia.

[317] St Mark's Episcopal Church (Philadelphia, Pa.), Church Records, 1847–1945, Baptisms, p. 171, Samuel Getty, 26 Sep. 1870; "Pennsylvania and New Jersey, U.S., Church and Town Records, 1669-2013," database, *Ancestry.com* (https://www.ancestry.com/).

[318] City of Philadelphia, Return of Deaths, Samuel Getty; City Archives, Philadelphia.

39.   iii.   ELLEN "NELLIE" JANE GETTY b. 8 Sep. 1871,[319] bapt. Philadelphia in St. Stephen's Episcopal Church 26 Nov. 1871;[320] m. SAMUEL JACKSON BOWKER;[321] d. of fatty degeneration of the heart [heart failure] there 21 Mar. 1914, age 42,[322] bur. there Cedar Hill Cemetery.[323]

40.   iv.   EMMA BRADLEY GETTY, b. 2 Feb. 1874;[324] m. BENJAMIN AYERS HAINES;[325] d. of cirrhosis of the liver in Philadelphia 13 Dec. 1935.[326]

41.   v.   ROBERT H. GETTY, JR. [sic], b. 1876[327] or 1877;[328] d. of phthisis (tuberculosis) in Philadelphia 8 Dec. 1898,[329] age 21, and bur. there in North Cedar Hill Cemetery.[330]

Generation Three

9. MARK M.[3] RILEY (*Samuel Warner*[2], *William*[1] *Riley*), was born probably in Upper Providence Township, Montgomery County, Pennsylvania,[331] in February 1859[332] and was baptized as an adult at Trinity Christian Church, Collegeville, Montgomery County, Pennsylvania, on 13 June 1882.[333] Mark died of "cholera morbus [severe gastroenteritis] followed by heart failure"[334] in South Bethlehem (later part of Bethlehem),[335] Northampton County, Pennsylvania, 7 August 1906, age ca. 47,[336] and was buried in Saint Michael's Cemetery, Bethlehem.[337] He married in

---

[319] Ibid., Return of Births from [blank] to the [blank], name of child [blank], 9 Sep. 1871, parents Robert & Mary Getty.

[320] St. Stephen's Episcopal Church (Philadelphia, Pa.), Baptisms, p. 53, no. 63, Ellen Jane Getty; "Pennsylvania and New Jersey, U.S., Church and Town Records, 1669-2013," digital images, *Ancestry.com* (https://www.ancestry.com/).

[321] "Ellen J. Bowker [death notice]," *The Philadelphia Inquirer*, 24 Mar. 1914, p. 16, col. 5, "...wife of Samuel J. Bowker...." 1900 U.S. census, Philadelphia Co., Pa., pop. sch., Philadelphia, ED 527, p. 8, dwell. 162, fam. 166, Ellen J. Bowker, wife, in the household of Samuel J. Bowker; NARA T623, roll 1465. Married eleven years. Register of Wills, City and County of Philadelphia, 23 May 2022, letter, reporting negative marriage-record search for Samuel Bowker-Ellen Getty, 1889.

[322] Pennsylvania death certificate no. 3962, Ellen J. Bowker (1914). *The Philadelphia Inquirer*, 24 Mar. 1914.

[323] *Find A Grave*, database and images (http://findagrave.com), Ellen Jane Bowker, memorial no. 186,920,018.

[324] St. Stephen's Episcopal Church (Philadelphia, Pa.), Church Records 1823–1941, Baptisms, no. 150, p. 70, Emma B. Getty, b. 2 Feb. 1874, bapt. 31 May 1874; "Pennsylvania and New Jersey, U.S., Church and Town Records, 1669-2013," digital images, *Ancestry.com* (https://www.ancestry.com/).

[325] "Pennsylvania, Philadelphia Marriage Indexes, 1885-1951," database and digital images, *FamilySearch.org* (https://www.familysearch.org/), Benjamin Ayres Haines-Getty [sic], license no. 60540, m. 1893.

[326] Pennsylvania death certificate no. 23730, Emma Haines (1935); Vital Statistics, Harrisburg.

[327] *Find A Grave*, database and images (http://findagrave.com), Robert Getty, Jr., memorial no. 223,690,324.

[328] City of Philadelphia, Return of Deaths, Robert Getty, Jr., 8 Dec. 1898; *FamilySearch.org* (https://www.familysearch.org/). Philadelphia, Pa., City Archives, 1 Jun. 2022, email reporting negative birth-record search for Robert S. or H. Getty, Jun. – Aug. 1877.

[329] "Robert H. Getty [death notice]," *The Philadelphia Inquirer,* 12 Dec. 1896, p. 15, col. 1. Ibid., "Robert H. Getty [In Memoriam]," 8 Dec. 1898, p. 12, col. 2.

[330] *Find A Grave*, Robert Getty, Jr., memorial no. 223,690,324.

[331] 1860 U.S. census, Montgomery Co., Pa., Upper Providence, p. 571, dwell. 939, fam. 1044.

[332] 1900 U.S. census, Northampton Co., Pa., Lower Saucon Twp., ED 117, p. 25, dwell. 485, fam. 509.

[333] Trinity Christian Church (Collegeville, Pa.), Church Records, 1863-1897, Baptisms, p. 187, Mark M. Riley, 13 Jun. 1882; "Pennsylvania and New Jersey, U.S., Church and Town Records, 1669-2013," digital images, *Ancestry.com* (https://www.ancestry.com/).

[334] Pennsylvania death certificate no. 78795, Mark Rieley [sic] (1906); Vital Statistics, Harrisburg, informant, Thos. J. McGiven (?). Birthplace incorrectly given as Ireland.

[335] *Wikipedia* (https://en.wikipedia.org/), "Bethlehem, Pennsylvania," rev. 03:41, 20 Sep. 2021.

[336] "Death of Mark Riley," *The Allentown Leader*, 8 Aug. 1906. "A brother, Henry, of Atlantic City also survives."

[337] *Find A Grave*, Mark Riley, memorial no. 131,643,396.

Philadelphia, Philadelphia County, Pennsylvania,[338] ca. 1882[339] CATHERINE "KATE" SIMON, daughter of Abraham/Urban and Margaret/Magdalena (–?–) Simon/Simons.[340] She was born in Philadelphia June 1862[341] and died of coronary sclerosis [atherosclerosis] and diabetes mellitus in Bethlehem on 15 October 1947[342] and was buried with her husband.[343]

Mark apparently converted to Roman Catholicism, based on his burial in a Catholic cemetery.[344] The family home in Bethlehem was occupied from at least 1916 until Catherine's death in 1947, but there was no payment of real estate taxes.[345] At the time of his death, Mark was the "chief clerk in the rolling department of the [Bethlehem] steel mill."[346] Widowed at age 44,[347] Catherine probably depended on support from her adult children, since she lived with them for twenty-four years.[348] In 1920, daughters Estella, Mary, and Henrietta worked in area textile mills,[349] which employed girls not yet eighteen in the early twentieth century.[350]

---

[338] "Death of Mark Riley," *The Allentown Leader*, 8 Aug. 1906.

[339] "Mrs. Catharine Riley," *The Morning Call*, 16 Oct. 1947. Philadelphia, Pa., City Archives, 10 Apr. 2022, email reporting negative marriage-record search for Mark M. Riley & Catherine Simon, Jan. to Dec. 1881-1883.

[340] 1870 U.S. census, Philadelphia Co., Pa., pop. sch., Philadelphia, p. 196B, dwell. 190, fam. 240, Kate Simon in the household of Abraham Simon; NARA M593, roll 1390. Register of Wills, City and County of Philadelphia, probate case file no. 300, Margaret Simon, will, 25 Mar. 1880; Probate Court, Philadelphia. Named husband Urban Simon and children Kate and John Simon.

[341] 1870 U.S. census, Philadelphia Co., Pa., Philadelphia, p. 196B, dwell. 190, fam. 240.

[342] Pennsylvania death certificate no. 90554, Catherine Riley (1947); Vital Statistics. Harrisburg. "Mrs. Catharine Riley," *The Morning Call*, 16 Oct. 1947.

[343] *Find A Grave*, database and images (http://findagrave.com), Catherine Riley, memorial no. 148,160,252.

[344] *Find A Grave*, Mark Riley, memorial no. 131,643,396.

[345] Northampton Co., Pa., Appraisement Docket Book 6: 234, Catherine Riley, filed 15 Jul. 1949; Register of Wills, Easton. An attempt to collect back taxes on the property after Catherine's death was abandoned.

[346] "Death of Mark Riley," *The Allentown Leader*, 8 Aug. 1906. Bethlehem Steel was a major steel manufacturer. *Wikipedia* (https://en.wikipedia.org/), "Bethlehem, Pennsylvania," rev. 03:41, 20 Sep. 2021.

[347] 1910 U.S. census, Northampton Co., Pa., pop. sch., South Bethlehem, ED 117, p. 20A, dwell. 412, fam. 423; NARA T624, roll 1382.

[348] *Bethlehem, Pa. City Directory for 1923* (n. p.: Piedmont Directory Co., 1923), 521, "Riley Catharine C, wid Mark, h 218 Summit"; By the same title: (1927), 649; (1929), 717. *Bethlehem City Directory for 1937-38* (Philadelphia: R. L. Polk & Co., 1937), 464, "Riley Cath C (wid Martin [sic]) h218 Summit"; By the same title: (1939), 507; (1941), 482; (1943), 511; (1945), 549; (1947), 609. By the same title: (1923), 521, "Riley Henrietta Miss, emp Sauquoit Silk Mill, h 218 Summit"; (1927), 649; (1929), 717. *Bethlehem City Directory for 1937-38* (Philadelphia: R. L. Polk & Co., 1937), 464, "Riley Henrietta silkwkr Bethlehem Silk Co r218 Summit"; By the same title: (1939), 507; (1941), 483, "Riley Henrietta cooper Bethlehem Silk Co r 218 Summit"; (1943), 511; (1945), 549; (1947), 609. By the same title: (1923), 521, "Riley Mary Miss, h 218 Summit"; (1927), 649; (1929), 717; *Bethlehem City Directory for 1937-38* (Philadelphia: R. L. Polk & Co., 1937), 464, "Riley Mary E r218 Summit"; By the same title: (1939), 507; (1941), 483; (1943), 512; (1945), 550; (1947), 609.
By the same title: (1923), 521, "Riley Robt F, emp Lehigh University, h 218 Summit"; (1927), 649; (1929), 717,"Riley Robt F (Mary E), clk Lehigh Univ Library, h 218 Summit"; *Bethlehem City Directory for 1937-38* (Philadelphia: R. L. Polk & Co., 1937), 464, "Riley Robert F hlpr r218 Summit"; By the same title: (1939), 507, "Riley Robert F (Mary) order clk LU Library r218 Summit"; (1941), 483, "Riley Robt F (Mary E) handymn r 218 Summit"; (1943), 512; (1945), 550, "Riley Robt F (Mary E) library asst LU r 218 Summit"; (1947), 609, "Riley Robt F (Mary E) clk LU r 218 Summit." By the same title: (1923), 521, "Riley Stella A Miss, winder Sauquoit Silk Mill, h 218 Summit"; (1927), 650; (1929), 717.

[349] 1920 U.S. census, Northampton Co., Pa., pop. sch., Bethlehem, ED 78, p. 8A, dwell. 144, fam. 148, Stella, Loretta, and Mary Reely [sic] in the household of Catheryn Reely; NARA T625, roll 1608.

[350] Bonnie Stepenoff, "Child Labor in Pennsylvania Silk Mills: Protest and Change, 1900-1910," *Pennsylvania History* 59 (Apr. 1992): 101-21.

Children of Mark M. Riley and Catherine Simon, child i. born in Philadelphia[351] and children ii. to v. born in Bethlehem,[352] were (birth order of children vi. and vii. uncertain):[353]

42.   i.   WILLIAM RILEY, b. 19 Sep. 1883; d. in Rittersville Asylum[354] of epilepsy, which he had since childhood, in Hanover Twp., Lehigh Co., Pa., 27 Feb. 1913, age 29 yrs., 5 mo., and 8 da.[355]

43.   ii.   ESTELLA/STELLA A. RILEY, b. 16 May 1887; m. JAMES F. MCGINLEY;[356] d. of complications of bone graft surgery in Bethlehem 2 Feb. 1931, age 43,[357] and bur. there in Saint Michael's Cemetery.[358]

44.   iii.   MARY/MAMIE RILEY, b. 6 Sep. 1890; d. Bethlehem 11 Apr. 1974 or 15 Apr. 1974, age 83,[359] and bur. there in Holy Saviour Cemetery.[360]

45.   iv.   HENRIETTA/LORETTA RILEY, b. 16 Sep. 1892; d. Fountain Hill, Lehigh Co., Pa. 29 Aug. 1987, age 94,[361] and bur. in Bethlehem in Holy Saviour Cemetery.[362]

46.   v.   ROBERT FRANCIS RILEY, b. 2 April 1899; m. MARY E. MICHAEL;[363] d. carcinoma of the stomach Bethlehem 13 Mar. 1959, age 60,[364] and bur. there in Holy Saviour Cemetery.[365]

47.   vi.   FIRST UNNAMED RILEY CHILD.[366]

48.   vii.   SECOND UNNAMED RILEY CHILD.[367]

Foster child and paternal great-niece of Catherine (Simon) Riley and biological daughter of James F. McGettigan and Margaret Simon[368] was:

---

[351] *Philadelphia City Directory for 1884* (Philadelphia: James Gopsill, 1884), 1452, "Riley Mark, carpenter, h 1623 Carver"; By the same title: (1886), 1347, "Riley Mark, laborer, h r 35 Mill. Gtn. [Germantown]."

[352] "Mrs. Catharine Riley [obituary]," *The Morning Call*, 16 Oct. 1947.

[353] 1910 U.S. census, Northampton Co., Pa., South Bethlehem, ED 117, p. 20A, dwell. 412, fam. 423.

[354] "Allentown State Hospital," *Lehigh Valley History*, 10 Jul. 2010 (http://lehighvalleyhistory.blogspot.com/2010/07/allentown-state-hospital.html). Originally called the Pennsylvania Homeopathic Hospital for the Insane.

[355] Pennsylvania death certificate no. 11694, William Reilley [sic] (1913); Vital Statistics, Harrisburg. Birth calculated from age at death.

[356] "Death Calls Popular Bethlehem Resident [obituary of Estella A. McGinley]," *The Morning Call*, 3 Feb. 1931, p. 18, col. 2.

[357] Pennsylvania death certificate no. 55, Estella McGinley (1931); Vital Statistics, Harrisburg.

[358] *Find A Grave*, database and images (http://findagrave.com), Estelle A. McGinley, memorial no. 49,822,029.

[359] "Mary Riley [death notice]," *The Morning Call*, 14 Apr. 1974, p. 66, col. 5. Social Security Administration, "U.S., Social Security Death Index, 1935-2014," database, *FamilySearch.org* (https://www.familysearch.org/), Mary Riley, SS no. 180-40-0126, d. 15 Apr. 1974.

[360] *Find A Grave*, database and images (http://findagrave.com), Mary Riley, memorial no. 174,632,655.

[361] "Henrietta Riley [death notice]," *The Morning Call*, 30 Aug. 1987, p. 19, col. 4.

[362] *Find A Grave*, database and images (http://findagrave.com), Henrietta Riley, memorial no. 174,632,637.

[363] "Robert F. Riley [death notice]," *The Morning Call*, 14 Mar. 1959, p. 19, col. 3.

[364] Pennsylvania death certificate no. 71, Robert Frances Riley (1959); Vital Statistics, Harrisburg.

[365] *Find A Grave*, database and images (http://findagrave.com), Robert F. Riley, memorial no. 174,632,664.

[366] 1910 U.S. census, Northampton Co., Pa., South Bethlehem, ED 117, p. 20A, dwell. 412, fam. 423. Catherine gave birth to seven children, five of whom were living.

[367] Ibid.

[368] "Wedding Rites in Bethlehem," *The Morning Call*, 27 Oct. 1947, p. 6, col. 5, Solsky-McGettigan. Bride was the "...foster daughter of the late Mrs. Catherine Riley." Catherine (Simon) Riley was a sister of John Simon. 1870 U.S. census, Philadelphia Co., Pa., Philadelphia, p. 196B, dwell. 190, fam. 240. John B. Simon had a daughter, Margaret (Simon) McGettigan. Pennsylvania death certificate no. 84357, Mrs. Margaret McGattigan (1921); Vital Statistics, Harrisburg. Margaret (Simon) McGattigan was the mother of Dorothy McGattigan. 1920 U.S. census, Northampton Co., Pa., pop. sch., Bethlehem, ED 87, p. 1B, dwell. 12, fam. 15, Dorothy McGettigan [sic] and Margaret

49. viii. DOROTHY MARIE MCGETTIGAN, b. Bethlehem 23 Jun. 1919;[369] m. SERGIE A. SOLSKY;[370] d. there 11 May 1998.[371]

12. JACOB H.[3] RILEY (*Samuel Warner*[2], *William*[1] *Riley*), was born in Philadelphia, Philadelphia County, Pennsylvania,[372] on 5 February 1864[373] and died of "dilation heart [heart failure]" at the home of his daughter, Olive Urban,[374] in Zanesville, Muskingum County, Ohio, on 1 August 1931, age 67 years, 5 months, and 7 days.[375] Jacob was buried in Zanesville in Greenwood Cemetery.[376] He married in Belmont County, Ohio, on 3 March 1892 ADDA/ADA MAY SMITH,[377] daughter of George B. and Lydia (Bishop) Smith.[378] She was born in Barnesville, Belmont County, Ohio, on 6 March 1869 and died of lobar pneumonia in Zanesville on 4 December 1929, age 61 years, 8 months, and 29 days.[379] Adda was buried with her husband.[380]

Jacob left home at an early age, went west, and joined the Army.[381] In the early twentieth century, he was employed as a carpenter for the Baltimore & Ohio (B & O) Railroad in Zanesville,[382] and by 1920 was working as a foreman at a B & O shop in Keyser, Mineral

---

McGettigan in the household of James McGettigan; NARA T625, roll 1608. For Margaret's birth surname, Pennsylvania death certificate no. 84357, Mrs. Margaret McGettigan (1921); Vital Statistics, Harrisburg.

[369] Social Security Administration, "U.S., Social Security Death Index, 1935-2014," database, *FamilySearch.org* (https://www.familysearch.org/), Dorothy M. Solsky, SS no. 161-16-0585. Birth date 23 Jun. 1919. *Find A Grave*, database and images (http://findagrave.com), Dorothy Solsky, memorial no. 51,045,718.

[370] "Wedding Rites in Bethlehem," *The Morning Call*, 27 Oct. 1947.

[371] "Funeral notices [Dorothy M. Solsky]," *The Morning Call*, 12 May 1998, p. 27, col. 7.

[372] "U.S., Army, Register of Enlistments, 1798-1914," database, *Ancestry.com* (https://www.ancestry.com/); Jacob H. Riley, enlistments for 1885-1890, L-Z, p. 10, line 35.

[373] Ohio death certificate no. 50497 (1931), Jacob H. Riley.

[374] "Jacob H. Riley Dies Suddenly at Home Sunday," *The Times-Recorder*, 3 Aug. 1931.

[375] Ohio death certificate no. 50497 (1931), Jacob H. Riley. Informant, Mrs. Olive Urban.

[376] *Find A Grave*, database and images (http://findagrave.com), Jacob H. Riley, memorial no. 7,152,270. Indexed as Ada May Smith Riley.

[377] Belmont Co., Ohio, marriage Riley-Smith. "Licensed to Marry," *Belmont (Ohio) Chronicle*, 10 Mar. 1892.

[378] Ohio death certificate no. 79627, Ada May Riley (1929); Vital Statistics, Columbus. Informant J. H. Riley. 1870 U.S. census, Belmont Co., Ohio, pop. sch., Kirkwood, p. 71A, dwell. 95, fam. 100, Adda Smith in the household of George B. Smith; NARA M593, roll 1173.

[379] Ohio death certificate no. 79627 (1929), Ada May Riley.

[380] *Find A Grave*, database and images (http://findagrave.com), Ada May Smith Riley, memorial no. 7,152,270.

[381] 1870 U.S. census (2nd enumeration), Philadelphia Co., Pa., pop. sch., Philadelphia, p. 271B, line 33, dwell. 2007, Jacob H. Riley, age 5, in the household of Saml. W. Riley; NARA M593, roll 1434. Jacob not found in the 1880 enumeration. *Ancestry.com*=Search, Search for First and Middle Names=Jacob (exact, sounds like, and similar), Last Name=Riley (exact, sounds like, and similar), Birth Year=1865 ± 5, Location=[blank], Census & Voter Lists=1880s. In 1880, his father Samuel lived separately from other family members. 1880 U.S. census, Philadelphia Co., Pa., Philadelphia, ED 222, p. 319B, dwell. 146, fam. 163. Jacob was probably the twenty-year-old Pennsylvania-born farm laborer in Kansas in 1885. 1885 Kansas state census, Brown Co., pop. sch., Mission Twp., p. 151, dwell. [blank], line 2, Jacob Riley. *REGISTER of the Hospital Corps, U.S. Army, appointed under Act of Congress approved March 1, 1887*, p. 584, line 1; "U.S., Army, Register of Enlistments, 1798-1914," digital images, *Ancestry.com* (https://www.ancestry.com/). U.S. census, Logan Co., Okla. Terr., pop. sch., Guthrie, ED [blank], p. 226, line 42, Jacob H. Riley, Pvt., Co. B, 13th Inf.; NARA [blank], roll [blank], image 226 of 231.

[382] *Zanesville City Directory for 1900* (Akron, Ohio: Burch Directory Co., 1900), 340, "Riley Jacob H [Ada M] wks B & O Shops, res 35 Railroad." By the same title: (1901-02), 343; (1903-04), 385; (1905-06), 495; (1907-08), 402; (1910), 404; (1912), 409; (1914), 443.

County, West Virginia.[383] After his wife died, he returned to Zanesville and lived with his daughter Olive.[384] Jacob's estate, which was settled in 1932, consisted of a life insurance policy and back wages totaling $461; these covered his debts, and there were no distributions.[385]

Children of Jacob H. Riley and Adda/Ada M. Smith were:[386]

50. i. OLIVE SMITH RILEY, b. Barnesville, Belmont Co., Ohio, 17 July 1893;[387] m. JOHN H. URBAN;[388] d. of cardiopulmonary failure in Zanesville on 20 Nov. 1986, age 93, bur. there in Memorial Park Cemetery.[389]
51. ii. ROBERT ROY RILEY, b. Barnesville, Belmont Co., Ohio, 7 Mar. 1896;[390] m. (1) HARRIET "HATTIE" ANN (SEWELL) BROOKS[391] and (2) SARAH C. (RYAN) HOLMES;[392] d. of cancer of the prostate in Pontiac, Oakland Co., Mich. 17 Apr. 1976, age 80., and bur. Christian Memorial Cemetery, Avon Twp., Mich.[393]
52. iii. WALTER BENTON RILEY, b., Zanesville 22 Sep. 1899;[394] m. MINNIE LEE (HARRIS) BOYCE;[395] d. Keyser ca. 29 Oct. 1955, age 56.[396]

---

[383] 1920 U.S. census, Mineral Co., W.Va., pop. sch., New Creek, ED 84, p. 9A, dwell. 180, fam. 202; NARA T624, roll 1964. "Jacob H. Riley," *The Times Recorder,* 3 Aug. 1931.

[384] "United States Census, 1930," database and images, *FamilySearch.org* (https://familysearch.org) > Ohio Muskingum > Zanesville > ED 42 > image 4 of 56; citing NARA T626. Jacob H. Riley, son-in-law, in the household of John H. Urban.

[385] Muskingum County, Ohio, probate case file no. 33756, Jacob H. Riley (1931), will, 1 Jul. 1931; Probate Court, Zanesville. Heirs: Olive Urban, Zanesville, Ohio; Walter B. Riley, Keyser, W. Va.; and Robert Riley, Pontiac, Mich.

[386] Ibid.

[387] *Find A Grave.com*, database and images (https://www.findagrave.com/), Olive Urban, memorial no. 194,441,163.

[388] "Ohio, County Marriages, 1789-2016," digital images, *FamilySearch.org* (https://www.familysearch.org/); Urban-Riley, p. 324, no. 647, 24 Dec. 1913.

[389] Ohio death certificate no. 087419, Mrs. Olive S. Urban, 20 Nov. 1986; Vital Statistics, Columbus. *Find A Grave.com*, Olive Urban, memorial no. 194,441,163.

[390] Record of Births, Probate Court, Muskingum County, Ohio, 1896, p. 200, line 53, Robert Roy Riley; "Ohio, U.S., Births and Christenings Index, 1774-1973," digital images, *FamilySearch.org* (https://www.familysearch.org/).

[391] County of Wayne, Return of Marriages for the 1st Quarter Ending [blank] A. D. 1925, p. 32, no. 285026, Riley-Brooks, 7 Jan. 1925; "Michigan, U.S., Marriage Records, 1867-1952," digital images, *Ancestry.com* (https://www.ancestry.com/).

[392] Wood County Marriage Records, 1941-1942, p. 155, no. 310, Riley-Holmes, 7 Mar. 1941; "Ohio, County Marriages, 1789-2016," digital images, *FamilySearch.org* (https://www.familysearch.org/).

[393] Michigan death certificate no. 23967, Robert Roy Riley (1976); Vital Records and Health Statistics, Lansing.

[394] Record of Births, Probate Court, Muskingum County, Ohio, 1899, p. 204, line 29, Walter Reilly [sic]; "Ohio, U.S., Births and Christenings Index, 1774-1973," digital images, *FamilySearch.org* (https://www.familysearch.org/).

[395] Draft registration of son. "U.S., World War II Draft Cards Young Men, 1940-1947," digital images, *Ancestry.com* (https://www.ancestry.com/), Arthur Arnold Boyce. Contact person Mrs. Minnie Lee Riley, mother, Keyser, W.Va. For relationships, 1940 U.S. census, rural, Allegheny Co., Md., ED 1-40, p. 4B, dwell. 73, Walter B. Riley, husband, Arthur A. Boyce, son, in the household of Minnie Riley; NARA T726, roll m-t0627-01499. For Minnie's previous marriage, "U.S., World War I Draft Registration Cards, 1917–1918," digital images, *Ancestry.com* (https://www.ancestry.com/), Arthur Dorak Boyce, wife, Minnie Lee Boyce, Keyser, W.Va. For Minnie's birth surname, "West Virginia, U.S., Births Index, 1804-1938," database, *Ancestry.com* (https://www.ancestry.com/); Minnie L. Harris, 14 Mar. 1895, Grant, W. Va. "Deaths [obituary, Walter B. Riley]," *Cumberland (Md.) News,* 29 Oct. 1955, p. 13, col. 4. Negative search for death-entry, *West Virginia Archives and History* (https://archive.wvculture.org/) > Vital Research Records Search Selection…, Last Name=Riley, Year of Death=1955 (exact).

[396] "Deaths," *Cumberland News,* 29 Oct. 1955. Negative search for death-entry, *West Virginia Archives and History*, Walter B. Riley.

15. EMMA[3] RILEY (*Samuel Warner*[2], *William*[1] *Riley*), was born in Pennsylvania in June 1879[397] or June 1880[398] and died possibly in Atlantic City, Atlantic County, New Jersey, after 1941.[399] She married at St. Andrew's Lutheran Church, Atlantic City, on 15 October 1902 CHARLES WILLIAM ALBRECHT,[400] son of German-born[401] Bernhardt/Bernard Friedrich/Frederick and Wilhelmina/Mina C. (Weidenmann) Albrecht.[402] He was born in Philadelphia, Philadelphia County, Pennsylvania, on 10 June 1876[403] and died after 1930 and before 1935.[404]

Emma was enumerated in the household of her stepmother's relatives in Phillipsburg, Warren County, New Jersey, in 1895.[405] Enumerated as a twenty-year old hairdresser in 1900, she lived with her father and stepmother in Atlantic City.[406] In 1905, Emma and Charles lived near members of his family in Atlantic City.[407] Emma was prolific, giving birth to five sons in six years (see below). Charles was employed as a clerk and later as a carpenter in Pleasantville, Atlantic County, New Jersey.[408] In her widowhood, Emma resided in Pleasantville with her sons Harry and Robert.[409]

Children of Charles William Albrecht and Emma Riley, all born in Atlantic City, were:[410]

---

[397] 1900 U.S. census, Atlantic Co., N.J., Atlantic City, ED 10, p. 2, dwell. 20, fam. 20. Emma Riley (1879-1947), Family Tree ID LVMJ-NTN, "Family Tree," database, *FamilySearch.org* (https://www.familysearch.org/tree/person/details/ LVMJ-NTN), birthdate 6 Jun. 1879.

[398] 1905 New Jersey state census, Atlantic Co., Atlantic City, p. 6B, dwell. 43, fam. 45, Emma Albrecht.

[399] "Mrs. Laura E. Riley," *Tampa Bay Times*, 8 Apr. 1941. Survivors included a "daughter," Mrs. Emma Albrecht.

[400] New Jersey marriage certificate no. 12159 (1902), Albrecht-Riley.

[401] "Württemberg, Germany Emigration Index," database, *Ancestry.com* (https://www.ancestry.com/), Bernhardt Albrecht, b. 19 Jun. 1836, Heilbronn, Kingdom of Württemberg (now Baden-Württemberg, Germany), application date Sep. 1854, destination, North America.

[402] 1870 U.S. census, Philadelphia Co., Pa., pop. sch., Philadelphia, p. 191B, dwell. 1047, fam. 1256, household of Bernard Albrecht; NARA M593, roll 1391. 1880 U.S. census, Atlantic Co., N.J., pop. sch., ED 1, p. 48D, dwell. 33, fam. 907, Charles Albricht [sic] in the household of Bernard Albricht: NARA T9, roll 770. For mother's birth surname, New Jersey marriage certificate no. 12159 (1902), Albrecht-Riley.

[403] "Pennsylvania, Philadelphia City Births, 1860-1906," database with images, *FamilySearch.org* (https://www.familysearch.org/), Chas Albrecht. New Jersey marriage certificate no. 12159 (1902), Albrecht-Riley.

[404] 1930 U.S. census, Atlantic Co., N.J., pop. sch., Pleasantville, ED 63, p. 10A, dwell. 242, fam. 214, household of Charles Albrecht; NARA T626, roll 1310. *Atlantic City...Directory for 1935* (Atlantic City, N.J.: Atlantic Directories, 1935), 275, "Albrecht Emma (wid Chas W) r211 Woodland Av [Pleasantville]."

[405] 1895 New Jersey state census, Warren Co., pop. sch., Phillipsburg, p. 23, dwell. 164, fam. 175, Emma Riley, Elizabeth Cooke [sic] in the household of William Cooke. For relationships, Elizabeth Gilinger (17 Sep. 1825-5 Apr. 1919), Family Tree ID L786-X53, "Family Tree," database, *FamilySearch.org* (https://www.familysearch.org/tree/person/details/L786-X53).

[406] 1900 U.S. census, Atlantic Co., N.J., Atlantic City, ED 10, p. 2, dwell. 20, fam. 20.

[407] 1905 New Jersey state census, Atlantic Co., pop. sch., Atlantic City, p. 6B, dwell. 43, fam. 45; ibid., p. 6B, dwell. 41, fam. 43, Wilhelmina Albrecht, Frederick Albrecht, Minnie Albrecht, and Maud Albrecht. For sibling relationships, 1880 U.S. census, Atlantic Co., N.J., Atlantic City, ED 1, p. 48D, dwell. [blank], fam., 907, household of Bernard Albricht [sic].

[408] *Atlantic City Directory for 1904* (Philadelphia: James Gopsill, 1904) 27, "Albrecht Charles W. (Emma), clerk, h 1 Albrecht's pl." 1930 U.S. census, Atlantic Co., N.J., pop. sch., Pleasantville, ED 63, p. 10A, dwell. 242, fam. 214, household of Charles Albrecht; NARA T626, roll 1310.

[409] 1940 U.S. census, Atlantic Co., N.J., pop. sch., Pleasantville, ED 1-125, p. 7B, dwell. 32, household of Emma Albrecht; NARA T627, roll m-t0627-02303.

[410] 1910 U.S. census, Atlantic Co., N.J., pop. sch., Atlantic City, ED 16, p. 14B, dwell. 233, fam. 249, household of Charles Albrecht; NARA T624, roll 867. 1920 U.S. census, Atlantic Co., N.J., pop. sch., Atlantic City, ED 54, p. 7A, dwell. 167, fam. 168, household of Charles W. Albrecht; NARA T625, roll 1016.

53.   i.   BERNHARDT "BERNIE" WILLIAM ALBRECHT, b. 23 July 1903;[411] m. EDITH/EDYTHE SAMPSON;[412] d. Somers Point, Atlantic Co., N.J. 9 Dec. 1977 and bur. Atlantic City Cemetery, Pleasantville, N.J.[413]

54.   ii.   CHARLES WALTER ALBRECHT, b. 20 Sep. 1904;[414] m. MARY BARBARA ALICE STUCK;[415] d. probably Carrolton, Greene Co., Ill.,[416] Apr. 1974, age 69,[417] and bur. Rose Lawn Memorial Gardens, Bethalto, Madison Co., Ill.[418]

55.   iii.   GEORGE FRANCIS ALBRECHT, b. 30 Mar. 1906;[419] m. MABEL CATHERINE ROHM;[420] d. Atlantic City 7 May 1967, age 61, and bur. Blain Cemetery, Blain, Perry Co., Pa.[421]

56.   iv.   HARRY NEWCOMET ALBRECHT, b. 28 Apr. 1907;[422] m. BERTHA CONNELLY;[423] d. Atlantic City 2 Feb. 1976, age 69, bur. Atlantic City Cemetery, Pleasantville, N.J.[424]

57.   v.   FREDRICK ALFRED ALBRECHT, b. 19 May 1908;[425] m. EVELYN MARIE OLSEN;[426] d. Otego, Otsego Co., N.Y., 3 Mar. 1995, age 86,[427] and bur. Laurel Memorial Park and Crematory, Egg Harbor Twp., Atlantic Co., N.J.[428]

[411] "U.S., World War II Draft Cards Young Men, 1940-1947," digital images, *Ancestry.com* (https://www.ancestry.com/), Bernhardt William Albrecht.

[412] For wife's birth surname, 1940 U.S. census, Atlantic Co., N.J., pop. sch., Pleasantville, ED 1-129, p. 4A, dwell. 67, Bernhardt Albrecht, son-in-law, in the household of Ella G. Sampson; NARA T627, roll m-t0627-02303.

[413] New Jersey death certificate no. 57736, Bernhardt W. Albrecht (1977); Vital Statistics and Registrar, Trenton. *Find A Grave*, database and images (http://findagrave.com), Bernhardt Albrecht, memorial no. 178,247,307.

[414] "U.S., World War II Draft Cards Young Men, 1940-1947," digital images, *Ancestry.com* (https://www.ancestry.com/), Charles Walter Albrecht.

[415] "Mary Barbara Alice (Stuck) Albrecht…," *St. Louis Post-Dispatch*, 21 Mar. 2002.

[416] "Robert S. Albrecht [funeral announcement]," *Arizona Republic (Phoenix, Ariz.)*, 8 Dec. 1972, p. 61, col. 2.

[417] Social Security Administration, "U.S., Social Security Death Index, 1935-2014," database, *Ancestry.com* (https://search.ancestry.com/), Charles Albrecht, SS no. 148-10-7811.

[418] *Find A Grave*, database and images (http://findagrave.com), Charles W. Albrecht, memorial no. 87,291,470.

[419] "U.S., World War II Draft Cards Young Men, 1940-1947," digital images, *Ancestry.com* (https://www.ancestry.com/), George Francis Albrecht.

[420] "Mable Rohm Albrecht [obituary]," *The Perry County Times (New Bloomfield, Pa.)*, 29 July 1965, p. 12, col. 4.

[421] New Jersey death certificate no. 21118, George F. Albrecht (1967); Vital Statistics and Registrar, Trenton. "Blain [death notice of George Albrecht]," *The Perry County Times*, 11 May 1967, p. 9, col. 4. Ibid., "Blain [burial notice of George Albrecht]," 18 May 1967, p. 6, col. 6.

[422] "U.S., World War II Draft Cards Young Men, 1940-1947," digital images, *Ancestry.com* (https://www.ancestry.com/), Harry Newcomet Albrecht.

[423] Index of Marriages in New Jersey 1941, Bride Index, Albrecht-Connelly, 1941; "New Jersey, U.S., Marriage Index, 1901-2016," digital images, *Ancestry.com* (https://www.ancestry.com/).

[424] New Jersey death certificate no. 05459, Harry N. Albrecht (1976); Vital Statistics and Registrar, Trenton.

[425] "U.S., World War II Draft Cards Young Men, 1940-1947," digital images, *Ancestry.com* (https://www.ancestry.com/), Frederick Alfred Albrecht. New Jersey Department of Health, Vital Statistics and Registry, 20 Jun. 2022, email reporting negative birth-record search for Frederick Alfred Albrecht.

[426] Index of Marriages in New Jersey 1936, Bride Index, Albrecht-Olson, 1936; "New Jersey, U.S., Marriage Index, 1901-2016," digital images, *Ancestry.com* (https://www.ancestry.com/).

[427] Social Security Administration, "U.S., Social Security Death Index, 1935-2014," database, *Ancestry.com* (https://search.ancestry.com/), Frederick A. Albrecht, SS no. 150-09-3059.

[428] *Find A Grave*, database and images (http://findagrave.com), Frederick Alfred Albrecht, memorial no. 13,8561,378.

58.   vi.   ROBERT SAMUEL ALBRECHT, b. 13 Jun. 1916;[429] m. (1) DORIS DIXSON,[430] (2) JUNE ANN
MERKEL,[431] and (3) SUSAN B. SMITH;[432] d. Phoenix, Maricopa Co., Ariz. 5 Dec. 1972, age 56,
and his body was cremated.[433]

16. WILLIAM R.[3] RILEY, SR. (*Christian Fulmer*[2], *William*[1] *Riley*), was born probably in Upper
Providence Township, Montgomery County, Pennsylvania,[434] on 7 June 1857,[435] died in
Chalfont, Bucks County, Pennsylvania, on 6 August 1933, age 76,[436] and was buried there in
Saint James Church Cemetery.[437] He married (1) ca. 1880[438] ELIZABETH/LIZZIE/ELIZA H.
HOUCK/HAUCK,[439] daughter of Peter and (−?−) (Small) Houck.[440] She was born in Pennsylvania
on 13 March 1854 and died in Chalfont on 23 July 1916, age 62,[441] and was buried with her
husband.[442] William married (2) in Bucks County on 1 Mar. 1918 LOUISA/LOUISE (PRAHL)
BRUNNER,[443] daughter of German-born[444] Adam and Ottile/Ottilie (Bauer) Prahl.[445] Louisa was

---

[429] "U.S., World War II Draft Cards Young Men, 1940-1947," digital images, *Ancestry.com*
(https://www.ancestry.com/), Robert Samuel Albrecht.

[430] Index of Marriages in New Jersey, 1941, image 153 of 686; "New Jersey, U.S., Marriage Index, 1901-2016,"
database, *Ancestry.com* (https://www.ancestry.com/), Robert S. Albrecht-Doris Dixson, 1941.

[431] "County Court. Marriage Licenses [Robert S. Albrecht-June Ann Merkel]," *Ft. Lauderdale (Fla.) News*, 3 Apr.
1951, p. 10, col. 3. Robert and June Ann divorced. "Texas, U.S., Select County Marriage Records, 1837-1965,"
database, *Ancestry.com* (https://www.ancestry.com/); Jane [sic] Ann Albrecht-John Tom Gibson, 1977, Gregg, Tex.

[432] Clerk of the Superior Court, Maricopa Co., Ariz. marriage no. 71-61795, Robert S. Albrecht-Susan B. Smith, 12
May 1971; Clerk's Office, Phoenix.

[433] "Robert S. Albrecht [obituary]," *Arizona Republic*, 8 Dec. 1972, p. 62, col. 4.

[434] Alderfer to Riley, 26 Sep. 1991.

[435] Circular to verify veteran's identity, Christian F. Riley, Sr., pension application no. S.C. 1,069,104, Civil War,
RG 15, NA-Washington.

[436] Pennsylvania death certificate no. 69925 (1933), William R. Riley.

[437] *Find A Grave*, database and images (http://findagrave.com), William R. Riley, memorial no. 99,593,969.

[438] 1910 U.S. census, Bucks Co., Pa., pop. sch., New Britain, ED 31, p. 2B, dwell. 46, fam. 52, Elizabeth Reilly
[sic], wife, in the household of Wm. R. Reilly; NARA T624, roll 1320. Marriage year calculated from number of
years married (30 years). Philadelphia, Pa., City Archives, 8 Feb. 2022, email reporting negative marriage-record
search for William R. Riley and Elizabeth Houck.

[439] *Find A Grave*, William R. Riley, memorial no. 99,593,969. Annotation gives wife's birth surname.

[440] Pennsylvania death certificate no. 70089 (1916), Elizabeth H. Riley. For spellings of wife's birth surname,
records of her daughters. Ibid., death certificate no. 4 (1921), Mary B. Worthington. Social Security Administration,
"U.S., Social Security Applications and Claims Index, 1936-2007," database, *Ancestry.com*, entry for Kathryn H.
Maurer, SS no. 197-14-2019.

[441] Pennsylvania death certificate no. 70089 (1916), Elizabeth H. Riley.

[442] *Find A Grave*, database and images (http://findagrave.com), Elizabeth H. Riley, memorial no. 97,783,124.

[443] Bucks Co., Pa., Index to Marriage Applications, 1885–1946, p. 2105, Riley-Brunner.

[444] For bapt. of Louisa's father, Adam Prahl, "Germany, Lutheran Baptisms, Marriages, and Burials, 1500-1971,"
database and digital images, *FamilySearch.org* (https://www.familysearch.org/), Adam Prahl, bapt., Heidelberg,
Grand Duchy of Baden, 20 Nov. 1831, son of Christian Friedrich and Anna Elisabetha Prahl.

[445] For father's name, Pennsylvania death certificate no. 69929, Louise Riley (1945); Vital Statistics, Harrisburg. For
mother's birth surname, "Mortuary Notices [Ottilie Prahl], *The Philadelphia Inquirer*, 13 Dec. 1906, p. 7, col. 4,
"…widow of the late Adam Prahl." For evidence of parental relationship, 1870 U.S. census, Philadelphia Co., Pa.,
pop. sch., Philadelphia, p. 193A, dwell. 394, fam. 415, Otto Prahl, son, age 4, Louisa Prahl, daughter, age 8, in the
household of Adam Prahl, b. Baden, and Ottile Prahl, b. Württemberg, his presumed wife; NARA M593, roll 1401.
For mother's birth surname, baptismal record of Louisa's brother Otto. First German Methodist Church
(Philadelphia, Pa.), Tauf [baptisms], p. 152, 1869, baptism of Otto Prahl, b. 25 Mar. 1866, bapt. 10 Mar. 1869;
"Pennsylvania and New Jersey, U.S., Church and Town Records, 1669-2013," database with images, *Ancestry.com*
(https://www.ancestry.com/). Named parents, Adam Prahl and Ottilie Bauer.

born in Philadelphia on 3 September 1861 and died there on 1 July 1945, age 84,[446] and was buried in Glenwood Memorial Gardens, Broomall, Delaware County, Pennsylvania.[447] Louisa married (1) George Brunner.[448]

William, probably named for his paternal grandfather, left Upper Providence[449] when he was about nine-years-old and moved with his family to Philadelphia.[450] At age 20, he was listed in a city directory as a blacksmith.[451] It is speculated that William and his brother, Henry/Harry, also a blacksmith, apprenticed and later worked with their father, Christian, whose blacksmith shop was on North Broad Street.[452] This is based on the proximity of their properties in the 1880s[453] (Figure 8). William worked at that trade in Philadelphia from 1877 to 1889.[454]

Five children of William and Elizabeth died of childhood diseases (see below). The parents left Philadelphia and went to nearby Bucks County, Pennsylvania, where William resumed his trade.[455] William's mother, Anna F. or T. (Landis) Riley, died at his home there in 1910.[456] Within a few years, the surviving children married,[457] Elizabeth died,[458] and William

[446] Pennsylvania death certificate no. 69929, Louise Riley (1945); Vital Statistics, Harrisburg.

[447] *Find A Grave*, database and images (http://findagrave.com), Louise Prahl Riley, memorial no. 228,865,637.

[448] The evidence for this marriage is indirect. Louisa was in George's household. 1900 U.S. census, Philadelphia Co., Pa., pop. sch., Philadelphia, ED 221, p. 6, dwell. 51, fam. 116, Louise Brunner in the household of George Brunner; NARA T623, roll 1457. George presumably died ca. 1915. *Philadelphia City Directory for 1901* (Philadelphia: James Gospill, 1901), 336, "Brunner Geo, barber, h 524 N 6th." By the same title: (1906), 399; (1907), 292. *Philadelphia City Directory for 1908* (Philadelphia: C.E. Howe,1908), 267, "Brunner Geo, barber, 524 N 6th." By the same title: (1909), 315; (1910), 305; (1911), 294; (1912), 300; (1916), 323, no listing for George.

[449] 1860 U.S. census, Montgomery Co., Pa., pop. sch., Upper Providence Twp., p. 555, dwell. 843, fam. 937, William Riley in the household of Christian Riley; NARA M653, roll 1145.

[450] "City Intelligence," *The Philadelphia Inquirer*, 4 Dec. 1866. 1870 U.S. census, Philadelphia Co., Pa., pop. sch., Philadelphia, p. 176A, dwell. 3, fam. 4, William Riley in the household of Christian Riley; NARA M593, roll 1404.

[451] Gopsill's *Philadelphia City Directory*, for (1877), 1222.

[452] Gopsill's *Philadelphia City Directory*, for (1880), 1423.

[453] For Christian's residence, Philadelphia City Death Certificates, 1803-1915," *FamilySearch.org*, Anna Elizabeth Riley. Father, Christian F. Riley, address, 2216 N. Broad St. For William's residence at 1509 French St., 1880 U.S. census, Philadelphia Co., Pa., Philadelphia, ED 595, p. 4D, dwell. 29, fam. 42. *Philadelphia City Directory for 1883* (Philadelphia: James Gopsill, 1883), 1354; By the same title: (1884), 1347; (1885), 1483; (1886), 1453; (1887), 1432; (1888), 1470; (1889), 1512; (1890), 1561, no listing for William Riley as blacksmith or horseshoer. For Henry's residence at 2216 North Broad St., Gopsill's *Philadelphia City Directory*, for (1877), 78; (1881), 1382.

[454] Gopsill's *Philadelphia City Directory*, for (1877), 1222; (1883), 1354; (1884), 1347; (1885), 1483; (1886), 1453; (1887), 1432; (1888), 1470; (1889), 1512; (1890), 1561, no listing for William Riley, blacksmith or horseshoer.

[455] 1900 U.S. census, Bucks Co., Pa., pop. sch., New Britain, ED 27, p. 10, dwell. 217, fam. 234, household of William R. Riley; NARA T623, roll 1385. 1910 U.S. census, Bucks Co., Pa., New Britain, ED 31, p. 2B, dwell. 46, fam. 52.

[456] Pennsylvania death certificate no. 77377 (1910), Anna Tyson Riley.

[457] Delaware County, Pennsylvania, Affidavit for Marriage License, case no. 15,626, Franklin Lynford Maurer-Kathryn H. Riley, 23 Mar. 1911; "Pennsylvania, U.S., Marriages, 1852-1968," database and digital images, *Ancestry.com* (https://www.ancestry.com/). "United States World War I Draft Registration Cards, 1917-1918," database and images, *FamilySearch.org* (https://www.familysearch.org/), card for Winfield Scott Riley.

[458] *Find A Grave*, Elizabeth H. Riley, memorial no. 97,783,124.

remarried.[459] In 1920, his second wife, Louisa, was a matron at the "Pa S of A [sic] Aged & Afflicted [Home]."[460] Louisa moved to Philadelphia in her widowhood.[461]

Children of William R. Riley, Sr. and Elizabeth/Lizzie/Eliza H. Houck/Hauck were:[462]

59.   i.   CHRISTIAN FULLMER/FULMER RILEY, b. Philadelphia 16 Nov. 1878;[463] m. (1) SARA "SADIE" LOUISE RANDALL[464] and (2) EMILE/EMILY/EMILIE SHUBERT;[465] d. there 16 Nov. 1964,[466] bur. Saint James Church Cemetery, Chalfont, Pa.[467]

60.   ii.   MARK RILEY, b. Philadelphia 26 Jun. 1880;[468] d. there of cholera infinitum, 13 Jun. 1882, age 2 yr., bur. Upper Providence Twp., Pa.[469]

61.   iii.   ANNA/ANNIE RILEY, b. Philadelphia 28 Sep. 1881;[470] d. there of measles 16 May 1887, age 6 yrs., bur. Upper Providence Twp., Pa.[471]

---

[459] Bucks Co., Pa., Index to Marriage Applications, 1885–1946, p. 2105, Riley-Brunner, 1 Mar. 1918; Family History Library (FHL) microfilm no. 007727321, viewed at *FamilySearch.org* (https://www.familysearch.org/ark:/61903/3:1:3Q9M-C9BL-F9RL-M?cc=1589502), image 99 of 323.

[460] 1920 U.S. census, Bucks Co., Pa., New Britain Twp., ED 17, p. 2A, dwell. 29, fam. 33. Later, they lived in Chalfont, Pa. 1930 U.S. census, Bucks Co., Pa., pop. sch., Chalfont, ED 27, p. 10, dwell. 34, fam. 34, household of William R. Riley; NARA T623, roll 2007.

[461] 1940 U.S. census, Philadelphia Co., Pa., pop. sch., Philadelphia, ED 51-1362, p. 11B, dwell. 183, Louisa Riley, in the household of Joseph Liggon; NARA T627, roll m-t0627-03730.

[462] 1910 U.S. census, Bucks Co., Pa., New Britain, ED 31, p. 2B, dwell. 46, fam. 52, indicating Elizabeth gave birth to ten children, five of whom were living. Birth order of child x. is uncertain.

[463] City of Philadelphia, Return of Births for the Month of November 1878, Christian Rily [sic]; City Archives, Philadelphia.

[464] Montgomery County Orphans' Court, Marriage License Docket, 1885–1905, vol. 30, no. 13.147, p. 88, Christian Fullmer Riley-Sara Louise Randall, 17 Jun. 1903; "Philadelphia, Pennsylvania, U.S., Marriage Index, 1885-1951," database and images, *Ancestry.com* (https://www.ancestry.com/). "Sarah L. Riley [obituary]," *The Philadelphia Inquirer*, 15 Apr. 1919, p. 20, col. 5. Died, 13 Apr. 1919. "…wife of Christian F. Riley and daughter of Emma and the Rev. F.W. Rendell [sic]…." For father's name, 1900 U.S. census, Philadelphia Co., Pa., pop. sch., Philadelphia, ED 13, p. 13, dwell. 290, fam. 310, Sadie Randall in the household of Frederick W. Randall, minister; NARA T623, roll 1384.

[465] St. Paul's Lutheran Church (Philadelphia, Pa.), Tauf [Birth] Register, 1922, entry for Robert Fullmer, Jr. [sic], , b. 11 Oct. 1921; "Pennsylvania and New Jersey, U.S., Church and Town Records, 1669-2013," database and images, *Ancestry.com* (https://www.ancestry.com/). Image 818 of 888. Son of "Rob. Fullmer Riley & Eṁa geb. [*geboren* = born] Schubert." "Pennsylvania, U.S., Veteran Compensation Application Files, WWII, 1950-1966," digital images, *Ancestry.com* (https://www.ancestry.com/), application for Robert Fullmer Riley, deceased, b. Philadelphia, 11 Oct. 1921, service no. 0868526, 10 May 1950. Parents, Christian Fullmer and Emilie Riley. Branch of service, Army Air, d. 5 Jan. 1945, "Central Pacific." For additional documentation of second wife, Emilie Riley, wife, in the household of Christian Riley, line 11, sheet 4, ED 51-808, Philadelphia, Philadelphia Co., Pa.; Seventeenth Census of the United States, 1950; RG 29, Records of the Bureau of the Census; NARA, Washington, D.C.

[466] Pennsylvania death certificate no. 22464, Christian F. Riley (1964); Vital Statistics, Harrisburg.

[467] *Find A Grave*, database and images (http://findagrave.com), Christian F. Riley, memorial no. 97,783,099.

[468] City of Philadelphia, Return of Births for the Month of June 1880, Mark Riley; City Archives, Philadelphia.

[469] "Pennsylvania, Philadelphia City Death Certificates, 1803-1915," database and digital images, *FamilySearch.org* (https://www.familysearch.org/), Mark Riley.

[470] City of Philadelphia, Return of Births for the Month of Sept 1881, Anna Riley; City Archives, Philadelphia.

[471] Philadelphia, Pennsylvania, Registration of Deaths, 1887, p. 238-39, Annie Riley; "Pennsylvania, Philadelphia City Death Certificates, 1803-1915," database and digital images, *FamilySearch.org* (https://www.familysearch.org/).

62. iv. WILLIAM R. RILEY, JR., b. Philadelphia 28 Feb. 1883;[472] d. there of scarlet fever 21 Nov. 1888, age 6 yr., bur. Upper Providence Twp., Pa.[473]

63. v. THOMAS JEFFERSON RILEY, b. Philadelphia 28 Dec. 1884;[474] m. MARY ELEANOR NEAL;[475] d. of carcinoma of the lung in Norwalk, Fairfield Co., Conn. 14 Jun. 1952, age 67, bur. there in Riverside Cemetery.[476]

64. vi. MAGGIE RILEY, b. Philadelphia 1 Nov. 1886;[477] d. there of lobar pneumonia 1 Apr. 1890, age 3 yr., 5 mo., bur. Mennonite Church Cemetery (place not specified).[478]

64. vii. KATHERINE/KATHRYN HAUCK RILEY, b. Line Lexington, Bucks, Co., Pa. 10 Nov. 1888;[479] m. FRANKLIN LINFORD/LYNFORD MAURER;[480] d. Lansdale, Montgomery Co., Pa. 5 Apr. 1957,[481] and bur. Saint James Church Cemetery, Chalfont, Pa.[482]

66. viii. MARY/MAY BERRY RILEY,[483] b. Pa. 8 Mar. 1892;[484] m. GEORGE HOWARD WORTHINGTON;[485] d. West Rockhill, Bucks Co., Pa. 16 Jan. 1921 of thrombosis of pulmonary artery following curettage of retained placenta, age 28,[486] and bur. Lansdale Cemetery, Lansdale, Pa.[487] George m. (2) Margaret Houck.[488]

---

[472] City of Philadelphia, Returns of Births for February 1883, William R. Riley, 28 Feb. 1883; City Archives, Philadelphia.

[473] "Pennsylvania, Philadelphia City Death Certificates, 1803-1915," database and digital images, *FamilySearch.org* (https://www.familysearch.org/), William Riley.

[474] City of Philadelphia, Birth Return for December 1884, Thomas J. Riley; City Archives, Philadelphia.

[475] "Invited to Rio Grande Wedding [wedding announcement]," *The Philadelphia Inquirer*, 8 Feb. 1908, p. 14, col. 3. Rio Grande is an unincorporated community within Middle Twp. and Lower Twp., Cape May Co., N.J. *Wikipedia* (https://en.wikipedia.org/), "Rio Grande, New Jersey," rev. 01:53, 9 Jun. 2021.

[476] Connecticut death certificate no. [blank], Thomas Jefferson Riley (1952); Town Clerk's Office, Norwalk.

[477] City of Philadelphia, Return of Births For the Month of November 1886, Maggie Riley; City Archives, Philadelphia.

[478] "Pennsylvania, Philadelphia City Death Certificates, 1803-1915," database and digital images, *FamilySearch.org* (https://www.familysearch.org/), Maggie Riley.

[479] Delaware County, Pennsylvania, Affidavit for Marriage License, no. 15,626, Franklin Lynford Maurer-Kathryn H. Riley, 23 Mar. 1911; "Philadelphia, Pennsylvania, U.S., Marriage Index, 1885-1951," database and digital images, *Ancestry.com* (https://www.ancestry.com/). Social Security Administration, "U.S., Social Security Applications and Claims Index, 1936-2007," database, *Ancestry.com* (https://www.ancestry.com/), Kathryn H. Maurer, SS no. 197-14-2019, b. Philadelphia, Pa., 10 Nov. 1888, parents, William R. Riley and Elizabeth Hauck [sic].

[480] Delaware County Affidavit for Marriage License, Maurer-Riley, *Ancestry.com*. Pennsylvania death certificate no. 013781-66, F. Linford Maurer (1966); Vital Statistics, Harrisburg. Son of Franklin P. Maurer and Emma Hines.

[481] Pennsylvania death certificate no. 105, Kathryn Hauck Maurer (1957); Vital Statistics, Harrisburg. "Died [death notice of Kathryn (sic) H. (nee Riley) Maurer]," *The Philadelphia Inquirer*, 7 Apr. 1957, p. 74, col. 8. "…wife of E. Linford Maurer…"

[482] *Find A Grave*, database and images (http://findagrave.com), Kathryn H. Maurer, memorial no. 97,782,995.

[483] For middle name, Pennsylvania birth certificate no. 11047, Charles Robert Worthington (1913); Vital Records, Harrisburg. Parents, George Howard Worthington and Mary Berry Riley.

[484] Pennsylvania death certificate no. 4, Mary B. Worthington (1921); Vital Statistics, Harrisburg.

[485] State of Delaware, Register of Marriages, vol. 4, p. 85, no. 56486, Geo. H. Worthington-May B. Riley, 20 Mar. 1911; "Delaware, U.S., Marriage Records, 1806-1933," database and digital images, *Ancestry.com* (https://www.ancestry.com/). George was the son of Charles L. [sic] Worthington and Mary L. Fedigan.

[486] Pennsylvania death certificate no. 4 (1921), Mary B. Worthington.

[487] *Find A Grave*, database and images (http://findagrave.com), Mary B. Worthington, memorial no. 37,766,195.

[488] "Washington, D.C, U.S., Marriage Records, 1810-1953," database, *Ancestry.com* (https://www.ancestry.com/), George H. Worthington-Margaret Houck, 16 Oct. 1923. "Marriage Licenses," *Evening Star (Washington, D.C.)*, 17 Oct. 1923, p. 9, col. 2. "George H. Worthington of Lansdale, Pa., and Margaret Houck of Aldan, Pa."

67.   ix.   WINFIELD SCOTT RILEY, b. probably in the New Britain section of Line Lexington, Bucks, Co., Pa.[489] 18 Nov. 1893;[490] m. HANNAH/ANNA LOUISE SCHWAGER;[491] d. Holmes, Delaware Co., Pa. Sep. 1969[492] or 24 May 1969 and bur. in Arlington Cemetery, Drexel Hill, Pa.[493]

68.   x.   UNNAMED RILEY CHILD, d. probably before 1900.[494]

17. HENRY/HARRY LANDIS[3] RILEY (*Christian Fulmer[2]*, *William[1] Riley*), was born probably in Upper Providence Township, Montgomery County, Pennsylvania,[495] on 6 September 1858[496] and died in Atlantic City, Atlantic County, New Jersey, on 30 December 1937, age 81, and was buried in Laurel Memorial Park, Egg Harbor Township, New Jersey.[497] He married at the residence of a Presbyterian minister in Philadelphia, Philadelphia County, Pennsylvania, on 14 November 1881 EDWARDENE/EDITH/EDA MAGILL COPE,[498] probable daughter of Amandamus/Amandus B. F. and Anna Elizabeth (Funk) Cope.[499] She was born in Doylestown,

---

[489] Line Lexington is an unincorporated community split between the Bucks Co. townships of Hilltown and New Britain and the Montgomery Co. township of Hatfield. *Wikipedia* (https://en.wikipedia.org/), "Line Lexington, Pennsylvania," rev. 03.21, 6 Mar. 2021.

[490] "United States World War I Draft Registration Cards, 1917-1918," *FamilySearch.org*, Winfield Scott Riley.

[491] Hannah Louise Schwager (1883-1944), "Public Profile," database, *GENi.com* (https://www.geni.com/), updated 16 May 2020. Wife of Winfred Scott Riley. Years of birth and death on this website conflict with engraving on tombstone. *Find A Grave*, database and images (http://findagrave.com), Anna E. [sic] Riley, memorial no. 135,451,105.

[492] Social Security Administration, "U.S., Social Security Death Index, 1935-2014," database, *Ancestry.com* (https://search.ancestry.com/), entry for Winfield Riley, SS no. 202-18-0763. Last known address, Holmes, Pa.

[493] *Find A Grave*, database and images (http://findagrave.com), Winfield S. Riley, memorial no. 135,451,133.

[494] Death of child x. is based on the absence of a child younger than child ix. in the 1900 census. 1900 U.S. census, Bucks Co., Pa., New Britain, ED 27, p. 10, dwell. 217, fam. 234.

[495] Alderfer to Riley, 26 Sep. 1991. 1860 U.S. census, Montgomery Co., Pa., Upper Providence Twp., p. 555, dwell. 843, fam. 937.

[496] Circular to verify veteran's identity, Christian F. Riley, Sr., pension application no. S.C. 1,069,104, Civil War, RG 15, NA-Washington.

[497] First Presbyterian Church, Atlantic City, N.J., Register of Deaths, Henry Landis Riley.

[498] City of Philadelphia, Marriage Returns, 1 Oct. to 31 Dec. 1881, Harry L. Riley-Eda Cope; City Archives, Philadelphia.

[499] "Lancaster, Pennsylvania, U.S., Mennonite Vital Records, 1750-2014," database, *Ancestry.com* (https://search.ancestry.com/), Amandus B. F. Cope. For Edwardene's mother's birth surname, death certificates of her brothers. Pennsylvania death certificate no. 106746, Daniel Cope (1950); Vital Statistics, Harrisburg. Ibid., no. 71292, Clinton B. Cope (1952). Ibid., no. 37971, B. Frank Cope (1934). Ibid., no. 119667, Samuel Ellsworth Cope (1924). 1880 U.S. census, Montgomery Co., Pa., pop. sch., Upper Salford, ED 34, p. 201C, dwell. 138, fam. 156, household of Amandus Cope; NARA T9, roll 1159. "Died [death notice and Anna E. Cope]," *The Philadelphia Inquirer*, 6 Dec. 1898, p. 11, col. 8. Died at the "…home of her son, B. Frank Cope…."

Bucks County, Pennsylvania,[500] in December 1861,[501] 1863,[502] 28 December 1864,[503] ca. 1865,[504] or December 1866[505] and died after 1935 and before 1950.[506]

Henry, a blacksmith, lived on North Broad Street, Philadelphia, in 1877 and 1881.[507] He moved to Telford, Bucks County, Pennsylvania, in 1883 (birthplace of first child).[508] By 1901, he was in Atlantic City where he was employed as a blacksmith, machinist, and chauffer over the next three decades.[509]

Children of Henry/Harry Landis Riley and Edwardene/Edith/Eda Magill Cope were:[510]

---

[500] 1930 U.S. census, Atlantic Co., N.J., pop. sch., Atlantic City, ED 4, p. 23B, dwell. 654, fam. 655, Edwardine [sic] Riley in the household of Harry L. Riley; NARA T626, roll 1308. Birthplace, Doylestown, Pa. 1870 U.S. census, Bucks Co., Pa., pop. sch., Doylestown, p. 185B, dwell. 262, fam. 277, Edwardene Cope in the household of Franklin Cope; NARA M593, roll 1313.

[501] 1900 U.S. census, Atlantic Co., N.J., pop. sch., Atlantic City, ED 3, p. 8, dwell. 174, fam. 182, Edith Reley [sic], b. Dec. 1861, in the household of Harry L. Reley; NARA T623, roll 953.

[502] Philadelphia Marriage Return, Riley-Cope, 14 Nov. 1881. Bride, age 18 (calculated birth year 1863).

[503] 1870 U.S. census, Bucks Co., Pa., Doylestown, p. 185B, dwell. 262, fam. 277. Charles H. Price, Jr., *A Hartzell-Price Family History and Genealogy* (n.p.; by the author, 1972), 89, (https://www.ancestry.com/imageviewer/collections/14911/images/). Edwardene M. Cope (1864-deceased), Family Tree ID MY1C-H88, "Family Tree," database, *FamilySearch.org* (https://www.familysearch.org/tree/person/sources/MY1C-H88).

[504] 1920 U.S. census, Atlantic Co., N.J., pop. sch., Atlantic City, ED 6, p. 12B, dwell. 217, fam. 314, Edwardene Riley in the household of Harry L. Riley; NARA T625, roll 1015. 1930 U.S. census, Atlantic Co., N.J., Atlantic City, ED 4, p. 23B, dwell. 654, fam. 655.

[505] 1905 New Jersey state census, Atlantic Co., pop. sch., Atlantic City, ED 4, p. 43A, dwell. 372, fam. 389, Edwardeen [sic] Riley in the household of Harry L. Riley.

[506] *Atlantic City Directory of 1935* (Atlantic City, N.J.: Atlantic Directories, 1935), 204, "Riley Harry L (Edith) 9 N Irving ave." "Daniel Cope," *The Philadelphia Inquirer*, 31 Dec. 1950, p. 18, col. 4. Obituary of Edwardene's brother does not mention her as a surviving relative.

[507] Gopsill's *Philadelphia City Directory,* for (1877), 78, (1881), 1382.

[508] Pennsylvania birth certificate no. 33081, Craig Bispham Mickle (1911); Vital Statistics, Harrisburg. Mother, Florence Riley, b. Telford, Pa.; "Pennsylvania, U.S., Birth Certificates," database and images, *Ancestry.com* (https://search.ancestry.com/).

[509] *Atlantic City Directory for 1901* (Philadelphia: James Gopsill's Sons, 1901), 303, "Riley Harry L (Edith), blacksmith, h 209 N S Carolina av"; ibid., "Riley Harry L (Riley & Weer), h 118 St. James pl"; By the same title: (1904), 346, "Riley Harry L, machinist, h 117 Mt. Vernon av"; (1906), 408, "Riley Harry L., blacksmith, h 27½ S Virginia av"; *Atlantic City Directory for 1908* (Philadelphia: C.E. Howe, 1908), 474, "Riley Harry L. (Edwardene), chauffer, h 27½ S Virginia"; By the same title: (1909), 532, "Riley Harry L., chauffer, h 29 Caspian av"; (1911), 610, "Riley Harry L. (Edwardene), machinist, h 6A Virginia Apartments"; (1913), 677, "Riley Harry L. (Edwardine), machinist, h 319 N Vermont ave"; (1914), 688; (1915), 741, "Riley Harry L (Edwardene M), blacksmith, h 106 N Rhode Island ave"; (1916), 748, "Riley Harry (Edith) blacksmith h 22 Taylor ave"; (1917), 734; (1918), 662, "Riley Harry (Edwardinie) blksmh h 243 S Congress"; (1920), 674; (1921), 744. *Atlantic City Directory for 1923* (Philadelphia: R. L. Polk & Co., 1923), 915, "Riley Harry L (Edwardine), watchmn, h 12 N Maryland"; By the same title: (1924), 1015, "Riley Harry L (Edwardine M), blksmith Seashore Machine Works h3C The Presston apts"; (1925), 743; (1926), 791; (1927), 779; (1930), 601, "Riley Harry L (Edwardene) mach h9A Irving av"; (1931), 627; *Atlantic City Directory of 1935* (Atlantic City, N.J.: Atlantic Directories, 1935), 204, "Riley Harry L (Edith) 9 Irving av."

[510] 1905 New Jersey state census, Atlantic Co., Atlantic City, ED 4, p. 43A, dwell. 372, fam. 389.

69.   i.   FLORENCE VIRGINIA RILEY, b. Telford, Bucks Co., Pa.[511] 20 Apr. 1883;[512] m. HARRY SHERATS/ SHERDTS[513] MICKLE;[514] d. Somers Point, Atlantic Co., N.J. 26 Jun. 1963, bur. Laurel Memorial Park, Pomona, N.J.[515]

70.   ii.   STELLA CUSHMAN RILEY, b. Atlantic City 6 Mar. 1885;[516] m. GEORGE CROSBY AMOLE;[517] d. there Jul. 1951.[518]

21. CHARLES BRADFORD[3] "BRAD" RILEY (*Christian Fulmer[2]*, *William[1]* *Riley*), was born in Philadelphia, Philadelphia County, Pennsylvania, on 2 June 1865[519] or 22 June 1865[520] and died probably in Atlantic City, Atlantic County, New Jersey, after 13 April 1940[521] and before 31 December 1940, and was buried in Atlantic City Cemetery, Pleasantville, New Jersey.[522] Charles married in Atlantic City on 7 March 1885 MARGARET "MAGGIE" T. PETERS,[523] daughter of Uriah G. and Catherine/Catharina S.A. (Peter) Peters.[524] She was born probably in Cinnaminson, Burlington County, New Jersey,[525] in August 1869.[526] Margaret was baptized at St. Paul's Methodist Church, Atlantic City, on 2 February 1883, age 15,[527] died in 1945, and was buried with her husband.[528] Charles married (2) ca. 1926 as her fourth husband ORA LOUISE MAY

---

[511] Pennsylvania birth certificate no. 33081 (1911), Craig Bispham Mickle.

[512] New Jersey death certificate no. 26914, Florence Virginia Mickle (1965); Vital Statistics, Trenton.

[513] For middle name, "U.S., World War I Draft Registration Cards, 1917-1918," database and images, *Ancestry.com* (https://search.ancestry.com/), Harry Sherats Mickle. Names of wife, Florence Mickle.

[514] New Jersey Department of Health and Senior Services, Vital Records, Marriage Records, Brides Indexes, 1904 - 1909, R-S, Harry Mickle-Florence Riley, 1907; "New Jersey, U.S., Marriage Index, 1901–2016," database, *Ancestry.com* (https://www.ancestry.com/).

[515] New Jersey death certificate no. 26914 (1965), Florence Virginia Mickle.

[516] New Jersey birth certificate no. R25, Stella Cushman Riley, 6 Mar. 1885; Vital Statistics and Registry, Trenton.

[517] "U.S., World War I Draft Registration Cards, 1917-1918," database and images, *Ancestry.com* (https://search.ancestry.com/), George Crosby Amole. Name of wife, Stella Amole.

[518] Deaths, 1951, Stella R. Amole, annotation gives place of death; "New Jersey Death Index, 1901-2017," database and images, *Ancestry.com* (https://search.ancestry.com/).

[519] Circular to verify veteran's identity, Christian F. Riley, Sr., pension application no. S.C. 1,069,104, Civil War, RG 15, NA-Washington.

[520] Social Security Administration, "U.S., Social Security Death Index, 1935-2014," database, *Ancestry.com,* Charles Bradford Riley, SS no. 155-01-7384.

[521] 1940 U.S. census, Atlantic Co., N.J., Atlantic City, ED 1-27, p. 8A, dwell. 204.

[522] *Find A Grave*, Charles B. Riley, memorial no. 184,888,841.

[523] "New Jersey, U.S., Marriage Records, 1670-1965," database, *Ancestry.com*, Chas. B. Riley-Marg T. E. Peters. 1930 U.S. census, Atlantic Co., N.J., pop. sch., Northfield, ED 61, p. 7B, dwell. 171, fam. 174, Ora May Riley, wife, in the household of Charles B. Riley; NARA T626, roll 1310. Charles was age 19 at first marriage. New Jersey State Archives, 17 Dec. 2021, letter reporting negative marriage-record search for Charles Riley and Margaret Peters.

[524] 1870 U.S. census, Burlington Co., N.J., pop. sch., Cinnaminson, p. 292A, dwell. 393, fam. 367, Margaret Peters in the household of Uriah Peters; NARA M593, roll 854. For mother's birth surname, "Public Member Trees," database, *Ancestry.com* (http://www.ancestry.com/), "Peter, Hickman, Kekuhaupio, Jenkins, Gebler, Bader, Schoenewolf Family Tree," family tree by kepi527, profile for Catharine S. A. Peter (1832-1905).

[525] 1870 U.S. census, Burlington Co., N.J., Cinnaminson, p. 292A, dwell. 393, fam. 367.

[526] 1900 U.S. census, Atlantic Co., N.J., pop. sch., Atlantic City, ED 3, p. 16, dwell. 347, fam. 372, household of Maggie Riley; NARA T632, roll 953.

[527] St. Paul's Methodist Church (Atlantic City, N.J.), Church Register, Baptisms, Maggie Peters, 2 Feb. 1883; "New Jersey, U.S., United Methodist Church Records, 1800-1970," database and images, *Ancestry.com* (https://www.ancestry.com).

[528] *Find A Grave*, database and images (http://findagrave.com), Margaret E. [sic] Riley, memorial no. 184,888,842.

(TYSON) KELLEY BACON CONRAD,[529] daughter of Jesse James, Sr. and Mary Elizabeth (Benn) Tyson.[530] She was probably born in Bart, Lancaster County, Pennsylvania,[531] on 1 October 1877 and died of breast cancer, age 57, at the home of her son in Wilmington, New Castle County, Delaware, on 30 January 1935.[532] Ora married (1) Albert James Kelley, Sr.,[533] (2) James A. Bacon,[534] and (3) Isaac W. Conrad.[535]

Charles, who was in Atlantic City by 1893, was employed as a plumber, property man, and theatrical agent.[536] Charles become separated or divorced from Margaret by 1900-1901, leaving her with three minor children.[537]

Children of Charles Bradford Riley and Margaret T. Peters, all born in Atlantic City, were:[538]

---

[529] New Castle County, Deed Book 398: 122, Ora L. Riley and Charles B. Riley to Arthur V. Yearsley, 24 Feb. 1927; Recorder of Deeds, Wilmington; "Delaware, U.S., Land Records, 1677-1947," database and images, *Ancestry.com* (https://www.ancestry.com/). "…Ora L. Riley (formerly Ora L. Conrad) and Charles B. Riley, her husband of Northfield [N.J.]…." conveyed a parcel of land. "Mrs. O. L. Riley [obituary]," *The News Journal (Wilmington, Del.),* 31 Jan. 1935, p. 2, col. 5. Ora had moved from Wilmington, Del. to Northfield, N.J. where her husband lived. 1930 U.S. census, Atlantic Co., N.J., Northfield, ED 61, p. 7B, dwell. 171, fam. 174. New Jersey State Archives, 21 Dec. 2021, letter reporting negative marriage-record search for Charles Bradford Riley and Ora Conrad.

[530] Delaware death certificate no. 160 (1935), Ora May Riley.

[531] 1880 U.S. census, Lancaster Co., Pa., Bart, ED 175, p. 516A, dwell. 133, fam. 133.

[532] Delaware death certificate no. 160 (1935), Ora May Riley. "Mrs. O. L. Riley," *The News Journal,* 31 Jan. 1935.

[533] Delaware marriage certificate no. 769, Albert James Kelley, Jr.-Lillian Dorothy Smith (1918); Vital Statistics, Dover; "Delaware Marriage Records, 1913–1954," database and digital images, *FamilySearch.org* (https://www.familysearch.org/). Parents of groom, Albert James Kelley Sr. and Ora Tyson.

[534] Ibid., certificate no. 234, James A. Bacon-Ora L. Kelley, (1919).

[535] Ibid., certificate no. 149, Isaac W. Conrad-Ora L. Bacon (1937).

[536] *Atlantic City Directory for 1893* (Philadelphia: James Gopsill's Sons, 1893), 215, "Riley Charles B., plumber, h 17 S Presbyterian av"; By the same title: (1898), 222, "Riley Charles B., plumber, h 8 Moore av"; (1899), 247, "Riley Charles B., plumber, h 131 N New Jersey av"; ibid., "Riley Charles B., plumber, h r 121 S New Jersey av"; (1901), 303, "Riley Charles D. [sic] (Margaret) plumber h 171 Westminster av"; Ibid. "Riley Charles B. plumber h 118 St James pl"; (1904), 346. *Atlantic City Directory for 1909* (Philadelphia: C.E. Howe Co., 1909), 532, "Riley Charles B. propertyman h 118 St James' pl"; By the same title: (1910), 619, "Riley Charles B. h 310 Beach ave"; (1911), 610; (1912), 644, "Riley Charles B., plumber, h 310 Beach ave"; (1914), 688, "Riley Charles B propertyman h 230 S Congress ave"; (1915), 740; (1916), 748; (1917-18), 734; (1918-19), 661; (1919-20), 674; (1921), 744; (1922), 829. *Atlantic City Directory for 1923* (Philadelphia: R.L. Polk & Co., 1923), 914, "Riley Chas B, property master Apollo Theater r 230 S Congress ave"; By the same title: (1924), 1013; (1925), 742; no listing after 1925.

[537] 1900 U.S. census, Atlantic Co., N.J., Atlantic City, ED 3, p. 16, dwell. 347, fam. 672, household of Maggie Riley, "widowed," and residing with her children. Gopsill's *Atlantic City Directory*, for (1901), 303; ibid. "Riley Charles B. plumber h 118 St James pl." Separate listings suggest the couple was separated or divorced.

[538] 1900 U.S. census, Atlantic Co., N.J., Atlantic City, ED 3, p. 16, dwell. 347, fam. 672.

71.   i.   MABLE ELIZABETH RILEY,[539] b. Jun. 1886,[540] Jun. 1887,[541] or 21 Jun 1887;[542] may have m. EDWARD ROYER NAPPELL;[543] d. Atlantic City Oct. 1975[544] bur. Atlantic City Cemetery, Pleasantville, N.J.[545]

72.   ii.   CHARLES WILLIAM "BILL" RILEY, b. 7 Apr. 1889;[546] m. ALICE H. MATHIS;[547] d. 1949.[548]

73.   iii.   JESSIE LEWIS RILEY, b. 30 Nov. 1891;[549] m. (1) LAURA E. or H. DEVENDORF,[550] divorced 1940,[551] and (2) ALICE ANDREWS;[552] d. Atlantic City 23 Oct. 1953, age 61, bur. Atlantic City Cemetery, Pleasantville.[553]

22.   VIRGINIA "JENNIE" GERTRUDE[3] RILEY (*Christian Fulmer[2], William[1] Riley*), was born in Philadelphia, Philadelphia County, Pennsylvania, on 3 February 1867[554] and died in Atlantic City, Atlantic County, New Jersey.[555] Death due to acute pulmonary edema was on 7 July 1920, age 53 years, 5 months, 4 days, and burial was in Pleasantville Cemetery, Pleasantville, New

---

[539] For middle name, "U.S., World War I Draft Registration Cards, 1917-1918," database and images, *Ancestry.com* (https://search.ancestry.com/), Edward Royce Nappell. Nearest relative, Mable Elizabeth Nappell.

[540] 1900 U.S. census, Atlantic Co., N.J., Atlantic City, ED 3, p. 16, dwell. 347, fam. 372. New Jersey Department of Health, Vital Statistics and Registry, 20 Jun. 2022, email reporting negative birth-record search for Mable Riley.

[541] 1905 New Jersey state census, Atlantic Co., pop. sch., Atlantic City, ED 2, p. 7B, dwell. 140, fam. 176, Mable Riley in the household of Maggie Riley.

[542] Mable E. Riley (1887-1975), Family Tree ID G7QT-2VL, "Family Tree," database, *FamilySearch.org* (https://www.familysearch.org/tree/person/details/G7QT-2VL).

[543] *Find A Grave*, database and images (http://findagrave.com), Edward Royce Nappell, memorial no. 209,174,718. Annotation names wife. New Jersey State Archives, 21 Dec. 2021, letter reporting negative marriage-record search for Edward Royce Nappell-Mable Elizabeth Riley.

[544] Social Security Administration, "U.S., Social Security Death Index, 1935-2014," database, *Ancestry.com* (https://search.ancestry.com/), Mable Nappell, Oct. 1975, SS no. 156-20-8972. Annotation gives place of death. New Jersey Department of Health, Vital Statistics and Registry, 25 Apr. 2022, letter reporting negative death-record search for Mable Elizabeth Nappel [sic].

[545] *Find A Grave*, database and images (http://findagrave.com), Mabel Nappell, memorial no. 209,174,991.

[546] New Jersey birth certificate, R59, Charles W. Riley, 7 Apr. 1889; Vital Records and Registry. Trenton.

[547] Marriages, Bride Index, 1910–1914, William Riley-Alice H. Mathis, m. 1912; "New Jersey, U.S., Marriage Index, 1901-2016," database and images, *Ancestry.com* (https://www.ancestry.com/).

[548] *Find A Grave*, database and images (http://findagrave.com), William Riley, memorial no. 191,899,160. New Jersey Department of Health, Vital Statistics and Registry, 20 Mar. 2022, letter reporting negative death-record search for Charles William Riley.

[549] New Jersey birth certificate no. R72, Jesse Riley, 30 Nov. 1891; Vital Records and Registry, Trenton.

[550] "Philadelphia, Pennsylvania, U.S., Marriage Index, 1885-1951," database, *Ancestry.com* (https://www.ancestry.com/), Jesse Riley-Laura Devendorf.

[551] Social Security Administration, "U.S., Social Security Death Index, 1935-2014," database, *Ancestry.com* (https://search.ancestry.com/), Laura Riley, 1973, SS no. 157-28-6514, Oct. 1973. The divorce occurred after the 5 Apr. 1940 census enumeration. 1940 U.S. census, Atlantic Co., N.J., Atlantic City, ED 1-3, p. 4A, dwell. 57, Laura Riley, wife, in the household of Jesse Riley; NARA T627, roll m-t0627-02300.

[552] "New Jersey, U.S., Marriage Index, 1901-2016," database, *Ancestry.com* (https://search.ancestry.com/), Jess L. Riley-Alice Andrews, m. 1940. First Methodist Episcopal Church (Atlantic City, N.J.), Church Records, Baptisms, Nancy Ann Riley of Brigantine, N.J., b. 18 Nov. 1959. Mother's name "Alice Andrews Riley."

[553] New Jersey death certificate no. 3816, Jesse C. [sic] Riley (1953); Vital Records and Registrar, Trenton. *Find A Grave*, database and images (http://findagrave.com), Jesse C. [sic] Riley, memorial no. 192,169,119.

[554] Circular to verify veteran's identity, Christian F. Riley, Sr., pension application no. S.C. 1,069,104, Civil War, RG 15, NA-Washington.

[555] *Atlantic City Directory for 1921* (Philadelphia: James Gospill's Sons, 1921), 385, "Freeman Harry G (Virginia) plumber h 15 N North Carolina"; (1922), 420. No listings for Virginia as spouse of Harry G. Freeman in Atlantic City directories after 1921. *Atlantic City Directory for 1923* (Philadelphia: R. L. Polk Co., 1923), 463.

Jersey.[556] She married in Atlantic City on 21 June 1886, HARRY GRANT FREEMAN, SR.,[557] son of Albert Allen and Hannah Jane (Poist) Freeman.[558] He was born in Philadelphia on 26 December 1864 and died in Atlantic City on 17 May 1940, age 75, and was buried in Atlantic City Cemetery, Pleasantville.[559]

Harry, a plumber and steamfitter, was listed in Atlantic City directories from 1893 to at least 1925.[560]

Children of Harry Grant Freeman, Sr. and Virginia Gertrude Riley, all born in Atlantic City, were:[561]

74. i. MAY SLOAN FREEMAN, b. 1 Feb. 1887;[562] d. from burns due to clothes catching on fire in Atlantic City 18 Sep. 1892, age 5 yr., 8 mo.[563]

75. ii. ALBERT ALLEN FREEMAN, b. 27 Mar. 1888;[564] m. as her second husband[565] GERTRUDE MAY (JONES) HAWKES;[566] d. Atlantic City 24 May 1951, age 63, bur. Atlantic City Cemetery, Pleasantville, N.J.[567]

---

[556] New Jersey death certificate no. [blank], Virginia G. Freeman (1920); Vital Statistics and Registrar, Trenton.

[557] New Jersey marriage return, F20 (1886), Freeman-Riley.

[558] For father's name, New Jersey death certificate no. [blank], Harry Grant Freeman (1940); Vital Records and Registrar, Trenton. For parents' names, 1880 U.S. census, Philadelphia Co., Pa., pop. sch., Philadelphia, ED 588, p. 278C, dwell. 81, fam. 86, Harry G. Freeman, son, in the household of Albert A. Freeman; NARA T9, roll 1186. "Official List of Deaths [death notice of Hanna Jane Freeman]," *The Philadelphia Inquirer*, 9 Apr. 1903, p. 15, col. 6.

[559] New Jersey death certificate no. [blank] (1940), Harry Grant Freeman. Wesley United Methodist Church (Pleasantville, N.J.), Church Record, Funerals, Harry G. Freeman; "Pennsylvania and New Jersey, U.S., Church and Town Records, 1669-2013," database and images, *Ancestry.com* (https://search.ancestry.com/). The church record gives place and date of birth. This could not be verified with a birth record. Philadelphia, Pa., City Archives, 7 Apr. 2022, email reporting negative birth-record search for Harry Grant Freeman.

[560] *Atlantic City Directory for 1893* (Philadelphia: James Gospill's Sons, 1893), 90. "Freeman Harry G., plumber, h 31 S Presbyterian av"; By the same title: (1894), 71, "Freeman Harry G., plumber, h 218 N North Carolina av"; (1897), 93, "Freeman Harry G., fitter, h 31 S Presbyterian av"; (1898), 94; (1899), 105, "Freeman Harry G., steamfitter, h 133 N Mass. av"; (1901), 127, "Freeman Harry G. (Jennie G.), fitter, h 133 N Mass. av"; (1902), 164, "Freeman Harry G. (Virginia), steam fitter, h 10 Bartlett's av"; (1903), 153; (1904), 158; (1905), 169; (1906), 202; (1907), 206. *Atlantic City Directory for 1908* (Philadelphia: C. E. Howe Co., 1908), 234; (1909), 256; (1910), 291; (1911), 289; (1912), 302; (1913), 316; (1914), 310; (1915), 382; (1916). 388, "Freeman Harry G (Virginia) plumber h 15 N North Carolina ave"; (1917), 382; (1918-19), 345; (1920), 356; (1921), 385; (1922), 420. *Atlantic City Directory for 1923* (Philadelphia: R. L. Polk Co., 1923), 463." No listings for Virginia Freeman after 1921.

[561] Birth records for children ii. and iii. show born in N.J. New Jersey birth registration no. F49, Allen Freeman (1888); State Archives, Trenton. Ibid., birth registration no. F67, Virginia Gertrude Freeman (1891). However, another record says they were b. Pa. 1915 New Jersey state census, Atlantic Co., pop. sch., Atlantic City, p. 8, dwell. 10, fam. 77, household of Harry G. Freeman.

[562] New Jersey birth registration, May S. Freeman (1887); State Archives, Trenton.

[563] New Jersey death report no. F61, May Sloan Freeman (1893); State Archives, Trenton.

[564] New Jersey birth registration no. F49, Allen Freeman (1888). "U.S., World War II Draft Registration Cards, 1942," database and images, *FamilySearch.org* (https://www.familysearch.org/), Albert Allen Freeman.

[565] St. Anna's Church of the Redemption (Philadelphia, Pa.), Parish Register, 1894–1956, Marriages, p. 228-29, George L. Hawkes-Gertrude Jones, 5 Nov. 1912; "Pennsylvania and New Jersey, U.S., Church and Town Records, 1669-2013," database and images, *Ancestry.com* (https://search.ancestry.com/). 1920 U.S. census, Philadelphia Co., Pa., pop. sch., Philadelphia, ED 774, p. 1A, dwell. 5, fam. 5, Gertrude May Hawkes, daughter, and George L. Hawkes, son-in-law, in the household of Albert P. Jones; NARA T625, roll 1628.

[566] "Philadelphia, Pennsylvania, U.S., Marriage Index, 1885-1951," database, *Ancestry.com* (https://search.ancestry.com/), Albert A. Freeman-Gertrude M. Jones [sic], cert. no. 491447. Married 1924.

[567] New Jersey death certificate no. 17509, Albert Allen Freeman (1951); Vital Records and Registry, Trenton.

76. iii. VIRGINIA GERTRUDE FREEMAN, b. 5 Feb. 1891;[568] d. Pleasantville, Atlantic Co., N.J. 16. Oct. 1938, age 47.[569]

77. iv. HARRY GRANT FREEMAN, JR., b. 24 May 1892;[570] m. (1) ESTHER BOWERS[571] and (2) HELEN W. (JACHEN) MEAK;[572] bur. Pleasantville 16 Aug. 1957, age 64.[573]

78. v. SERVETUS CARLILE FREEMAN, b. 19 Apr. 1894;[574] m. as her second husband, ANNIE/ANNA/ANE ALBERTINE KRISTINE ESTHER (NEILSEN) ANDERSON/ANDERSEN;[575] d. Atlantic City 17 Mar. 1956, age 62, bur. Atlantic City Cemetery, Pleasantville.[576]

79. vi. LILLIAN MAY/MAE FREEMAN, b. 11 Apr. 1898;[577] m. ALEXANDER QUIGLEY GIBSON, JR.;[578] d. Atlantic City 26 Oct. 1973, age 75, bur. Laurel Memorial Park, Pomona, N.J.[579]

---

[568] New Jersey birth registration no. F67, Virginia Gertrude Freeman (1891).

[569] Wesley United Methodist Church (Pleasantville, N.J.), Church Record, Funerals, Miss Virginia Freeman, 16 Oct. 1938; "Pennsylvania and New Jersey, U.S., Church and Town Records, 1669-2013," database and images, *Ancestry.com* (https://search.ancestry.com/). Notation, "Sister to Mrs. Alex. Gibson."

[570] New Jersey birth registration no. F36, Harry Freeman (1892); State Archives, Trenton. Parents Harry Freeman and Virginia Riley. "U.S., World War I Draft Registration Cards, 1917–1918," digital images, *Ancestry.com* (https://www.ancestry.com/), Harry Grant Freeman.

[571] New York City death certificate no. 4147, Esther Freeman (1941); Municipal Archives, New York City. 1940 U.S. census, Queens Co., N.Y., pop. sch., Queens, ED 41-1685, p. 3B, dwell. 64, Esther Freeman, wife, in the household of Harry Freeman, Jr.; NARA T627, roll m-t0627-02751.

[572] "Delaware, U.S., Marriage Records, 1750-1954," database and digital images, *Ancestry.com* (https://www.ancestry.com/), Harry Grant Freeman-Helen W. Meak. "Weddings [Mrs. Helen W. Meak(,) Mr. Harry Freeman]," *The Morning News (Wilmington, Del.)*, 19 Jun. 1947, p. 10, col. 4. Helen W. Freeman, wife, in the household of Harry G. Freeman, line 3, sheet 4, ED 1-68, Pleasantville, Atlantic Co., N.J.; Seventeenth Census of the United States, 1950; Record Group 29, Records of the Bureau of the Census; NARA, Washington, D.C. For second wife's mother's birth surname, Delaware Marriage Records, vol. 64, p. 20, Edwin E. Jochen-Maude Wainwright, 3 Jul. 1894; "Delaware, U.S., Marriage Records, 1744-1912," database and digital images, *Ancestry.com* (https://www.ancestry.com/).

[573] *Find A Grave*, database and images (http://findagrave.com), Harry Grant Freeman, memorial no. 197,480,645.

[574] New Jersey birth registration no. F8, male Freeman child (1894); State Archives, Trenton. "U.S., World War I Draft Registration Cards, 1917–1918," database and digital images, *Ancestry.com* (https://www.ancestry.com/), Survetus Carlile Freeman.

[575] Index of Marriages in New Jersey, Bride Index, 1930-5, Survetus Freeman-Annie Anderson, 1935; "New Jersey, U.S., Marriage Index, 1901-2016," database and digital images, *Ancestry.com* (https://www.ancestry.com/). For previous marriage, "Denmark, Church Records, 1812-1918," database and digital images, *Ancestry.com* (https://www.ancestry.com/) > Ålborg Amt > Nørresundby Sogn [Parish], 1907-1919, Anders Andersen-Ane Albertine Kristine Esther Neilsen, m. Nørresundby Sogn [Parish], Danmark [Denmark], 3 Feb. 1913.

[576] New Jersey death certificate no. 08923, Servetus Freeman (1956); Vital Statistics and Registry, Trenton.

[577] New Jersey birth return no. F20, female Freeman child (1898); State Archives, Trenton.

[578] The evidence for the marriage is based on a burial record for Lillian's sister, Virginia, which mentions the name of Lillian's husband. Wesley United Methodist Church (Pleasantville, N.J.), Funerals, Miss Virginia Freeman. "United States World War II Draft Registration Cards, 1942," digital images, *Ancestry.com* (https://www.ancestry.com/), Alexander Quigley Gibson, Sr. Name of nearest relative, Mrs. Lillian Mae Gibson. Lillian Gibson, wife, in the household of Alexander Gibson, line 22, sheet 6, ED 1-90, Ventnor, Atlantic Co., N.J.; Seventeenth Census of the United States, 1950; Record Group 29, Records of the Bureau of the Census; NARA, Washington, D.C. For Alexander, Jr.'s parents, City of Philadelphia, Return of Births for the month of June 1901, Alexander Gibson, 3 Jun. 1901, parents, Alexander and Clara Gibson; City Archives, Philadelphia.

[579] New Jersey death certificate no. 49905, Lillian M. Gibson (1973); Vital Records and Registry, Trenton.

80. vii. CHARLES EDWARD FREEMAN, b. 28 Sep. 1899;[580] m. LILLIAN E. HALL;[581] d. Atlantic City 16 Sep. 1966, age 66, bur. Absecon Presbyterian Church Cemetery, Absecon, N.J.[582]

81. viii. HAZEL NOLL FREEMAN, b. 3 Nov. 1904;[583] d. Atlantis, Palm Beach Co., Fla. 18 Sep. 1967, age 63.[584]

23. JACOB DAVID[3] RILEY (*Christian Fulmer[2]*, *William[1] Riley*), was born in Philadelphia, Philadelphia County, Pennsylvania, on 17 November 1868[585] and died in Northfield, Atlantic County, New Jersey, on 22 April 1949.[586] He married in Atlantic City, Atlantic County, New Jersey, on 28 October 1894 MAMIE/MAMYE/MAME CARTER SHOWELL,[587] daughter of John Adams and Catherine (Woolbert) Showell.[588] She was born in Atlantic City on 4 December 1872 and died in Northfield on 27 June 1952.[589]

Jacob's name appeared in the 1895 *Atlantic City Directory* as a plumber and later as an inspector and foremen for the city's water department.[590] He moved to Northfield by 1940.[591] His widow Mamie lived there with her son-in-law.[592]

---

[580] New Jersey birth return no. [blank], Charles Freeman (1899); State Archives, Trenton. For middle name, "U.S., World War I Draft Registration Cards, 1917–1918," digital images, *Ancestry.com* (https://www.ancestry.com/), Charles Edward Freeman.

[581] "New Jersey, U.S., Marriage Index, 1901-2016," database and digital images, *Ancestry.com* (https://www.ancestry.com/), Charles Freeman-Lillian E. Hall, 1918. Lillian E. Freeman, wife, in the household of Charles E. Freeman, line 20, sheet 10, ED 22-33, Atlantic City, Atlantic Co., N.J.; Seventeenth Census of the United States, 1950; Record Group 29, Records of the Bureau of the Census; NARA, Washington, D.C. *Find A Grave*, database and images (http://findagrave.com), Lillian E. Freeman, memorial no. 50,653,302. Annotation gives birth surname as Hall.

[582] New Jersey death certificate no. 42898, Charles E. Freeman (1966); Vital Records and Registrar, Trenton. *Find A Grave*, database and images (http://findagrave.com), Charles E. Freeman, memorial no. 50,653,251.

[583] New Jersey birth certificate no. 439, Hazel Noll Freeman (1904); State Archives, Trenton.

[584] Florida death certificate no. 67-046754, Hazel N. Freeman (1967); Vital Statistics, Jacksonville.

[585] Circular to verify veteran's identity, Christian F. Riley, Sr., pension application no. S.C. 1,069,104, Civil War, RG 15, NA-Washington. New Jersey death certificate no. 12030 (1949), Jacob D. Riley.

[586] New Jersey death certificate no. 12030 (1949), Jacob D. Riley.

[587] New Jersey marriage return, R63 (1894), Riley-Showell. "MARRIED RILEY-SHOWELL…," *The Philadelphia Inquirer*, 2 Nov. 1894, p. 9, col. 6. Mayme Carter Showell, Family Tree ID 9N89-P1R, "Family Tree," database, *FamilySearch.org*.

[588] New Jersey death certificate no. 21722, Mame Carter Riley, 23 Jun. 1952; Vital Statistics and Registry, Trenton.

[589] Ibid.

[590] *Atlantic City Directory for 1895* (Philadelphia: James Gospill's Sons,1895), 206, "Riley Jacob, plumber, h 822 Arctic av"; By the same title: (1897), 228, "Riley Jacob D., plumber, h 113 N Rhode Island av"; (1898), 222; (1899), 249; (1901), 303, "Riley Jacob D. (Mayme), plumber, h 113 N Rhode Island av"; (1902), 348; (1903), 336; (1904), 347, "Riley Jacob D. (Mary), inspector, h 424 Madison av"; (1905), 378; (1906), 408; (1907), 414; (1909), 474, "Riley Jacob D. (Mary), meter inspector, h 113 N Rhode Island av"; (1909), 532. *Atlantic City Directory for 1910* (Philadelphia: C. E. Howe Co., 1910), 620; By the same title: (1911), 610; (1912), 645; (1913), 678; (1913), 689; (1915), 741; (1916), 748; (1917), 734; (1918), 662; (1920), 674, "Riley Jacob D (Mayme C) foreman h 121 N Massachusetts"; (1921), 744; (1922), 830. *Atlantic City Directory for 1923* (Philadelphia: R. L. Polk & Co., 1923), 915; By the same title: (1924), 1015; (1925), 743, "Riley Jacob D (Mamie C), formn h 44 N Montgomery av"; (1926), 794; (1927), 779; (1928), 767; (1929), 667; (1930), 601; (1931), 628; (1938), 640; (1941), 418; (1946), 584.

[591] 1940 U.S. census, Atlantic Co., N.J., pop. sch., Northfield, ED 1-118, p. 12A, dwell. 251, household of Jacob D. Riley; NARA T627, roll m-t0627-0230.

[592] Mame Riley in the household of Giles T. Gilmour, line 21, sheet 387, ED 1-61, Northfield, Atlantic Co., N.J.; Seventeenth Census of the United States, 1950; RG 29, Records of the Bureau of the Census; NARA, Washington, D.C.

Children of Jacob David Riley and Mamie Carter Showell, all born in Atlantic City,[593] were:

82.   i.   EMILY/EMMA GERTRUDE RILEY a.k.a GERTRUDE EMILY RILEY,[594] b. 17 Aug. 1895;[595] m. (1) THOMAS CHILES GILMOUR[596] and (2) TILFORD DAVIS NEVILLE;[597] d. of encephalomalacia in Los Angeles, Los Angeles Co., Calif. 10 Nov. 1965, age 70,[598] bur. Pomona Cemetery, Pomona, Calif.[599]

83.   ii.   ROY WOOLBERT RILEY, b. 6 Apr. 1898;[600] m. (1) ADELE L. SMITH[601] and (2) BERTHA MIRIAM (NICHOLSON) SAGE BEHRMAN;[602] d. San Diego, San Diego Co., Calif., 4 Sep. 1991.[603]

16. ELMIRA/ELMYRA/ELLA/ADA BREESE/BRACE[3] RILEY (*Christian Fulmer*[2], *William*[1] *Riley*), was born in Philadelphia, Philadelphia County, Pennsylvania, on 14 March 1871[604] and died in Ventnor, Atlantic County, New Jersey, 22 September 1943.[605] She married (1) in Atlantic City,

---

[593] Gospill's *Atlantic City Directory,* for (1895), 206, (1897), 228, (1898), 222, (1899) 249.

[594] New Jersey birth return R12, Emily Gertrude Riley, 17 Aug. 1895; Vital Records and Registry, Trenton.

[595] "New Jersey, U.S., Births and Christenings Index, 1660-1931," database, *Ancesty.com* (https://search.ancestry.com/), Emily G. Riley.

[596] "Philadelphia, Pennsylvania, U.S., Marriage Index, 1885-1951," database, *Ancesty.com* (https://search.ancestry.com/), Thomas C. Gilmour-Emma G. Riley, 1920, license no. 419321.

[597] Marriage Index, Brides, 1960-69, p. 9,328, Tilford D. Neville-Gertrude Gilmour, m. 13 Nov. 1963, Los Angeles, Calif.; "California, U.S., Marriage Index, 1960-1985," database and images, *Ancestry.com* (https://www.ancestry.com/). Annotation gives place of marriage. For groom's middle name, "Marriage Licenses," *Progress-Bulletin (Pomona, Calif.)*, 21 Nov. 1963, p. 19, col. 1.

[598] California death certificate no. 7053-45408, Gertrude Emily Neville (1965); Los Angeles County Registrar-Recorder/County Clerk, Norwalk.

[599] "Gertrude Neville [obituary]," *Chino (Calif.) Champion*, 17 Nov. 1965, p. 19, col. 1.

[600] New Jersey birth return R20, Roy W. Riley, 6 Apr. 1898; Vital Records and Registry, Trenton.

[601] *1938 Directory for Atlantic City* (Philadelphia: R.L. Polk Co., 1938), 640, "Riley Roy W (Adele S [sic]), cash Hotel Strand r Northfield." "U.S., World War II Draft Cards Young Men, 1940-1947," database and images, *Ancestry.com* (https://www.ancestry.com/), Roy Woolbert Riley. Named Mrs. Adele Riley. 1940 U.S. census, Monroe Co., Pa., pop. sch., East Stroudsburg, ED 45-5, p. 14A, dwell. 292, Adele Riley, wife, in the household of Roy W. Riley; NARA T627, roll m-t0627-03575. Adele Riley, wife, in the household of Roy W. Riley, line 20, sheet 11, ED 45-36, Stroud [Stroudsburg], Monroe Co., Pa.; Seventeenth Census of the United States, 1950; Record Group 29, Records of the Bureau of the Census; NARA, Washington, D.C. For spousal relationship, North Carolina death certificate no. 020856, David Woolbert Riley (1992); "North Carolina Deaths, 1931-1994," database and images, *FamilySearch.org* (https://familysearch.org). Parents, Roy Woolbert Riley and Adell [sic] Smith. Another record suggests that Roy W. Riley married Adele L. Smith in Florida in 1959. Marriage Index, p. 1038, Roy W. Riley, cert. no. 28819, Sep. 1959, Seminole Co.; "Florida, U.S., Marriage Indexes, 1822-1875 and 1937-2001," database, *Ancestry.com* (https://www.ancestry.com/). Ibid, Adele L. Smith, p. 1143. This marriage record suggests that the couple was either divorced, had remarried, or was not legally married the first time.

[602] Roy Woolbert Riley (1998-1991), Family Tree ID KFR2-GMB, "Family Tree," database, *FamilySearch.org,* (https://www.familysearch.org/tree/person/details/KFR2-GMB). For second wife's first marriage, "Indiana, U.S., Select Marriage Index, 1748-1933," database, *Ancestry.com* (https://www.ancestry.com/), Paul W. Sage-Bertha Miriam Nicholson, m. 11 Oct. 1911. For second wife's second marriage, ibid., William F. Behrman-Bertha M. Sage, m. 15 Apr. 1921. "California, U.S., Death Index, 1940-1997," database, *Ancestry.com* (https://www.ancestry.com/), Bertha Nicholsen [sic] Riley, SS no. 55-410-4234.

[603] "California, U.S., Death Index, 1940-1997," database, *Ancestry.com* (https://www.ancestry.com/), Roy Woolbert Riley, SS no. 14-905-6611.

[604] Circular to verify veteran's identity, Christian F. Riley, Sr., pension application no. S.C. 1,069,104, Civil War, RG 15, NA-Washington. New Jersey birth certificate S22, Russell F. Sackett, 30 May 1889; Vital Records and Registry, Trenton. Mother, Ella B. Riley, b. Philadelphia, Pa.

[605] "Public Member Trees," database, *Ancestry.com*, "Smith/Schoepfin Tree2 Family Tree," profile for Elmira Breese Riley.

Atlantic County, New Jersey, on 20 July 1888 THOMAS RUTHERFORD SACKETT,[606] a painter,[607] son of Thomas Elgar and Elizabeth Ann (Hawkins) Sackett.[608] He was born in New York City[609] on 2 July 1857[610] and died in Mount Vernon, Westchester County, New York, on 3 February 1891, age 34.[611] Elmira married (2) in Atlantic City on 1 September 1892 WILLIAM THOMAS BRAIDWOOD,[612] a policeman,[613] son of John and Margaret (Grimes) Braidwood.[614] He was born in Baltimore City, Maryland,[615] on 23 February 1867 and died of pulmonary tuberculosis in Atlantic City on 1 August 1914, age 47, was buried in Pleasantville Cemetery, Pleasantville, New Jersey.[616] Elmira may have married (3) by 1915 J. JAMES ROGERS a.k.a. JAMES J. ROGERS a.k.a. JEROME J. ROGERS,[617] and may have married (4) by 1940 CORNELIUS/CORNELINE ERNEST FORT.[618]

[606] "New Jersey, Marriage Records, 1670-1965," database, *Ancestry.com* (https://www.ancestry.com/), Thomas R. Sackett-Elmira B. Riley, 20 Jul. 1888. First Methodist Episcopal Church (Atlantic City, N.J.), Marriage Record, Thomas Rutherford Sackett-Emma Brace [sic] Riley; "New Jersey, United Methodist Church Records, 1800-1970," digital imagers, *Ancestry.com* (https://www.ancestry.com/).

[607] *Philadelphia City Directory for 1887* (Philadelphia: James Gopsill's Sons, 1887), 1478, "Sackett Thomas, painter, h 668 N 8th."

[608] "Thomas R. Sackett (1857-?)," *The Sackett Family Association*," (https://sackettfamily.info/37752.htm#i137752).

[609] Birthplace based on birthplace of father. New Jersey birth certificate S22 (1888), Russell F. Sackett. Father, Thomas Sackett, b. New York City.

[610] "Thomas R. Sackett (1857-?)", *The Sackett Family Association*.

[611] Mount Vernon Trinity Church (Mount Vernon, N.Y.), Parish Register, Burials, 3: 314, Thomas R. Sackett; "New York, U.S., Episcopal Diocese of New York Church Records, 1769-1970," digital images, *Ancestry.com* (https://www.ancestry.com/).

[612] "New Jersey Marriages, 1678-1985," database, *FamilySearch.org* (https://www.familysearch.org/), Wm. T. Braidwood-Ella B. Riley [sic]. St. Paul's Methodist Church (Atlantic City, N.J.), Marriage Register, William T. Braidwood-Ella B. Sackett; "New Jersey, United Methodist Church Records, 1800-1970," database, *Ancestry.com* (https://www.ancestry.com/).

[613] *Atlantic City Directory for 1914* (Philadelphia: C. E. Howe, 1914), 1147, "Braidwood William T (Ella) policeman h 10 Woodland ave [Pleasantville, N.J.]."

[614] New Jersey death certificate no. [blank], Wm. T. Braidwood (1914); State Archives, Trenton.

[615] John was enumerated in the household of his probable maternal grandmother, Eliza Grimes. 1870 U.S. census, Baltimore City, Md., pop. sch., p. 307A, dwell. 832, fam. 1041, Wm Thos Bradewood [sic] in the household of Eliza Grimes; NARA M593, roll 580. "Died [Maggie J. Braidwood]," *The Baltimore (Md.) Sun*, 27 Mar. 1869, p. 2, col. 2. "...MAGGIE J., wife of John Braidwood, and daughter of the late Josiah Grimes....."

[616] New Jersey death certificate no. [blank] (1914), Wm. T. Braidwood.

[617] 1915 New Jersey state census, Atlantic Co., pop. sch., Atlantic City, p. 4A, dwell. 76, fam. 79, Ella Rogers [sic] in the household of Sophia Weaver. Ibid., p. 4A, dwell. 77, fam. 80 which listed J. James Rogers, Dahlgren A. Braidwood, Horace Mc. Braidwood, and Harold S. Braidwood. *Atlantic City Directory for 1916* (Philadelphia: C.E. Howe Co., 1916), 758; By the same title: (1918), 1109; ibid., (1109). 1920 U.S. census, Cape May Co., N.J., pop. sch., Middle Twp., ED 123, p. 1B, dwell. 16, fam. 16, Ella B. [sic] Rogers, housekeeper, Harold McQ. Braidwood, housekeeper's son, in the household of Cornealore E. Fort; NARA T625, roll 1025.

[618] 1940 U.S. census, Cape May Co., N.J., pop. sch., Avalon, ED 5-1, p. 2B, dwell. 6, Elmira Fort, "wife," in the household of Corneline Fort; NARA T628, roll m-t0627-02324.

Elmira was widowed twice.[619] After her second husband died ca. 1914, Elmira had two close male associates: James/Jerome Rogers and Cornelius/Corneline E. Fort. No record of a marriage to either man has been found.[620]

Elmira had a relationship with James was in the late 1910s. In 1915, Elmira was enumerated in Atlantic City as "Elmira Rogers," a married housewife, in the household of Sophia Weaver.[621] One line below was the household of J. James Rogers, a married theater superintendent.[622] In James's household were Elmira's three sons, Dahlgren, Horace, and Harold Braidwood. James with presumed wife Ella was listed in 1916 and 1918 city directories.[623] Dahlgren used the surname "Rogers" in a city directory listing.[624] In a military draft registration, Dahlgren gave as a contact "Mrs. J.J. Rogers."[625] By 1920, Elmira and James lived in separate households.[626]

Elmira was associated with Cornelius Fort from 1920 to 1940. Fort was widowed in 1924.[627] Elmira was enumerated with Cornelius three times: as housekeeper Ella "Rogers" in 1920,[628] as widow Ella Braidwood in 1930,[629] and as "wife" Elmira Fort in 1940.[630] Cornelius died in 1958.[631] Elmira's marital status with J. James Rogers and Cornelius Fort is uncertain.

Children of Thomas Rutherford Sackett and Elmira Breese Riley were:

---

[619] Mount Vernon Trinity Church (Mount Vernon, N.Y.), Thomas R. Sackett burial, 1891. Howe's *Atlantic City Directory*, for (1914), 1147, (1915), 216, no listing for William.

[620] "New Jersey Marriages, 1678-1985," database, *FamilySearch.org* (https://www.familysearch.org/), negative searches > Deceased Ancestor's Information, First Names=Elmira, Last Names=Riley, Alternate First Names=Ella and Elmyra, Alternate Last Names=Braidwood and Rogers. "New Jersey, U.S., Marriage Index, 1901-2016," database, *Ancestry.com* (https://www.ancestry.com/), negative searches using First & Middle Name(s)=Elmira, Elmyra, or Ella, Last Names=Braidwood and Rogers.

[621] 1915 New Jersey state census, Atlantic Co., pop. sch., Atlantic City, p. 4A, dwell. 76, fam. 79, Ella Rogers [sic] in the household of Sophia Weaver.

[622] Ibid., p. 4A, dwell.77, fam. 80.

[623] *Atlantic City Directory for 1916* (Philadelphia: C.E. Howe Co., 1916), 758; By the same title: (1918), 1109.

[624] Ibid., (1109).

[625] "U.S., World War I Draft Registration Cards, 1917-1918," digital images, *Ancestry.com* (https://www.ancestry.com/), Dahlgren Albertson Braidwood.

[626] 1920 U.S. census, Cape May Co., N.J., pop. sch., Middle Twp., ED 123, p. 1B, dwell. 16, fam. 16, Ella B. Rogers, housekeeper, in the household of Cornealore E. Fort; NARA T625, roll 1025. Ibid., Atlantic Co., N.J., Atlantic City, ED 28, p. 12B, dwell. 264, fam. 283, James J. Rogers.

[627] "U.S., World War I Draft Registration Cards, 1917-1918," digital images, *Ancestry.com* (https://www.ancestry.com/), Cornelius Ernest Fort. Nearest relative, Emma Martha Fort. "New Jersey, U.S., Death Index, 1901-2017," database and images, *Ancestry.com* (https://www.ancestry.com/), Martha E. Fort, Dec. 1924.

[628] 1920 U.S. census, Cape May Co., N.J., Middle Twp., ED 123, p. 1B, dwell. 16, fam. 16.

[629] "United States Census, 1930," database and images, *FamilySearch.org* (https://familysearch.org) > New Jersey > Cape May > Avalon > ED 1 > image 1 of 10; citing NARA T626. Ella B. Braidwood in the household of Cornelius E. Fort.

[630] 1940 U.S. census, Cape May Co., N.J., Avalon, ED 5-1, p. 2B, dwell. 6.

[631] Deaths, 1958, Cornelius E. Fort, Jun. 1958; "New Jersey, U.S., Death Index, 1901-2017," digital images, *Ancestry.com* (https://www.ancestry.com/).

84.   i.   RUSSELL FULMER SACKETT, b. Atlantic City 30 May 1888[632] or 30 May 1889;[633] m. ADA ISABEL TAYLOR;[634] d. Ventnor, Atlantic Co., N.J., 20 Mar. 1936, age 45, bur. Laurel Memorial Park, Pomona, N.J.[635] Ada was an Olympiad and successful businesswoman.[636]

85.   ii.   PEARL TYSON/MARIE SACKETT, b. Atlantic City 8 May 1891;[637] m. CHARLES LEEDS TAYLOR;[638] d. there 9 Jun. 1973, age 82, bur. Atlantic City Cemetery, Pleasantville, N.J.[639]

Children of William Thomas Braidwood and Elmira Breese (Riley) Sackett, all born in Atlantic City were:[640]

86.   iii.   WILLIAM T. BRAIDWOOD, b. 21 May 1897;[641] d. of diphtheria in Atlantic City 5 Jan. 1900, age 2 yr., 6 mo.[642]

87.   iv.   GEORGE BRAIDWOOD (twin), b. 29 Dec. 1898;[643] d. of cerebral meningitis in Atlantic City 18 Feb. 1900, age 1 yr., 2 mo.[644]

88.   v.   DAHLGREN ALBERTSON BRAIDWOOD (twin), b. 29 Dec. 1898;[645] d. Somers Point, Atlantic Co., N.J. 19 May 1961, age 62, bur. Atlantic City Cemetery, Pleasantville, N.J.[646]

---

[632] New Jersey birth certificate S22 (1888), Russell F. Sackett.

[633] "U.S., World War I Draft Registration Cards, 1917-1918," digital images, *Ancestry.com* (https://www.ancestry.com/), Russell Fulmer Sackett.

[634] First Presbyterian Church (Atlantic City, N.J.), Register of Marriages, Russell Fulmer Sackett-Ada Isabel Taylor, m. 20 Jul. 1924; "U.S., Presbyterian Church Records, 1701-1970," digital images, *Ancestry.com* (https://www.ancestry.com/). "New Yorker Marries Shore Swimming Star," *The Philadelphia Enquirer*, 23 Jul. 1924.

[635] New Jersey death certificate no. [blank], Russell Fulmer Sackett (1936); Vital Statistics and Registry, Trenton. "Russell F. Sackett...," *The Morning Post*, 21 Mar. 1936. First Presbyterian Church (Atlantic City, N.J.), Register of Burials, Russell F. Sackett, 20 Mar. 1936; "U.S., Presbyterian Church Records, 1701-1970," digital images, *Ancestry.com* (https://www.ancestry.com/).

[636] *Atlantic County Women's Hall of Fame* (https://acwhf.org/) > Menu > Honorees > 2003 > Ada Taylor Sackett.

[637] New Jersey birth certificate S24, Pearl Tyson Sackett, 8 May 1891; Vital Records and Registry, Trenton.

[638] St. Paul's Methodist Church (Atlantic City, N.J.), Marriage Record, Chas. L. Taylor-Marie Sackett, 30 May 1913; "New Jersey, United Methodist Church Records, 1800-1970," digital images, *Ancestry.com* (https://www.ancestry.com/). "New Jersey, Marriage Index, 1901-2016," digital images, *Ancestry.com* (https://www.ancestry.com/), Bride Index, 1910-1914, Charles L. Taylor-Pearl M. Sackett. Married 1914.

[639] New Jersey death certificate no. 27875, Pearl Marie Taylor (1973); Vital Statistics and Registry, Trenton.

[640] 1900 U.S. census, Atlantic Co., N.J., Atlantic City, ED 9, p. 10, dwell. 151, fam. 214, Ella and William Braidwood in the household of Christian Riley, Sr. Record states that Ella gave birth to five children, four of whom were living. 1905 New Jersey state census, Atlantic Co., ED 7, p. 15B, dwell. 221, fam. 278, Ella Braidwood in the household of Christian F. Riley. 1910 U.S. census, Atlantic Co., N.J., Atlantic City, ED 13, p. 5A, dwell. 68, fam., 82. Incorrectly states that Elmira gave birth to nine children, five of whom were living. Negative search for children born after 1905. "New Jersey, U.S., Births and Christenings Index, 1660-1931," database, *Ancestry.com* (https://www.ancestry.com/), Last Name=Braidwood, Location=Atlantic City, Atlantic, New Jersey, Year(s)=1905, 1906, 1907, 1908, 1909, and 1910.

[641] "New Jersey, U.S., Births and Christenings Index, 1660-1931," database, *Ancestry.com* (https://www.ancestry.com/), William T. Broidwood [sic].

[642] New Jersey death report B46, William Braidwood (1900); Vital Statistics and Registry, Trenton.

[643] New Jersey return of birth no. B48, George Braidwood (1898); State Archives, Trenton.

[644] New Jersey report of death no. B47, George Braidwood (1900); State Archives, Trenton.

[645] New Jersey return of birth no. B47, Dahlgren Braidwood (1898); State Archives, Trenton. For middle name, "U.S., World War I Draft Registration Cards, 1917-1918," digital images, *Ancestry.com* (https://www.ancestry.com/), Dahlgren Albertson Braidwood.

[646] New Jersey death certificate no. 20156, Dahlgren A. Braidwood (1961); Vital Records and Registry, Trenton.

89. vi. HORACE MCQUAID BRAIDWOOD, b. 25 Sep. 1901;[647] m. as her second husband[648] EUNICE SOOY (CONOVER) THOMAS;[649] d. Northfield, Atlantic Co., N.J. 5 Mar. 1983, age 81, bur. Atlantic City Cemetery, Pleasantville.[650]

90. vii. HAROLD SEEDS BRAIDWOOD, b. 17 Mar. 1903;[651] m. MARY BROWN,[652] divorced;[653] d. Philadelphia 30 Sep. 1953,[654] bur. Beverly National Cemetery, Beverly, New Jersey.[655] Harold was imprisoned for auto larceny in 1926.[656]

24. ABRAHAM "ABE" LANDIS[3] RILEY, SR. (*Christian Fulmer*[2], *William*[1] *Riley*), was born in Philadelphia, Philadelphia County, Pennsylvania, on 15 December 1874,[657] died in Atlantic City, Atlantic County, New Jersey, on 9 September 1939, age 64,[658] and was buried in Atlantic City Cemetery, Pleasantville, New Jersey.[659] He married in Atlantic City on 3 September 1902 LILLIE CAROLINIA/CAROLINE KESLER,[660] daughter of Felix John and Henrietta (Kuhl) Kesler.[661] She was born in Beardstown, Cass County, Illinois, on 13 December 1880,[662] died in Winslow Township, Camden County, New Jersey, on 16 February 1966, age 85,[663] and was buried with her husband.[664]

---

[647] New Jersey return of birth no. 29656, Horace McQuaid Braidwood (1901); State Archives, Trenton.

[648] "New Jersey, Marriage Index, 1901-2016," database and images, *Ancestry.com* (https://www.ancestry.com/), Bride Index, 1904-1909, Leon Thomas-Eunice Conover, m. 1906. "Public Member Trees," database, *Ancestry.com* (https://www.ancestry.com/), "ThomasConoverArcherStadlmeir," family tree by DAThomas, profile for Eunice Sooy Conover (1890-1961).

[649] *Find A Grave*, database and images (http://findagrave.com), Horace M. Braidwood, memorial no. 187,632,987. Annotation gives wife's name. "New Jersey, Death Index, 1901-2017," database and digital images, *Ancestry.com* (https://www.ancestry.com/), Eunice S. Braidwood, d. Apr. 1961, Galloway Twp., Atlantic Co., N.J.

[650] New Jersey death certificate no. 11076, Horace M. Braidwood (1983); Vital Records and Registry, Trenton. Informant, Rev. Norman Thomas, stepson. *Find A Grave*, Horace M. Braidwood, memorial no. 187,632,987.

[651] "U.S., World War II Draft Cards Young Men, 1940-1947," digital images, *Ancestry.com* (https://www.ancestry.com/), Harold Braidwood.

[652] "Philadelphia, Pennsylvania, Marriage Index, 1885-1951," database, *Ancestry.com* (https://search.ancestry.com/), Harold Braidwood-Mary Brown, m. 1923.

[653] "Philadelphia, Pennsylvania, Marriage Index, 1885-1951," database, *Ancestry.com* (https://search.ancestry.com/), Miller [sic]-Mary E. Braidwood, m. 1935. "United States Census, 1930," database and images, *FamilySearch.org* (https://familysearch.org) > Pennsylvania > Philadelphia > Philadelphia > ED 902 > image 44 of 48; citing NARA T626. Harold Braidwood in the household of Mable Bobly.

[654] Pennsylvania death certificate no. 90379, Harold Braidwood (1953); Vital Statistics, Harrisburg.

[655] *Find A Grave*, database and images (http://findagrave.com), Harold Seeds Braidwood, memorial no. 401,074.

[656] "Pennsylvania, U.S., Prison, Reformatory, and Workhouse Records, 1829-1971," database and images, *Ancestry.com* (https://www.ancestry.com/), Western State Penitentiary, Harold Seeds Braidwood.

[657] "United States World War I Draft Registration Cards, 1917-1918," database and images, *FamilySearch.org*, Abraham Landis Riley.

[658] New Jersey death certificate, no. [blank] (1939), Abraham Landis Riley.

[659] *Find A Grave*, Abraham Landis Riley, memorial no. 232,425,171.

[660] New Jersey marriage certificate no. 12107 (1902), Riley-Kesler.

[661] Cass Co., Ill., Birth Return no. 989 (1880), Lillie Caroline Riley; Clerk's Office, Virginia.

[662] Ibid.

[663] New Jersey death certificate, no. 6421 (1966), Lillie C. Riley; Vital Records and Registrar, Trenton.

[664] *Find A Grave*, database and images (http://findagrave.com), Lillie Caroline Riley, memorial no. 232,565,040.

Abraham was first enumerated in Atlantic City in 1885.[665] He was an electrician and later an electrical inspector for the City of Atlantic City[666] (Figure 12). Their residence was above a gas station, located in Atlantic City at the terminus of the White Horse Pike, a major route connecting the Camden, New Jersey, area and Atlantic City[667] (Figure 13). Lillie was the owner of the gas station, sold patent medicines and "varieties," and took in boarders.[668]

Children of Abraham Landis Riley, Sr. and Lillie Carolinia/Caroline Kesler, all born in Atlantic City,[669] were:

91.   i.   ABRAHAM LANDIS RILEY, JR., b. 28 Jun. 1904;[670] m. ELEANOR MARGUERITE CAMPBELL;[671] d. Galloway Twp., Atlantic Co., N.J. 20 Jan. 1983, age 78,[672] bur. Atlantic City Cemetery, Pleasantville, N.J.[673]

[665] 1885 New Jersey state census, Atlantic Co., pop. sch., Atlantic City, p. 191, dwell. 1258, fam, 1286, Abraham Rieley [sic], in the household of Christian Rieley.

[666] *Atlantic City Directory for 1897* (Philadelphia: James Gospill's Sons, 1897), 227, "Riley Abraham A. [sic], electrician, h r S 121 New York av"; (1898), 222; (1899), 249; (1901), 303, "Riley Abram L., electrician, h 118 St. James pl"; (1902), 348; (1904), 346, "Riley Abraham, electrician, h 4 Bartlett av"; (1909), 531, "Riley Abraham L. (Lillie), electrician, h 725 N Ohio ave." *Atlantic City Directory for 1910* (Philadelphia: C. E. Howe Co., 1910), 619; By the same title: (1911), 609; (1912), 644; (1913), 677; (1913), 688; (1915), 740; (1916), 748; (1917), 734; (1918), 661; (1920), 674; (1921), 744; (1922), 829. *Atlantic City Directory for 1923* (Philadelphia: R. L. Polk & Co., 1923), 914, "Riley Abrahaam [sic] L (Lillie C), elec inspr Electrical Bureau City Hall and auto supplies 725 N Ohio"; By the same title: (1924), 1014; (1925), 742, "Riley Abr inspr City Elec Bureau h Indiana av at Absecon blvd"; (1926), 794; (1927), 778; (1930), 600, Riley Abr L (Lillian) gas and oil ss Absecom [sic] blvd and Indiana av h do"; (1931), 627; (1938), 640. Edwin G. Riley [HAGERSTOWN, MD.] to Russell E. Wigh, M.D., letter, 28 Mar. 1988, copy in author's possession. Riley's father was an electrician. Wigh was a college classmate of Edwin G. Riley. *Scarlet Letter [Yearbook of Rutgers University] Nineteen Thirty-Four* (New York: Schilling Press, 1934), 266.

[667] *Wikipedia* (https://en.wikipedia.org/), "U.S. Route 30 in New Jersey," rev. 15:57, 29 Sep. 2021.

[668] *Atlantic City Directory for 1909* (Philadelphia: James Gospill's Sons, 1909), 532, "Riley Lillie, patent medicines, 725 N Ohio ave." *Atlantic City Directory for 1911* (Philadelphia: C. E. Howe Co., 1911), 532, "Riley Lillie C, varieties, 725 N Ohio ave." *Atlantic City Directory for 1930* (New Brunswick, N.J.: R.L. Polk, 1930), 600, "Riley Abr L (Lillian) gas and oil ss Absecon blvd and Indiana av h do." *Atlantic City Directory for 1941* (Philadelphia: R.L. Polk & Co., 1941), 418, "Riley Lillie C (wid Abr L Riley; Riley's Esso Station) h Absecon Blvd nw cor N Indiana av." Marion (Riley) Mitchell [ADDRESS FOR PRIVATE USE], Northfield, N.J., interview by author, 2 Feb. 2022; recording privately held by author. Mrs. Mitchell, a granddaughter of Lillie Riley, recalls visiting the gas station as a child and stated Lillie took in boarders.

[669] Birth places inferred from parents' residence. 1900 U.S. census, Atlantic Co., N.J., pop. sch., Atlantic City, ED 19, p. 21A, dwell. 434, fam. 430 [sic], household of Abraham L. Riley. 1915 New Jersey state census, Atlantic Co., pop. sch., Atlantic City, p. 3A, dwell. 24, fam. 31, household of Abraham L. Riley.

[670] Abraham Landis Riley, SS no. 135-28-5516, 26 Feb. 1952, Application for Account Number (Form SS-5), Social Security Administration, Baltimore, Maryland.

[671] Staten Island [New York], Marriage License Index, Grooms Index, no. 771, A. Landis Riley, Jr., 23 August 1934; "New York, New York, Marriage License Indexes, 1907–2018," database, *Ancestry.com* (https://www.ancestry.com/).

[672] New Jersey death certificate no. 0004, Abraham Landis Riley, Jr. (1983); Vital Statistics and Registry, Trenton.

[673] *Find A Grave*, database and images (http://findagrave.com), Abraham Landis Riley, Jr., memorial no. 232,642,075.

92.   ii.   HENRIETTA KESLER RILEY, b. 12 Feb. 1907;[674] m. WALTER LEROY CAMP, JR., divorced;[675] d. Weathersfield, Parker Co., Tex., 28 July 1999, age 92,[676] bur. Atlantic City Cemetery, Pleasantville, N.J.[677]

93.   iii.   EDWIN GLOVER RILEY, b. 14 May 1911;[678] m. GERTRUDE AMELIA PFANNER;[679] d. Panorama City, Los Angeles Co., Calif., 16 July 1989, age 78,[680] bur. San Gabriel Cemetery, San Gabriel, Calif.[681]

28. CHARLES MORRIS[3] RILEY, SR. (*Mark Morris[2], William[1] Riley*), was born probably in Upper Providence Township, Montgomery County, Pennsylvania,[682] on 19 December 1861,[683] was baptized as an adult on 14 April 1909 at St. Peter's Episcopal Church, Phoenixville, Chester County, Pennsylvania,[684] and died in an automobile accident of "acute cardiac dilation en route on Lincoln Highway [U.S. Route 30]" in Salisbury, Lancaster County, Pennsylvania, on 3 September 1927, age 65.[685] Charles was buried in Morris Cemetery, Phoenixville, Chester County, Pennsylvania.[686] In 1866, the year Charles's father died, the court appointed Joseph Fitzwater as his guardian.[687] Charles married after 1900[688] and before 1910,[689] as her second husband,[690] MARY "MINNIE" E. (MCADAMS) HARRIS, daughter of John Robertson and Mary (Patterson) McAdams.[691] Mary, Charles Riley's wife, was born probably in Phoenixville in

---

[674] Henrietta Riley Camp, SS no. 145-20-9441, 24 Mar. 1944, Application for Account Number (Form SS-5), Social Security Administration, Baltimore, Maryland.

[675] Superior Court of New Jersey in Chancery, Docket M-5145-51 (1953), Camp v. Camp, Records Management Center, Trenton.

[676] Texas Department of Health, Records and Statistics, Deaths for 1999, p. 353, Henrietta Riley Camp; "Texas, Death Index, 1903–2000," database, *Ancestry.com* (https://www.ancestry.com/).

[677] *Find A Grave*, database and images (http://findagrave.com), Henrietta Kesler (Riley) Camp, memorial no. 232,425,414.

[678] City of Atlantic City, N.J. birth certificate no. [blank], Edwin Glover Riley (1911); Vital Statistics, Atlantic City.

[679] "NYC Grooms Records Index," database, *Italian Genealogy Group* (www.italiangen.org), Edwin G. Riley, Cert. no. 301 (1935). Ibid., "NYC Brides Records Index," Gertrude Pfanner, Cert. no. 301 (1935).

[680] California death certificate no. 33332, Edwin G. Riley (1989); Los Angeles County Registrar-Recorder/Clerk's Office, Norwalk. "Dr. Edwin G. Riley, Public Health Physician," *The Baltimore Sun,* 21 Jul. 1989.

[681] *Find A Grave*, database and images (http://findagrave.com), Dr. Edwin G. Riley, memorial no. 154,292,227.

[682] Birthplace based on location of father's residence. 1860 U.S. census, Montgomery Co., Pa., Upper Providence Twp., p. 571, dwell. 936, fam. 1040, Mark M. Riley in the household of William Riley.

[683] Pennsylvania death certificate no. 85057 (1927), Charles Morris Riley.

[684] St. Peter's Episcopal Church, Charles Morris Riley baptism.

[685] Pennsylvania death certificate no. 42 (1927), Charles Morris Riley.

[686] *Find A Grave*, database and images (http://findagrave.com), Charles Morris Riley, memorial no. 35,381,220.

[687] Montgomery County Register of Wills, Proceedings Index, petition and guardianship appointment, 19: 31, Charles M. Riley, minor, 12 Nov. 1866; "Pennsylvania, U.S., Wills and Probate Records, 1683-1993," digital images, *Ancestry.com* (https://www.ancestry.com/).

[688] 1900 U.S. census, Montgomery Co., Pa., pop. sch., Upper Providence Twp., ED 266, p. 14, dwell. 244, fam. 261, Mary Harris, wife, in the household of James Harris; NARA T623, roll 1444. Also enumerated was Charles's sister, Martha A. Riley, and an unidentified girl, Blanche Riley, age 14, b. Pa., Oct. 1885.

[689] Pennsylvania death certificate no. 27771 (1910), Mary Riley. Informant, Charles Riley, Mont Clare, Pa.

[690] "New Jersey, U.S., Marriage Index, 1901-2016," database, *Ancestry.com* (https://www.ancestry.com/), James R. Harris-Mary McAdams, m. 18 Mar. 1894, Camden, N.J.

[691] Pennsylvania death certificate no. 27771 (1910), Mary Riley. Parents, John McAdams and Mary Patterson. 1880 U.S. census, Chester Co., Pa., pop. sch. Phoenixville, ED 87, p. 286C, dwell. 52, fam. 53, Mary McAdam [sic], daughter, in the household of John McAdam; NARA T9, roll 1115. John McAdams's middle name is found in a

January 1870[692] or on 21 October 1870 and died of septicemia following a miscarriage in Phoenixville on 27 March 1910, age 39.[693] Mary was buried there in Morris Cemetery.[694]

Before he was eighteen, Charles left home and worked for a nearby farmer.[695] He was listed as a widower in the 1900 census,[696] but the identity of his presumed first wife is unknown.[697] Charles's fifty-seven-year-old arthritic sister, Martha Alice Riley, moved into the household to provide care to the children and stepchildren.[698] Charles apparently lived his entire life in Upper Providence Township as a blacksmith in a machine shop and in an iron works.[699]

Children of John Robertson Harris, Sr. and Mary/Minnie E. McAdams and presumed adopted children (i. to v.) of Charles Morris Riley, Sr. were:[700]

94. i. JESSIE B. HARRIS, b. Phoenixville 2 Oct. 1884;[701] m. BENJAMIN CLARENCE SHANNON;[702] d. Jacksonville, Duval Co., Fla. 10 Mar. 1955, age 70, and her body was cremated.[703]

---

record of his son. "Pennsylvania, U.S., World War I Veterans Service and Compensation Files, 1917-1919, 1934-1948," digital images, *Ancestry.com* (https://www.ancestry.com/). Lemuel George Harris, 5 Feb. 1934.

[692] 1870 U.S. census, Chester Co., Pa., pop. sch., Phoenixville, p. 626A, dwell. 846, fam. 845, Mary McAdams, age 7 mo., in the household of John McAdams; NARA M593, roll 1324. Based on the date of the enumeration, 8 Aug. 1870, Mary's birth month was calculated as Jan. 1870.

[693] Pennsylvania death certificate no. 27771 (1910), Mary Riley.

[694] *Find A Grave*, database and images (http://findagrave.com), Mary E. Riley, memorial no. 35,381,221.

[695] 1880 U.S. census, Montgomery Co., Pa., pop. sch., Upper Providence Twp., ED 33, p. 183B, dwell. 74, fam. 87, C.M. Riley in the household of Jacob Umstead; NARA T9, roll 1159.

[696] 1900 U.S. census, Montgomery Co., Pa., Upper Providence Twp., ED 266, p. 3, dwell. 39, fam. 44, Charles M. Riley in the household of Abraham H. Hallman. Also enumerated was Blanche Riley, age 14.

[697] Negative searches, "Pennsylvania, U.S., Marriages, 1852-1968," *Ancestry.com* (https://www.ancestry.com/): First & Middle Name(s)=Charles Morris; Last Name=Riley; Birth=1861±5 yrs. "Pennsylvania, U.S., County Marriage Records, 1845-1963," *Ancestry.com* (https://www.ancestry.com/): First & Middle Name(s)=Charles Morris; Last Name=Riley; Birth=1861±5 yrs.

[698] 1910 U.S. census, Montgomery Co., Pa., pop. sch., Upper Providence Twp., ED 158, p. 10B, dwell. 194, fam. 203, Martha A. Riley, sister, in the household of Charles M. Riley; NARA T624, roll 1380.

[699] 1910 U.S. census, Montgomery Co., Pa., Upper Providence Twp., ED 158, p. 10B, dwell. 194, fam. 203. 1920 U.S. census, Montgomery Co., Pa., pop. sch., Upper Providence Twp., ED 187, p. 17B, dwell. 362, fam. 365, household of Charles M. Riley; NARA T625, roll 1605.

[700] 1920 U.S. census, Montgomery Co., Pa., Upper Providence Twp., ED 187, p. 17B, dwell. 362, fam. 365. Naomi M. Harris and Dorothy B. Harris listed as stepdaughters. "Phoenixville Man Dies in Machine," *Sunday News (Lancaster, Pa.)*, 4 Sep. 1927. "He was accompanied by a stepson, Harris Riley [sic]...." This is incorrect.

[701] Pennsylvania Probate Court (Chester County), Probate Records N-R, will of Charles Morris Riley, made 16 Apr. 1927; "Pennsylvania, U.S., Wills and Probate Records, 1683-1993," digital images, *Ancestry.com* (https://www.ancestry.com/). Charles Morris Riley of Phoenixville, Pa. named daughter Jessie B. Shannon of Somers Point, N.J.

[702] "U.S., World War I Draft Registration Cards, 1917-1918," digital images, *Ancestry.com* (https://www.ancestry.com/), Benjamin Clarence Shannon. Nearest relative, Jessie Shannon. 1910 U.S. census, Philadelphia Co., Pa., pop. sch., Philadelphia, ED 191, p. 8B, dwell. 2, fam. 131, Jessie Shannon, wife, in the household of Benjamin Shannon; NARA T624, roll 1390.

[703] Florida death certificate no. 7258 (1955), Jesse B. Shannon.

95.   ii.   LEMUEL GEORGE HARRIS, b. Philadelphia 6 Sep. 1895;[704] m. HELEN ELIZABETH SCHOFSTALL;[705] d. New Haven, New Haven Co., Conn. 2 Jun. 1966, age 70,[706] bur. Arlington National Cemetery, Arlington, Va.[707]

96.   iii. JAMES ROBERTSON HARRIS, JR., b. Philadelphia 2 Dec. 1896;[708] m. FLORENCE M. WHITWORTH;[709] d. Narberth, Montgomery Co., Pa. 2 Feb. 1949,[710] bur. Oakland Cemetery, Philadelphia.[711]

97.   iv.   DOROTHY BARBARA HARRIS, b. Philadelphia 5 Feb. 1900;[712] m. SILAS LEE MOSES;[713] d. Upper Darby Twp., Delaware Co., Pa. 10 Jan. 1960,[714] bur. Arlington Cemetery, Drexel Hill, Pa.[715]

98.   v.   NAOMI M. HARRIS a.k.a. MILDRED NAOMI HARRIS,[716] b. Mont Clair, Upper Providence Twp., Montgomery Co., Pa. 19 May 1902;[717] m. COURTNEY M. OGBORN, JR.;[718] d. probably Wynnewood, Montgomery Co., Pa. 22 Apr. 1988.[719]

Children of Charles Morris Riley, Sr. and Mary "Minnie" E. (McAdams) Harris were:[720]

---

[704] City of Philadelphia, Return of Births…for the Month of September 1895, Lemuel George Harris; City Archives, Philadelphia.

[705] "Pennsylvania, U.S., World War I Veterans Service and Compensation Files, 1917-1919, 1934-1948," *Ancestry.com*, Lemuel George Harris. Gives birth surname of wife.

[706] "Connecticut Death Index, 1949-2012," database, *Ancestry.com* (https://www.ancestry.com/), Lemuel G. Harris, file no. 12049. "Died [death notice of Lemuel G. Harris]," *The Philadelphia Inquirer*, 4 Jun. 1966, p. 14, col. 5.

[707] *Find A Grave*, database and images (http://findagrave.com), Lemuel G. Harris, memorial no. 126,295,796.

[708] City of Philadelphia, Return of Births…for the Month of December 1896, James Robertson Harris (1896); City Archives, Philadelphia.

[709] "Died [death notice of James R. Harris]," *The Philadelphia Inquirer*, 6 Feb. 1949, p. 59, col. 7. Wife's name, Florence Whitworth. Ibid., "Died [death notice of Florence M. Harris]," 9 Mar. 1998, p. 72, col. 4.

[710] Pennsylvania death certificate no. 14873, James R. Harris (1949); Vital Statistics, Harrisburg.

[711] Oakland Cemetery, Philadelphia, Pa., 1911-1982, p. 161, James R. Harris; "Pennsylvania and New Jersey, U.S., Church and Town Records, 1669-2013," database and images, *Ancestry.com* (https://www.ancestry.com/).

[712] City of Philadelphia, Return of Births…for the Month of February 1899, Dorothy Barbara Harris (1899); City Archives, Philadelphia.

[713] "New York, New York, U.S., Marriage License Indexes, 1907-2018," database and images, *Ancestry.com* (https://www.ancestry.com/), S. Lee Moses-Dorothy Harris, Manhattan, 12 Jun. 1922. For husband's first name, "U.S., World War II Draft Cards Young Men, 1940-1947," digital images, *Ancestry.com* (https://www.ancestry.com/), Silas Lee Moses. Contact person, Dorothy Harris Moses, Drexel Hill, Pa.

[714] Pennsylvania death certificate no. 4323, Dorothy Harris Moses (1960); Vital Statistics, Harrisburg. "Died [death notice of Dorothy Moses]," *The Philadelphia Inquirer*, 12 Jan. 1960, p. 27, col. 7.

[715] *Find A Grave*, database and images (http://findagrave.com), Dorothy H. Moses, memorial no. 121,546,947.

[716] St. Peter's [Episcopal] Church (Phoenixville, Pa.), Parish Register 1909–1943, confirmation, "Third Sunday after Easter 1917," p. 185, Mildred Naomi Harris; "Pennsylvania and New Jersey, U.S., Church and Town Records, 1669-2013," database and digital images, *Ancestry.com* (https://www.ancestry.com/).

[717] Social Security Administration, "U.S., Social Security Applications and Claims Index, 1936-2007," database, *Ancestry.com* (https://www.ancestry.com/), Naomi Harris Ogborn, SS no. 170-50-7981.

[718] *Johnstown (Pa.) City Directory for 1938-39* (Pittsburgh: R.L. Polk, 1938), 385, "Ogborn Courtney M (Naomi H) chemist h148 State (Smt. [Southmont])." 1940 U.S. census, Cambria Co., Pa., Southmont, ED 11-144A, p. 9B, dwell. 194.

[719] Social Security Administration, "U.S., Social Security Death Index, 1935-2014," database, *Ancestry.com* (https://www.ancestry.com/), Naomi H. Ogborn, SS no. 170-50-7981. Last residence, Wynnewood, Pa.

[720] Pennsylvania Probate Court (Chester Co.) will of Charles Morris Riley; "Pennsylvania, U.S., Wills and Probate Records, 1683-1993," digital images, *Ancestry.com* (https://www.ancestry.com/). Named were Jessie B. Shannon and Charles Morris Riley, Jr. 1910 U.S. census, Montgomery Co., Pa., Upper Providence Twp., ED 158, p. 10B, dwell. 194, fam. 203.

99. vi. HAROLD G. RILEY, b. ca. 1905;[721] d. probably bef. 1908.[722]
100. vii. CHARLES MORRIS RILEY, JR., b. Mont Clair, Upper Providence Twp. 27 Oct. 1908;[723] m. ELIZABETH FRANCIS (–?–);[724] d. of atherosclerotic heart disease, Philadelphia, Philadelphia Co., Pa. 17 Jun. 1963, age 54.[725]

30. JESSE MARK[3] RILEY (*Mark Morris*[2], *William*[1] *Riley*), was born in Mont Clare, Upper Providence Township, Montgomery County, Pennsylvania, on 15 August 1866[726] and died in Linden, Union County, New Jersey, on 16 May 1943 and was buried in Morris Cemetery, Phoenixville, Chester County, Pennsylvania.[727] Joseph Fitzwater was appointed his guardian in 1866.[728] He married in Collegeville, Montgomery County, Pennsylvania, on 7 January 1892 SALLIE/SARAH/SARA S. BECHTEL,[729] daughter of Abraham Detweiler and Emma H. a.k.a Hanna Emma (Seasholtz) Bechtel.[730] Sallie was born in Upper Providence Township on 5 January 1870, died of a cerebral hemorrhage in Phoenixville on 28 December 1942, age 72,[731] and was buried with her husband.[732]

Jesse was born one month before his father died.[733] He was raised by his mother who resided in the households of her Billew and Dettra kinfolk.[734] Jesse lived in Phoenixville prior to 1900, based on the birth places of children i. to iii (see below). After 1902, he resided in the Mont

---

[721] 1910 U.S. census, Montgomery Co., Pa., Upper Providence Twp., ED 158, p. 10B, dwell. 194, fam. 203, Harold D. Riley, son, in the household of Charles M. Riley.

[722] Death date based on a sibling's birth record stating the number of children born to the mother. "Pennsylvania, U.S., Birth Certificates, 1906-1911," digital images, *Ancestry.com* (https://www.ancestry.com/), Charles Morris Riley, b. 27 Oct. 1908. Seven children, six of whom were living.

[723] "Pennsylvania, U.S., Birth Certificates, 1906-1911," *Ancestry.com*, Charles Morris Riley. "U.S., World War II Draft Cards Young Men, 1940-1947," digital images, *Ancestry.com* (https://www.ancestry.com/), Charles Morris Riley. Contact person, Mrs. Elizabeth Francis Riley.

[724] Ibid.

[725] Pennsylvania death certificate no. 064296-63, Charles M. Riley (1963); Vital Statistics, Harrisburg. "Died [death notice of Charles M. Riley]," *The Philadelphia Inquirer*, 19 Jun. 1963, p. 20, col. 8.

[726] Social Security Administration, "U.S., Social Security Applications and Claims Index, 1936-2007," database, *Ancestry.com* (https://www.ancestry.com/), Jesse Mark Riley, SS no. 204-05-6643. Gives date and place of birth.

[727] *Find A Grave*, database and images (http://findagrave.com), Jesse M. Riley, memorial no. 192,065,352. Clipping in an unknown newspaper in the annotation gives death place.

[728] Montgomery County Register of Wills, Proceedings Index, petition and guardianship appointment, 19: 244, Jesse M. Riley; "Pennsylvania, U.S., Wills and Probate Records, 1683-1993," digital images, *Ancestry.com* (https://www.ancestry.com/).

[729] Montgomery County Register of Wills, Marriage License Docket, 1885-1901, application for marriage and marriage license, Jesse M. Riley-Sallie S. Bechtel, m. 21 Mat 1892; "Pennsylvania, U.S., Wills and Probate Records, 1683-1993," digital images, *Ancestry.com* (https://www.ancestry.com/). Filed in book 22: 4190.

[730] Pennsylvania death certificate no. 109799, Sarah B. Riley (1942); Vital Statistics, Harrisburg. Jacob Clymer Justice of the Peace Dockets, General Records, Marriages, p. 18, Abraham D. Bechtel-Emma H. Seasholtz [no date]; "Pennsylvania and New Jersey, U.S., Church and Town Records, 1669-2014," digital images, *Ancestry.com* (https://www.ancestry.com/).

[731] Pennsylvania death certificate no. 109799 (1942), Sarah B. Riley. "Deaths [death notice of Sarah B. Riley]," *The Mercury (Pottstown, Pa.)*, 31 Dec. 1942, p. 11, col. 1.

[732] *Find A Grave*, database and images (http://findagrave.com), Sarah B. Riley, memorial no. 192,065,340.

[733] *Find A Grave*, Jesse M. Riley, memorial no. 192,065,352.

[734] 1870 U.S. census, Montgomery Co., Pa., pop. sch., Upper Providence Twp., p. 377A, dwell. 517, fam. 566, household of Sarah Riley; NARA M593, roll 379.

Clare section of Upper Providence Township[735] and was employed in an iron works as a clerk, bookkeeper, and cashier.[736] The iron works was likely in Phoenixville, which was across the Schuylkill River bridge from where Jesse lived.[737]

Children of Jesse Mark Riley and Sallie S. Bechtel were:[738]

101. i. VERE BECHTEL RILEY, b. Phoenixville 28 Jun. 1893;[739] m. ESTHER LANSDOWNE MILLER;[740] d. Mount Holly, Burlington Co., N.J. 2 Mar. 1967, age 73.[741]

102. ii. WALTER BECHTEL RILEY, b. Phoenixville 28 Aug. 1894;[742] m. HANNAH "STELLA" DETWILER MILLER;[743] d. of acute coronary insufficiency [atherosclerosis] in Phoenixville 23 Apr. 1962, age 62, bur. Morris Cemetery, Phoenixville.[744]

103. iii. EMMA BECHTEL RILEY, b. Phoenixville 1897[745] or 25 Sep. 1900;[746] m. JOHN DEWEY MCCARRAHER;[747] d. of cerebral hemorrhage from a skull fracture caused by an automobile accident near Cuyahoga Falls, Summit Co., Ohio, 29 Sep. 1950, age 50 or 53,[748] bur. Morris Cemetery, Phoenixville.[749]

---

[735] "Deaths [obituary of Mrs. Jesse M. Riley]," unknown newspaper, 29 Dec. 1942. Newspaper clipping; Riley Family History, privately held by Deborah (Le Van) Swift [ADDRESS FOR PRIVATE USE] Las Vegas, Nev., 2022. Inherited by Ms. Swift from her mother, Barbara (Martin) Le Van, who inherited it from her mother, Helen Bechtel (Riley) Martin.

[736] 1900 U.S. census, Montgomery Co., Pa., pop. sch., Upper Providence Twp., ED 266, p. 16, dwell. 399, fam. 316, household of Jesse Riley; NARA T623, roll 1444. 1910 U.S. census, Montgomery Co., Pa., Upper Providence Twp., ED 158, p. 6A, dwell. 101, fam. 109. 1920 U.S. census, Montgomery Co., Pa., pop. sch., Upper Providence Twp., ED 187, p. 13B, dwell. 274, fam. 277, household of Jesse M. Riley; NARA T625, roll 1605. 1930 U.S. census, Montgomery Co., Pa., pop. sch., Upper Providence Twp., ED 15, p. 6A, dwell. 97, fam. 101, household of Jesse M. Riley; NARA T626, roll 2085.

[737] 1930 U.S. census, Montgomery Co., Pa., Upper Providence Twp., ED 15, p. 6A, dwell. 97, fam. 101. Jesse's residence was Bridge St., Mont Clare.

[738] 1900 U.S. census, Montgomery Co., Pa., Upper Providence Twp., ED 266, p. 16, dwell. 399, fam. 316. 1910 U.S. census, Montgomery Co., Pa., Upper Providence Twp., ED 158, p. 6A, dwell. 101, fam. 109.

[739] "Pennsylvania, U.S., World War I Veterans Service and Compensation Files, 1917-1919, 1938-1848," digital images, *Ancestry.com* (https://www.ancestry.com/), Vere Bechtel Riley. Birthplace based on residence of parents. 1900 U.S. census, Montgomery Co., Pa., Upper Providence Twp., ED 266, p. 16, dwell. 399, fam. 316.

[740] Marriage Records, Chester Co., 1915–1920, Vere Bechtel Riley-Esther Lansdowne Miller, 28 Jun. 1917; "Pennsylvania, U.S., Marriages, 1852-1968," digital images, *Ancestry.com* (https://www.ancestry.com/).

[741] "U.S., Veterans Administration Master Index, 1917-1940," database, *Ancestry.com* (https://www.ancestry.com/), Vere Bechtel Riley. Social Security Administration, "U.S., Social Security Death Index, 1935-2014," database *FamilySearch.org* (https://www.familysearch.org/), Vere Riley. "Riley," unknown newspaper; Riley Family History, privately held by Deborah (Le Van) Swift. New Jersey Department of Health, Vital Statistics and Registry, 23 Mar. 2022, letter reporting negative death-record search for Vere Riley.

[742] Pennsylvania death certificate no. 035657-62, Walter B. Riley (1962); Vital Statistics, Harrisburg.

[743] Trinity Reformed Church (Philadelphia, Pa.), Marriage Records, no. C219, Walter Bechtel Riley-Hanna Detweiler Miller, 25 Jun. 1919; "Pennsylvania and New Jersey, U.S., Church and Town Records, 1669-2013," digital images, *Ancestry.com* (https://www.ancestry.com/).

[744] Pennsylvania death certificate no. 035657-62 (1962), Walter B. Riley. "Deaths," *The Philadelphia Inquirer*, 24 Apr. 1962.

[745] Chester Co., Birth Records, 1893-1906, Emma Riley, Book 1: 223; "Chester County, Pennsylvania, U.S., Birth Index, 1852 - 1855, 1893 - 1907," database, *Ancestry.com* (https://www.ancestry.com/).

[746] Ohio death certificate no. 65367, Emma Riley McCarraher (1950); Vital Statistics, Columbus.

[747] Chester County, Marriage Records, 1920-1925, no. 25,114, John Dewey McCarraher-Emma Bechtel Riley, 10 June 1924; "Pennsylvania, U.S., Marriages, 1852-1968," digital images, *Ancestry.com* (https://www.ancestry.com/).

[748] Ohio death certificate no. 65367 (1950), Emma Riley McCarraher. "Youth Fleeing Cops Causes Fatal Crash Involving Wedding Party," *The Daily Times (New Philadelphia, Ohio)*, 30 Sep. 1950, p. 10, cols. 5-6.

[749] *Find A Grave*, database and images (http://findagrave.com), Emma McCarraher, memorial no. 192,122,415.

104. iv. HAROLD B. RILEY, b. probably Mont Clare, Upper Providence Twp.,[750] 1902; d. 1902, bur. Morris Cemetery, Phoenixville.[751]

105. v. HELEN BECHTEL RILEY, b. Mont Clare, Upper Providence Twp. 8 Aug. 1908;[752] m. BENJAMIN YOST MARTIN;[753] d. probably Upper Darby Twp., Delaware Co., Pa. 24 Jan. 1996, age 88, bur. Morris Cemetery, Phoenixville.[754]

106. vi. GEORGE BECHTEL RILEY, b. Mont Clare, Upper Providence Twp., Pa. 16 Oct. 1913;[755] m. (1) MARY LOUISE YENCHICK[756] and (2) KATHERINE MAE DAY;[757] d. Port Charlotte, Charlotte Co., Fla. 26 Nov. 1996, age 83, cremated Southeastern Crematory, Punta Gorda, Fla.[758] bur. Morris Cemetery, Phoenixville.[759]

32. ROBERT WILEY³ BROWN (*Lydia Ann²*, *William¹ Riley*), was born in Philadelphia, Philadelphia County, Pennsylvania, on 2 December 1869[760] or 28 December 1869 and was baptized there with his brother Edward Henry at the Port Richmond Methodist Episcopal Church on 26 May 1872.[761] Robert died probably in Atlantic City, Atlantic County, New Jersey,[762] on 14 April 1941, age 72, and was buried in Laurel Memorial Park and Crematory, Egg Harbor Township, New Jersey.[763] He married in Philadelphia on 7 Jun. 1899 MARGARET/MAGGIE J. CHRISTIAN,[764] daughter of

---

[750] Birthplace based on residence of parents. 1900 U.S. census, Montgomery Co., Pa., Upper Providence Twp., ED 266, p. 16, dwell. 399, fam. 316.

[751] *Find A Grave*, database and images (http://findagrave.com), Harold B. Riley, memorial no. 192,065,365.

[752] Pennsylvania Birth Certificate, no. 128523, Helen Riley (1908); Vital Statistics, Harrisburg.

[753] "Philadelphia, Pennsylvania, U.S., Marriage Index, 1885-1951," database, *Ancestry.com* (https://www.ancestry.com/), Benjamin Y. Martin-Helen B. Riley, 1931. 1940 U.S. census, Montgomery Co., Pa., pop. sch., Lower Merion Twp., ED 46-83, p. 7A, dwell. 139, Helen Martin, wife, in the household of Benjamin Martin; NARA T627, roll m-t0627-03580. For their middle names, "Barbara Anne Martin Le Van [obituary]," *Erie (Pa.) Times-News*, 18 Mar. 2016. Viewed at *GenealogyBank.com* (https://www.genealogybank.com/).

[754] Social Security Administration, "United States Social Security Death Index," database, *FamilySearch.org* (https://www.familysearch.org/), Helen R. Martin. Deborah (Le Van) Swift [ADDRESS FOR PRIVATE USE], Las Vegas, Nev., interview by author, 23 Nov. 2021. Ms. Swift, a granddaughter of Helen (Riley) Martin, consulted notes of her mother, Barbara Anne (Martin) LeVan.

[755] Pennsylvania birth certificate no. 216354, George B. Riley (1913); Vital Statistics, Harrisburg. For middle name, "U.S., World War II Draft Cards Young Men, 1940-1947," digital images, *Ancestry.com* (https://www.ancestry.com/), George Bechtel Riley.

[756] "New York, New York, U.S., Marriage License Indexes, 1907-2018," digital images, *Ancestry.com* (https://www.ancestry.com/), Grooms, Brooklyn, 1933, George B. Riley. Ibid., Brides, Brooklyn, 1933, Mary L. Yenchick. Marriage record of son states Mary's middle name. Virginia marriage certificate no. 26136, Norman A. Riley-Maureen M. Sauers, 4 Sep. 1954; "Virginia, U.S., Marriage Records, 1936-2014," digital images, *Ancestry.com* (https://www.ancestry.com/).

[757] "Florida, U.S., Marriage Indexes, 1822-1875 and 1927-2001," database, *Ancestry.com* (https://www.ancestry.com/), George Bechtel Riley-Katherine Mae Day, Lake Co., 17 Jun. 1996.

[758] Florida death certificate no. 96 136538, George Bechtel Riley (1996); Vital Statistics, Jacksonville. "George B. Riley [obituary]," *Sarasota (Fla.) Herald-Tribune*, 30 Nov. 1996, p. 7B, col. 1. "…his wife, Katherine Day…."

[759] *Find A Grave*, database and images (http://findagrave.com), George B. Riley, memorial no. 192,072,546.

[760] Philadelphia Birth Return, Robt. W [Brown], 27 Dec. 1869.

[761] Port Richmond Methodist Episcopal Church (Philadelphia, Pa.), Baptisms, Robert Wiley Brown, 26 May 1872.

[762] *Atlantic City Directory for 1941* (New York: R. L. Polk, 1941), 90, "Brown Robt (Margt) carp contr h 126 Adriatic av h do."

[763] *Find A Grave*, Robert W. Brown, memorial no. 138,488,529.

[764] "Pennsylvania, U.S., Marriages, 1852-1968," database, *Ancestry.com* (https://www.ancestry.com/), Brown-Christian, 7 Jun. 1899. Social Security Administration, "U.S., Social Security Applications and Claims Index, 1936-2007," database, *Ancestry.com* (https://www.ancestry.com/), Robert William Brown, SS no. 150-07-4639. 1915 New Jersey state census, Atlantic Co., Atlantic City, p. 8A, dwell. 86, fam. 183.

Joseph and Margaret (Potts) Christian.[765] She was born in Marlton, Evesham Township, Burlington County, New Jersey,[766] on 8 August 1876[767] and died in Atlantic City in January 1954.[768]

After his 1899 marriage, Robert was a clerk in Philadelphia.[769] He moved to Atlantic City about 1907 and was employed as a clerk, notary, auto body worker, and carpet contractor.[770] Margaret resided in Atlantic City until her death.[771]

Children of Robert Wiley Brown and Margaret/Maggie Christian, birth order of child ii. uncertain, were:[772]

[765] 1880 U.S. census, Camden Co., N.J., pop. sch., Delaware (now Cherry Hill Twp.), ED 59, p. 455B, dwell. 93, fam. 4, Maggie Christian, daughter, in the household of Jos. Christian; NARA T9, roll 774. Mother's name documented in her son's death certificate. Virginia death certificate no. 4222, Harry Clayton Christian (1952); Vital Statistics, Richmond; "Virginia, Death Certificates, 1912-1987," digital images, *FamilySearch.org* (https://www.familysearch.org/). Mother, Margaret Potts. For relationship to Margaret (Christian) Brown, "Harry C. Christian [obituary]," *The Times-Dispatch (Richmond, Va.)*, 16 Feb. 1952, p. 9, col. 4. Survivors, "…a sister, Mrs. Margaret Brown, of Atlantic City, N.J.…."

[766] New Jersey birth certificate [blank], Ruth Williams Brown (1919); State Archives, Trenton. Gives mother's birthplace as Marlton, N.J.

[767] "Public Member Trees," database, *Ancestry.com* (http://www.ancestry.com/), "Constance Hollis Family Tree" family tree by Constance Hollis, profile for Margaret Christian (1876-unknown). 1915 New Jersey state census, Atlantic Co., pop. sch., Atlantic City, ED Third Ward, p. 8A, dwell. 86, fam. 183, Margaret Brown in the household of Robt W. Brown.

[768] "New Jersey, U.S., Death Index,1901-2017," database, *Ancestry.com* (http://www.ancestry.com/), Margaret J. Brown, file no. 28. Annotation gives death place. *Atlantic City Directory for 1954* (Pittsburgh: R. L. Polk, 1954), 50, "Brown Margt (wid Robt) h126 Adriatic av"; By the same title: (1955), 49, no listing for Margt Brown.

[769] 1900 U.S. census, Philadelphia Co., Pa., pop. sch., Philadelphia, ED 790, p. 10B, dwell. 175, fam. 187, Robert W. Brown, son-in-law, and Margaret Brown, daughter, in the household of Margaret Christian; NARA T623, roll 1473. *Philadelphia City Directory for 1905* (Philadelphia: James Gospill's Sons, 1905), 352, "Brown Robt W., clerk, h 2334 E Sergeant"; By the same title: (1906), 392, "Brown Robt W clerk h 2561 N 18th."

[770] *Atlantic City Directory for 1907* (Philadelphia: James Gopsill's Sons, 1907), 115, "Brown Robert W. (Margaret), clerk, h 27 Haddon av." *Atlantic City Directory for 1908* (Philadelphia: C.E. Howe Co., 1908), 124; By the same title: (1909), 134; (1911), 114, "Brown R Wiley (Margaret) h 3 Union National Bank Bldg"; (1913), 155, "Brown Robert W (Margaret) (Savage and Brown) h 1523 Atlantic ave"; (1914), 156, "Brown Robert W (Margaret) (Savage and Brown) and sec and treas Elite Amusement Co h 1523 Atlantic ave"; (1915), 228, "Brown Robert W (Margaret) (Brown's Baths) h 1523 Atlantic ave"; (1916), 231, "Brown Robert W (Margaret) clerk h 100 N Dover ave"; (1917). 227; (1920), 216, "Brown Robert W (Margaret) h 3020 Fairmont"; (1922), 241, "Brown Robert W (Margaret) asst mgr h 322 French." *Atlantic City Directory for 1923* (Philadelphia: R.L. Polk & Co., 1923), 266; (1924), 284; (1925), 206; (1926), 216; (1927), 197; (1928), 182; (1929), 178; (1930), 159; (1931), 165. *Atlantic City…Directory for 1938* (Atlantic City, N.J.: Atlantic Directories, 1938), 144, "Brown Renwick body and woodwkr Wm Mall Auto Body Shop r30 Parkside." *Atlantic City Directory for 1931* (Philadelphia: R.L. Polk & Co., 1931), 165, "Brown Robert W (Margt) carp contr 126 Adriatic av h do." *Atlantic City…Directory for 1935* (Atlantic City, N.J.: Atlantic Directories, 1935), 32; (1938), 114. *Atlantic City Directory for 1941* (New York: Polk & Co., 1941), 90.

[771] "New Jersey, U.S., Death Index,1901-2017," database, *Ancestry.com*, Margaret J. Brown. R. L. Polk, *Atlantic City Directory for,* (1954), 50, (1955), 49, no listing for Margt Brown.

[772] 1915 New Jersey state census, Atlantic Co., Atlantic City, ED Third Ward, p. 8A, dwell. 86, fam. 183. 1920 U.S. census, Atlantic Co., N.J., pop. sch., Atlantic City ED 38, p. 10A, dwell. 194, fam. 224, household of Robert W. Brown; NARA 625, roll 1015.

107. i.   WILLIAM R. BROWN a.k.a. RENWICK WILLIAM BROWN, b. Philadelphia 22 Dec. 1902,[773] bapt. there at Cumberland Street Methodist Episcopal Church, 5 Apr. 1903;[774] m. MARGARET GOLDIE (CRAMER) RUTTER;[775] d. there 28 Feb. 1983.[776]

108. ii. UNNAMED BROWN CHILD, b. aft. 1902;[777] d. bef. 1907.[778]

109. iii. SAVERY BRADLEY BROWN, b. Atlantic City 9 Dec. 1907,[779] bapt. there at Central Methodist Church 13 Jun. 1909;[780] m. HELEN WHALEY a.k.a. DOLORES A. WHALEY,[781] divorced,[782] and (2) DOROTHY (BROOME) LATIMER;[783] d. aft. 1957.[784]

---

[773] City of Philadelphia, Return of Births…for the Month of Dec. 1902, Renwick W. Brown (1902); City Archives, Philadelphia. "U.S., World War II Draft Cards Young Men, 1940-1947," digital images, *Ancestry.com* (https://www.ancestry.com/), Renwick William Brown.

[774] Cumberland Street Methodist Episcopal Church (Philadelphia, Pa.), 1885-1953, Record of Baptisms, Rennick [sic] William Brown; "Pennsylvania and New Jersey, U.S., Church and Town Records, 1669-2913," digital images, *Ancestry.com* (https://www.ancestry.com/).

[775] "Renwick W. Brown [death notice]," *The Philadelphia Inquirer*, 2 Mar. 1983, p. 18, col. 3. "…husband of Margaret Brown (nee Cramer)…." "Margaret G. Brown (nee Cramer) [death notice]," *Courier-Post (Camden, N.J.)*, 27 Jan. 1966, p. 10, col. 1. "…Margaret G. Brown (nee Cramer) wife of the late R. William Brown…." For wife's middle name, Social Security Administration, "U.S., Social Security Applications and Claims Index, 1936-2007," database, *Ancestry.com* (https://www.ancestry.com/), Margaret Goldie Brown. The name of a stepson in Renwick's household provides evidence of his wife's first marriage. 1940 U.S. census, Atlantic Co., N.J., pop. sch., Atlantic City, ED 1-17, p. 2B, fam. 42, William Ritter [sic], age 14, stepson, in the household of R. William Brown; NARA T627, roll m-t0627-02300. Stepson's burial information names his parents. *Find A Grave*, database and images (http://findagrave.com), William Riddle Rutter, memorial no. 214,399,540. Annotation, b. Atlantic City, N.J. to Margaret Cramer and William Rutter.

[776] Social Security Administration, "U.S., Social Security Death Index, 1935-2014," database, *Ancestry.com* (https://www.ancestry.com/), Renwick Brown, SS no. 150-07-6958. "Renwick W. Brown," *The Philadelphia Inquirer*, 2 Mar. 1983.

[777] Philadelphia Return of Births…for the Month of Dec. 1902, Renwick W. Brown (1902).

[778] New Jersey birth certificate no. 272, Savery Bradley Brown (1907); State Archives, Trenton. Number of children by this marriage, 3; number living, 2.

[779] Ibid.

[780] Central Methodist Church (Atlantic City, N.J.), Church Register, Record of Baptisms, 2 Sep. 1895–26 Feb. 1911, baptism, Bradley Brown. Parents, Robert W. and Mary [sic] Brown.

[781] Information about wife in a claim of a daughter. Social Security Administration, "U.S., Social Security Applications and Claims Index, 1936-2007," database, *Ancestry.com* (https://www.ancestry.com/), Dolores Helen Brown. Birth name of mother, Helen A. Whaley. For parental relationship, "Public Member Trees," database, *Ancestry.com* (https://www.ancestry.com/), "Herbert Family Tree" family tree by Kandi Stowers, profile for Dolores Helen Brown (1928-1999).

[782] Virginia certificate of marriage no. 10301, Savery Bradley Brown-Dorothy Broome Latimore, m. Richmond, Va., 20 Apr. 1942; "Virginia, U.S., Marriage Records, 1936-2014," database and digital images, *Ancestry.com* (https://www.ancestry.com/). Bride and groom had both been divorced.

[783] Ibid. The New Church Register of the Westminster Presbyterian Church (Atlantic City, N.J.), Book 1, Roll of Infant Church Members, no. 434, Ronald B. Brown, b. 17 Apr. 1943; "U.S., Presbyterian Church Records, 1701-1970," digital images, *Ancestry.com* (https://www.ancestry.com/). Image 210 of 306. Parents, Bradley and Dorothy Brown. Bradley S. Brown, line 215, sheet 12, ED 22-17, Atlantic City, Atlantic Co., N.J.; Seventeenth Census of the United States, 1950; Record Group 29, Records of the Bureau of the Census; NARA, Washington, D.C. Dorothy Brown, wife, age 37, Joan Latimer, stepdaughter, age 19, and Ronald Brown, son, age 7, in the household of Bradley Brown, age 42, mechanic for pin ball machine company.

[784] *Atlantic City Directory for 1957* (R. L. Polk, 1957), 46, "Brown Bradley S (Dorothy) mech h215 Tomlin av". Negative searches, "New Jersey, U.S., Death Index, 1901-2017," database, *Ancestry.com* (https://www.ancestry.com/), First & Middle Names(s)=Bradley, Last Name=Brown, Birth Year=1907. Negative search, "United States Social Security Death Index," database, *FamilySearch.org* (https://www.familysearch.org/), First Names=Bradley, Last Names=Brown, Year Birth=1907±2 yrs.

110. iv. ROBERT WILLIAM BROWN, JR. [sic], b. Atlantic City 14 Feb. 1912,[785] bapt. there at Central Methodist Church, 9 Jun. 1912;[786] m. (1) JEAN G. SEARLES[787] and possibly (2) RUTH (−?−);[788] d. in an automobile accident in Langhorne, Bucks Co., Pa. 20 Nov. 1988.[789]

111. v. RUTH WILLIAMS BROWN, b. Atlantic City 18 Jan. 1919;[790] m. PARK WAYNE SPENCE;[791] d. Bridgeton, Cumberland Co., N.J. Jul. 1966.[792]

37. MARY ANNE[3] GETTY (*Mary Rebecca*[2], *William*[1] *Riley*), was born in Philadelphia, Philadelphia County, Pennsylvania, on 23 February 1867 and was baptized there at St. Stephen's Episcopal Church on 26 November 1871.[793] Mary Anne died in Philadelphia on 12 December 1936, age 69 years, 9 months, and 20 days,[794] and was buried there in North Cedar Hill Cemetery.[795] She married there at St. Mark's Episcopal Church on 7 February 1885 WILLIAM HENRY EMMITT, a weaver,[796] son of William and Rebecca (Clark) Emmitt.[797] He was born in Philadelphia on

---

[785] New Jersey birth certificate no. [blank], Robert W. Brown, Jr. (1912); Vital Records and Registrar, Trenton.

[786] Central Methodist Church (Atlantic City, N.J.), Record of Baptisms, Robert Royal [sic] Brown; "New Jersey, U.S., United Methodist Church Records, 1800-1970," digital images, *Ancestry.com* (https://search.ancestry.com/).

[787] Index of Marriages in New Jersey, Brides Index, 1946, Robert W. Brown-Jean Searles; "New Jersey, U.S., Marriage Index, 1901-2016," database and digital images, *Ancestry.com* (https://search.ancestry.com/).

[788] Robert's first wife d. 1981. Index of Deaths for 1981, p. 161, Jean G. Brown, d. 23 Nov. 1981 in Atlantic City; "New Jersey, U.S., Death Index, 1901-2017," digital images, *Ancestry.com* (https://search.ancestry.com/). "Levittown man killed in crash in Bucks County," *The Philadelphia Inquirer*, 22 Nov. 1988, p. 16, col. 1. "…injuries to his wife, Ruth…."

[789] "Levittown man killed in crash…," *The Philadelphia Inquirer*, 22 Nov. 1988. Social Security Administration, "U.S., Social Security Death Index, 1935-2014," database, *Ancestry.com* (https://www.ancestry.com/), Robert W. Brown.

[790] New Jersey birth certificate [blank] (1919), Ruth Williams Brown.

[791] Index of Marriages in New Jersey, Brides Index, 1937, Park W. Spence-Ruth Brown [no date]; "New Jersey, U.S., Marriage Index, 1901-2016," digital images, *Ancestry.com* (https://www.ancestry.com/). Social Security Administration, "U.S., Social Security Death Index, 1935-2014," digital images, *Ancestry.com* (https://www.ancestry.com/), Ruth Spence, SS no. 150-09-6660. "U.S., World War II Draft Cards Young Men, 1940-1947," digital images, *Ancestry.com* (https://www.ancestry.com/), Park Wayne Spence. Relative, wife, Mrs. Ruth Williams Spence.

[792] Death Index for 1966, p. 725, Ruth W. Spence; "New Jersey, U.S., Death Index, 1901-2017," database and digital images, *Ancestry.com* (https://www.ancestry.com/). Death place, Bridgeton, N.J. "U.S., Social Security Death Index, 1935-2014," *Ancestry.com* (https://www.ancestry.com/), Ruth Spence.

[793] St. Stephen's Episcopal Church (Philadelphia, Pa.), Baptisms, p. 52, no. 62, Mary Anne Getty; "Pennsylvania and New Jersey, U.S., Church and Town Records, 1669-2013," database and digital images, *Ancestry.com* (https://www.ancestry.com/).

[794] Pennsylvania death certificate no. 24715, Mary Ann Emmitt. St. Mark's Episcopal Church (Philadelphia, Pa.), Church Records, Burials, p. 476, Mary A. Emmitt; "Pennsylvania and New Jersey, U.S., Church and Town Records, 1669-2013," database and digital images, *Ancestry.com* (https://www.ancestry.com/). "Mary A. Emmitt [death notice]," *The Philadelphia Inquirer*, 15 Dec. 1936, p. 35, col. 2. "…MARY A. EMMITT (nee Getty), widow of William H. Emmitt and daughter of the late Robert and Mary A Getty (nee Carey [sic])…."

[795] *Find A Grave*, database and images (http://findagrave.com), Mary Ann Emmitt, memorial no. 183,355,048.

[796] St. Mark's Episcopal Church (Philadelphia, Pa.), Marriages 1884-85, no. 649, William Emmitt-Mary Ann Getty; "Pennsylvania and New Jersey, U.S., Church and Town Records, 1669-2013," database and digital images, *Ancestry.com* (https://www.ancestry.com/). City of Philadelphia, Return of Marriages, 1 Jan. to 1 Apr. 1885, William Emmitt-Mary Ann Getty, 7 Feb. 1885; City Archives, Philadelphia. Groom was a weaver.

[797] Pennsylvania death certificate no. 23736, William Emmitt (1930); Department of Vital Statistics, Harrisburg.

14June 1863[798] and died there of a cerebral hemorrhage on 27 November 1930, age 68,[799] and was buried with his wife.[800]

As a thirteen-year-old girl, Mary Anne worked in the textile industry.[801] Two decades later her children, ages fourteen and fifteen, were also employed in that trade.[802] Philadelphia was the "…great seat of Hand-Loom Manufacturing and Weaving in America…" in mid-century.[803] In the early twentieth century, Mary ran boarding houses in Philadelphia[804] and Atlantic City.[805] The family lived in the Frankford neighborhood of Philadelphia where her husband William worked for many years as a dyer of textiles.[806] William witnessed his granddaughter's 1909 baptism in an Episcopal church;[807] he was later baptized in that denomination.[808]

Children of William Henry Emmitt and Mary Anne Getty were:[809]

[798] City of Philadelphia, Return of Births…from the "5th day of 6 mo. to the 14th day of same 1863," Wm. Henry Emmitt, 14 Jun. 1863; City Archives, Philadelphia.

[799] Pennsylvania death certificate no. 23736 (1930), William Emmitt.

[800] *Find A Grave*, database and images (http://findagrave.com), William Emmitt, memorial no. 183,355,077.

[801] 1880 U.S. census, Philadelphia Co., Pa., Philadelphia, ED 481, p. 286B, dwell. 227, fam. 230.

[802] 1900 U.S. census, Philadelphia Co., Pa., Philadelphia, ED 518, p. 12, dwell. 295, fam. 238.

[803] Elizabeth M. Geffen, "Industrial Development and Social Crisis, 1841-1854," in Russell F. Weigley, ed., *Philadelphia: A 300-Year History* (New York: W.W. Norton, 1982), 326-37.

[804] 1910 U.S. census, Philadelphia Co., Pa., pop. sch., Philadelphia, ED 467, p. 5B, dwell. 113, fam. 120 [boarding house], Mary A. Emmitt; NARA T624, roll 1397. 1930 U.S. census, Philadelphia Co., Pa., pop. sch., Philadelphia, ED 875, p. 2A, dwell. 31, fam. 36, William H. Emmitt; NARA T626, roll 2106. Four boarders were enumerated.

[805] 1920 U.S. census, Atlantic Co., N.J., pop. sch., Atlantic City, ED 14, p. 9B, dwell. 75, fam. 174 [boarding house] William H. Emitt [sic], hotel proprietor; NARA T625, roll 1015. *Atlantic City Directory for 1920* (Philadelphia: C.E. Howe, 1920), 324, "Emmitt Mary A (The Frankford) h 37 S North Carolina"; By the same title: (1920), 324, "Emmitt Wm H (Mary A) 37 S North Carolina"; (1921), 320, "Emmitt Mary A (The Frankford) h 37 S North Carolina."

[806] *Philadelphia City Directory for 1893* (Philadelphia: James Gopsill's Sons, 1893), 573, "Emmitt William, dyer, h 1516 Deal, Fkd [Frankford]"; By the same title: (1894), 588; (1895), 551; (1896), 574; (1897), 585; (1898), 643; (1899), 669; (1900), 666; (1901), 742; (1902), 709; (1905), 771; (1906), 795. *Philadelphia City Directory for 1907* (Philadelphia: C.E. Howe Co., 1907), 559, "Emmitt Wm confectioner 4264 Fkd av"; By the same title: (1908), 581, "Emmitt Wm, dyer, h 4308 Penn Fkd"; (1909), 624, "Emmitt Wm h 4952 Hawthorne Fkd"; (1910), 609, "Emmitt Wm dyer h 2739 Kirkbridge Bdg [Bridesburg]"; (1911), 581, "Emmitt Wm H 1659 Church"; (1912), 601; (1916), 564, "Emmitt Wm H dyer h 4637 Penn Fkd"; (1918), 593; (1919), 429; (1921), 418, "Emmitt Wm pipeftr h 4621 Edmund Fkd." *Philadelphia City Directory for 1922* (Philadelphia: R.L. Polk & Co., 1922), 437. By the same title: (1923), 299, "Emmitt Wm H dyer h4618 Penn Fkd"; (1924), 493; (1925), 502; (1930), 477. *Philadelphia City Directory for 1912* (Philadelphia: C.E. Howe Co., 1912), 601, "Emmitt Mary A boarding 1659 Church Fkd"; (1914), 402, "Emmitt Mary A boarding 4620 Penn Fkd"; (1917), 385, "Emmitt Mary A boarding 4637 Penn Fkd."

[807] St. Mark's Episcopal Church (Philadelphia, Pa.), Baptisms, Helen Elva Royal, bapt. 24 Jan. 1909, b. 22 Nov. 1908; "Pennsylvania and New Jersey, U.S., Church and Town Records, 1669-2013," digital images, *Ancestry.com* (https://www.ancestry.com/).

[808] Ibid., Baptisms, p. 72, William H. Emmitt, bapt. 3 Oct. 1929.

[809] 1900 U.S. census, Philadelphia Co., Pa., pop. sch., Philadelphia, ED 518, p. 12, dwell. 295, fam. 238, household of William Emmitt; NARA T623, roll 1465.

112.   i.   MARY/FANNIE REBECCA EMMITT, b. Philadelphia 3 Sep. 1885;[810] m. ELMER JOHN ROYAL;[811] d. there of a cerebral embolus due to rheumatic endocarditis 5 Jun. 1937, age 52, bur. there in East Cedar Hill Cemetery.[812]

113.   ii.   WILLIAM GETTY EMMITT, b. Philadelphia, 11 Jan. 1887;[813] m. SYLVANIA B. WALL;[814] d. of chronic nephritis in Plumstead Twp., Bucks Co., Pa. 14 Sep. 1945, age 58,[815] bur. Cedar Hill Cemetery, Philadelphia.[816]

39. ELLEN "NELLIE" JANE[3] GETTY (*Mary Rebecca*[2], *William*[1] *Riley*), was born in Philadelphia, Philadelphia County, Pennsylvania, 8 September 1871 and was baptized there at St. Stephen's Episcopal Church on 26 November 1871.[817] Ellen died of "fatty degeneration of the heart [heart failure]" there on 21 March 1914, age 42,[818] and was buried there in Cedar Hill Cemetery.[819] She married probably in Philadelphia[820] ca. 1889[821] SAMUEL JACKSON BOWKER,[822] son of Samuel and Mary A. (Gorman) Bowker.[823] He was born in Philadelphia on 9 September 1866[824] and died there of chronic myocarditis on 5 December 1937, age 71,[825] and was buried with his wife.[826] Samuel married (2) Rachel Balt (Allen) Beam.[827]

---

[810] City of Philadelphia, Return of Births for the Month of September 1883, [blank] Emmitt, 3 Sep. 1883; City Archives, Philadelphia. Parents, William and Fannie. Father's occupation, weaver.

[811] "Philadelphia, Pennsylvania, U.S., Marriage Index, 1885-1951," database, *Ancestry.com* (https://search.ancestry.com/), Elmer J. Royal-Mary R. Emmitt, 1906.

[812] Pennsylvania death certificate no. 57763, Mary R. Royal (1937); Vital Statistics, Harrisburg. "Mary R. Royal [death notice]," *The Philadelphia Inquirer*, 8 Jun. 1937, p. 33, col. 8.

[813] St. Mark's Episcopal Church (Philadelphia, Pa.), Baptisms, William Getty Emmitt, bapt. 24 Apr. 1887; "Pennsylvania and New Jersey, U.S., Church and Town Records, 1669-2013," digital images, *Ancestry.com* (https://www.ancestry.com/). "U.S., World War II Draft Registration Cards, 1942," digital images, *Ancestry.com* (https://www.ancestry.com/), William Getty Emmitt. Contact person, Mrs. Sylvania Emmitt.

[814] Delaware Register of Marriages for the Year 1911, p. 95, no. 56794, Wm. G. Emmitt-Sylvania B. Wall, 19 Jun. 1911, [no town]; "Delaware, U.S., Marriage Records, 1806-1933," digital images, *Ancestry.com* (https://www.ancestry.com/).

[815] Pennsylvania death certificate no. 157, William G. Emmitt (1945); Vital Statistics, Harrisburg. This source incorrectly gives his date of birth as 11 Jan. 1892.

[816] *Find A Grave*, database and images (http://findagrave.com), William Emmitt, memorial no. 210,466,534.

[817] St. Stephen's Episcopal Church (Philadelphia, Pa.), baptism, Ellen Jane Getty, 26 Nov. 1871.

[818] Pennsylvania death certificate no. 3962 (1914), Ellen J. Bowker. *The Philadelphia Inquirer*, 24 Mar. 1914.

[819] *Find A Grave*, Ellen Jane Bowker, memorial no. 186,920,018.

[820] *Philadelphia City Directory for 1889* (Philadelphia: James Gopsill, 1889), 15, "Bowker Samuel J., molder, h 2526 E Orthodox Bdg [Bridesburg]"; By the same title: (1890), 230, "Bowker Samuel J., moulder, h 4754 Tacony W Hall [Whitehall]"; (1892), 209, "Bowker Samuel J., clerk, h 4623 Edmund, Fkd"; (1894), 216, "Bowker Samuel J., clerk, h 4552 Mulberry, Fkd"; (1896), 211, "Bowker Saml J., ins, h 4552 Mulberry, Fkd"; (1898), 237, "Bowker Saml. J., conductor, h 4552 Mulberry, Fkd."

[821] 1900 U.S. census, Philadelphia Co., Pa., Philadelphia, ED 527, p. 8, dwell. 162, fam. 166.

[822] Ibid. "Ellen J. Bowker [death notice]," *The Philadelphia Inquirer*, 24 Mar. 1914, p. 16, col. 5. "...wife of Samuel J. Bowker...."

[823] Pennsylvania death certificate no. 110432, Samuel Jackson Bowker (1937); Vital Statistics, Harrisburg.

[824] "Pennsylvania, Philadelphia City Births, 1860-1906," database, *FamilySearch.org* (https://www.familysearch.org/), Saml. Jackson Bowker.

[825] Pennsylvania death certificate no. 110432 (1937), Samuel Jackson Bowker. "Samuel J. Bowker [death notice]," *The Philadelphia Inquirer*, 7 Dec. 1937, p. 33, col. 4.

[826] *Find A Grave*, database and images (http://findagrave.com), Samuel Jackson Bowker, memorial no. 186,919,956.

[827] "Philadelphia, Pennsylvania, U.S., Marriage Index, 1885-1951," database, *Ancestry.com* (https://www.ancestry.com/), Samuel J. Bowker-Rachel B. Beam, 1915. For second wife's birth name, Frankford Methodist Episcopal Church (Philadelphia, Pa.), Records of Baptisms, July 4, 1830 to July 18, 1864, Rachel Balt

In 1900, Ellen worked in a textile mill as a winder, and Samuel was a cloth weaver.[828] Later, he was employed as a mail carrier.[829]

Children of Samuel Jackson Bowker and Ellen Jane Getty were:[830]

114.   i.   HOWARD WARREN BOWKER, b. Philadelphia 12 July 1890;[831] m. MARION ELIZABETH GILMOUR;[832] d. there of pneumonia complicating cerebral thrombosis, 17 Sep. 1942, age 52,[833] bur. Arlington Cemetery, Drexel Hill, Pa.[834]

115.   ii.   WALTER IRVIN BOWKER, b. Philadelphia 1 Sep. 1892;[835] m. HELEN R. GREEN;[836] d. there of carcinoma of the bladder 22 Apr. 1954, age 61, said to be bur. Evergreen Cemetery, Bucks Co., Pa.[837]

116.   iii.   ALBERT BERTRAM BOWKER, b. Philadelphia 16 Aug. 1894;[838] m. SUSIE FLORENCE PLATT;[839] d. probably Philadelphia ca. 1921.[840]

[sic], bapt. 2 Nov. 1862, daughter of Henry C. and Catharine Allen; "Pennsylvania and New Jersey, U.S., Church and Town Records, 1669-2013," digital images, *Ancestry.com* (https://www.ancestry.com/). 1900 U.S. census, Philadelphia Co., Pa., pop. sch., Philadelphia, ED 526, p. 1, dwell. 8, fam. 2, R.B. Beam, wife, in the household of Has H. Beam; NARA T623, roll 1465. Pennsylvania death certificate no. 18481, Hassell Bean [sic] (1915); Vital Records, Harrisburg. Informant, Mrs. Rachel B. Bean.

[828] 1900 U.S. census, Philadelphia Co., Pa., Philadelphia, ED 527, p. 8, dwell. 162, fam. 166.

[829] 1920 U.S. census, Philadelphia Co., Pa., pop. sch., Philadelphia, ED 476, p. 11B, dwell. 259, fam. 264, household of Samuel J. Bowker; NARA T625, roll 1625.

[830] City of Philadelphia, Record of Birth, Miriam Drusilla Bowker, 27 "7th Month" 1907; City Archives, Philadelphia. Six children born, all of whom were living.

[831] City of Philadelphia, Registration of Births, 1890, Howard Bowker; City Archives, Philadelphia. Social Security Administration, "U.S., Social Security Applications and Claims Index, 1936-2007," database, *Ancestry.com* (https://www.ancestry.com/), Howard Warren Bowker, Apr. 1937.

[832] Office of the City Clerk, City of New York, Grooms' Marriage Index, Manhattan, Aug. – Oct. 1934, Howard W. Bowker, License no. 24908, 24 Oct. 1934; "New York, New York, U.S., Marriage License Indexes, 1907-2018," digital images, *Ancestry.com* (https://www.ancestry.com/). Ibid., Brides' Marriage Index, Manhattan, Marion E. Gilmour, License no. 24908, 24 Oct. 1934. Pennsylvania death certificate no. 054227-61, Marion Gilmour Bowker (1961); Vital Statistics, Harrisburg. Spouse, Howard E. Bowker.

[833] Pennsylvania death certificate no. 76584, Howard Warren Bowker (1942); Vital Statistics, Harrisburg. "Ellen J. Bowker [death notice]," *The Philadelphia Inquirer*, 24 Mar. 1914, p. 16. "BOWKER.-Sep. 17. HOWARD W., husband of Marion E. Bowker (nee Gilmour)."

[834] *Find A Grave*, database and images (http://findagrave.com), Howard Warren Bowker, memorial no. 69,507,160.

[835] City of Philadelphia, Return of Births for the month of Sept 1892, Walter E. [sic] Bowker; City Archives, Philadelphia. "U.S., World War II Draft Cards Young Men, 1940-1947," *Ancestry.com*), (https://www.ancestry.com/), Walter Irvin Bowker.

[836] 1920 U.S. census, Philadelphia Co., Pa., pop. sch., Philadelphia, ED 644, p. 3A, dwell. 71, fam. 74, Helen Bowker, wife, Earl Green, brother-in-law, in the household of Walter Bowker; NARA T625, roll 1625. Gilbert Cope, *Genealogy of the Darlington Family...* (West Chester, Pa.: By the family, 1900), 419-20. Among the children of John W. Green and Lillian Brinton were "...Helen R. 7 mo. [sic] 30, 1892; Earle H., 5 mo., 5, 1895...."

[837] Pennsylvania death certificate no. 7772, Walter Irvin Bowker (1954); Vital Statistics, Harrisburg.

[838] "U.S., World War II Draft Cards Young Men, 1940-1947," digital images, *Ancestry.com* (https://www.ancestry.com/), Albert Bertram Bowker.

[839] "Pennsylvania, County Marriages, 1885-1950," digital images, *FamilySearch.org* (https://www.familysearch.org/), Albert Bertram Bowker-Susie Florence Platt, 21 Nov. 1916. Presbyterian Church of Frankford (Philadelphia, Pa.), Church Records 1818–1981, Records of Marriages Performed by Rev. John B. Laird, 1895 -----, no. 250, Bowker-Platt, 22 Nov. 1916; digital images, *Ancestry.com* (https://www.ancestry.com/).

[840] 1920 U.S. census, Philadelphia Co., Pa., pop. sch., Philadelphia, ED 649, p. 7B, dwell. 152, fam. 152, Albert B. Bowker, son-in-law; NARA T625, roll 1625. *Philadelphia...City...Directory for 1921* (Philadelphia: C.E. Howe, 1921), 288, "Bowker Albert B clk h 1741 Foulkrod Fkd [Frankford]"; By the same title: (1922), 245, no listing.

117. iv.   ELISE MAY BOWKER, b. Philadelphia 22 Dec. 1896 and bapt. there at Orthodox Street Methodist Episcopal Church 2 Apr. 1899;[841] d. aft. 1910.[842]

118. v.   IRENE EDITH BOWKER, b. Philadelphia 7 Aug. 1898[843] and bapt. there at Orthodox Street Methodist Episcopal Church 2 Apr. 1899;[844] d. aft. 1910.[845]

119. vi.   MIRIAM DRUSILLA BOWKER, b. Philadelphia 27 July 1907[846] and bapt. there at St. Marks's Episcopal Church, 28 Feb. 1926;[847] m. JOHN WILLIAM RICHARD HARDING, JR.;[848] d. of cerebral hemorrhage in Roxboro, Person Co., N.C. 8 May 2001,[849] and cremated there at St. Marks's Episcopal Church Columbarium.[850]

40. EMMA BRADLEY[3] GETTY (*Mary Rebecca[2], William[1] Riley*), was born in Philadelphia, Philadelphia County, Pennsylvania, on 2 February 1874 and was baptized there on 31 May 1874 at St. Stephen's Episcopal Church.[851] She died of cirrhosis of the liver in Philadelphia on 13 December 1935, age 61.[852] She married there in 1893 BENJAMIN AYRES HAINES, JR.,[853] son of Benjamin, Sr. and Mary (McLean) Haines.[854] He was born there on 20 January 1872,[855] died there of "Myocardial Failure – Chronic Myocarditis" on 26 May 1931, age 59, and bur. there in East Cedar Hill Cemetery.[856]

---

[841] Orthodox Street Methodist Episcopal Church (Philadelphia, Pa.), Church Records 1875–1913, VII Record of Baptisms 1890–1913, p. 296, Elise May Bowker; "Pennsylvania and New Jersey, U.S., Church and Town Records, 1669-2013," digital images, *Ancestry.com* (https://www.ancestry.com/).

[842] 1910 U.S. census, Philadelphia Co., Pa., Philadelphia, ED 476, p. 8A, dwell. 188, fam. 188, Elise M. Bowker, daughter, in the household of Samuel J. Bowker.

[843] City of Philadelphia, Return of Births for the Month of August 1898, Irene E. [blank], 7 Aug. 1898; City Archives, Philadelphia. Parents, Saml J. and Ellen G. [sic] Bowker.

[844] Orthodox Street Methodist Episcopal Church (Philadelphia, Pa.), Church Records 1875–1913, VII Record of Baptisms 1890–1913, p. 296, Irene Edith Bowker; "Pennsylvania and New Jersey, U.S., Church and Town Records, 1669-2013," database, *Ancestry.com* (https://www.ancestry.com/). Parents, Samuel J. and Nellie Bowker.

[845] 1910 U.S. census, Philadelphia Co., Pa., Philadelphia, ED 476, p. 8A, dwell. 188, fam. 188, Irene E. Bowker, daughter, in the household of Samuel J. Bowker.

[846] Philadelphia Record of Birth. Miriam Drusilla Bowker, 27 "7th Month" 1907.

[847] St. Marks's Episcopal Church (Philadelphia, Pa.), Baptisms 1849–1948, Miriam Drusilla Bowker, p. 62; "Pennsylvania and New Jersey, U.S., Church and Town Records, 1669-2013," digital images, *Ancestry.com* (https://www.ancestry.com/).

[848] Ibid., Marriages, p. 91, John W. R. Harding, Jr.-Miriam Drusilla Bowker, 28 Jun. 1930. "Philadelphia, Pennsylvania, U.S., Marriage Index, 1885-1951," database, *Ancestry.com* (https://www.ancestry.com/).

[849] North Carolina death certificate no. 07570, Miriam Bowker Harding (2001); Person Co. Register of Deeds, Roxboro.

[850] *Find A Grave*, database and images (http://findagrave.com), Miriam Drusilla Harding, memorial no. 186,910,682.

[851] St. Stephen's Episcopal Church (Philadelphia, Pa.), Church Records 1823–1941, Baptisms, p. 70, Emma B. Getty; "Pennsylvania and New Jersey, U.S., Church and Town Records, 1669-2013," digital images, *Ancestry.com* (https://www.ancestry.com/).

[852] Pennsylvania death certificate no. 23730, Emma Haines (1935); Vital Statistics, Harrisburg.

[853] "Pennsylvania, Philadelphia Marriage Indexes, 1885-1951," database and digital images, *FamilySearch.org* (https://www.familysearch.org/), Benjamin Ayres Haines-Getty [sic].

[854] "Pennsylvania, Philadelphia City Births, 1860-1906," database, *FamilySearch* (https://familysearch.org/), Benjamin Haines.

[855] Ibid.

[856] Pennsylvania death certificate no. 12578, Benjamin A. Haines (1931); Vital Statistics, Harrisburg. "Benjamin A. Haines [death notice]," *The Philadelphia Inquirer*, 28 May 1931, p. 29, col. 5. "…husband of Emma B. Haines (nee Getty)…."

A resident of the Frankford neighborhood, Benjamin held various unskilled jobs.[857]

Children of Benjamin Ayres Haines, Jr. and Emma Bradley Getty were:[858]

120. i. ROBERT BENJAMIN HAINES, b. Philadelphia 19 Apr. 1894,[859] bapt. there with brothers Herbert and Russell at the Central United Methodist Church 7 Apr. 1901;[860] m. JULIA MARY STROUP;[861] d. there of carcinoma of the stomach 29 Dec. 1959,[862] bur. there in Cedar Hill Cemetery.[863]

121. ii. HERBERT AYRES HAINES, b. Philadelphia 22 Jun. 1896[864] and bapt. there at the Central United Methodist Church 7 Apr. 1901;[865] m. BERYL MYERS GRIFFITH;[866] d. probably Philadelphia[867] 20 Apr. 1976.[868]

---

[857] *Philadelphia City Directory for 1893* (Philadelphia: James Gopsill's Sons, 1893), 792, "Haines Benjamin, dyer, h 1695 Meadow, Fkd [Frankford]"; By the same title: (1894), 813, "Haines Benjamin A., dyer, h 4648 Hedge, Fkd"; (1895), 763, "Haines Benj, dyer, h 1516 Deal, Fkd"; (1897), 813, "Haines Benj A., Jr., dyer, h 4556 Mulberry, Fkd"; (1898), 891; (1899), 927, "Haines Benj, Jr., dyer, h 1828 Margaret, Fkd"; (1900), 926; (1901), 1029; (1902), 996, "Haines Benj, Jr., cegars [sic], h 1701 Oxford, Fkd"; (1905), 1062; (1906), 1086, "Haines Benj A Jr salesman h 1701 Oxford Fkd"; (1907), 755, "Haines Benj Jr produce h 1701 Oxford Fkd." *Philadelphia City Directory for 1908* (Philadelphia: C.E. Howe Co., 1908), 810, "Haines Benj A jr, produce, h 4451 Leiper Fkd"; By the same title: (1909), 844; (1910), 836; (1911), 793; (1912), 823; (1916), 746; (1918), 787; (1919), 551, "Haines Benj A ironwkr 4451 Leiper Fkd"; (1921); (1922), 565; (1923), 400; (1924), 601. *Philadelphia City Directory for 1925* (Philadelphia: R.L. Polk & Co., 1925), 614; By the same title: (1930), 619 [unreadable due to page fold].

[858] 1900 U.S. census, Philadelphia Co., Pa., pop. sch., Philadelphia, ED 530, p. 2, dwell. 38, fam. 40, household of Benjamin Haines; NARA T623, roll 1465.

[859] City of Philadelphia, Return of Births for the Months of March & April 1894, Robert Benjamin Haynes [sic]; City Archives, Philadelphia. "U.S., World War I Draft Registration Cards, 1917-1918," digital images, *Ancestry.com* (https://www.ancestry.com/), Robert Benjamin Haines. "U.S., World War II Draft Cards Young Men, 1940-1947," digital images, *Ancestry.com* (https://www.ancestry.com/), Robert Benjamin Haines. Contact person, Julia M. Haines.

[860] Central United Methodist Church (Philadelphia, Pa.), Church Records 1897–1913, Record of Baptisms, p. 256-57, Robert Benjamin Haines; "Pennsylvania and New Jersey, U.S., Church and Town Records, 1669-2013," digital images, *Ancestry.com* (https://www.ancestry.com/).

[861] New Jersey marriage certificate no. 667, Robert B. Haines-Julia M. Stroup (1922); State Archives, Trenton. For wife's middle name, Social Security Administration, "U.S., Social Security Applications and Claims Index, 1936-2007," database, *Ancestry.com* (https://www.ancestry.com/), Julia Mary Haines, SS no. 173-50-0786.

[862] Pennsylvania death certificate no. 116112, Robert B. Haines (1959); Vital Statistics, Harrisburg.

[863] *Find A Grave*, database and images (http://findagrave.com), Robert Benjamin Haines, memorial no. 195,144,609.

[864] "U.S., World War II Draft Registration Cards, 1942," digital images, *Ancestry.com* (https://www.ancestry.com/), Herbert Ayres Haines. Social Security Administration, "United States Social Security Death Index," database, *FamilySearch.org* (https://www.familysearch.org/), Herbert A. Haines.

[865] Central United Methodist Church (Philadelphia, Pa.), Church Records 1897–1913, Record of Baptisms, p. 256-57. Herbert Ayres Haines; "Pennsylvania and New Jersey, U.S., Church and Town Records, 1669-2013," digital images, *Ancestry.com* (https://www.ancestry.com/).

[866] "Pennsylvania, County Marriages, 1885-1950," database and images, *FamilySearch.org* (https://www.familysearch.org/), Herbert A. Haines-Beryl M. Griffith, m. 23 Oct. 1928. Holmesburg Methodist Episcopal Church (Philadelphia, Pa.), Church Records 1847–1949, Marriages, Haines-Griffith, m. 27 Oct. 1928; "Pennsylvania and New Jersey, U.S., Church and Town Records, 1669-2013," digital images, *Ancestry.com* (https://www.ancestry.com/).

[867] "Beryl G. Haines [death notice]," *Philadelphia Daily News*, 10 Feb. 1992, p. 24, col. 4. "HAINES BERYL G. (nee Griffith)…; wife of the late Herbert A. Haines."

[868] Social Security Administration, "United States Social Security Death Index," *FamilySearch.org*, Herbert A. Haines. "U.S., Department of Veterans Affairs BIRLS Death File, 1850-2010," database, *Ancestry.com* (https://www.ancestry.com/), Herbert Ayres Haines, SS no. 716-16-7129.

122. iii. RUSSELL ROY HAINES, SR., b. Philadelphia 23 Sep. 1897[869] and bapt. there at the Central United Methodist Church 7 Apr. 1901;[870] m. EVELYN/EVELYNN BANCROFT HOLLAND;[871] d. in Philadelphia of complications of carcinoma of the bladder 12 Apr. 1944, age 46,[872] and bur. there in Cedar Hill Cemetery.[873]

---

[869] Pennsylvania death certificate no. 8259, Russell R. Haines (1944); Department of Vital Statistics, Harrisburg.

[870] Central United Methodist Church (Philadelphia, Pa.), Church Records 1897–1913, Record of Baptisms, p. 256-57, Russell Roy Haines; "Pennsylvania and New Jersey, U.S., Church and Town Records, 1669-2013," digital images, *Ancestry.com* (https://www.ancestry.com/).

[871] "Pennsylvania, County Marriages, 1885-1950," database and digital images, *FamilySearch.org* (https://www.familysearch.org/), Russell Roy Haines-Evelynn Bancroft Holland, 3 Sep. 1926. "Philadelphia, Pennsylvania, U.S., Marriage Index, 1885-1951," database, *Ancestry.com* (https://www.ancestry.com/), Russell R. Haines-Evelyn B. Holland, m. 1926. For Evelynn's middle name, St Mark's Episcopal Church (Philadelphia, Pa.), Church Records, Baptisms 1849–1949, p. 68, Russell R. Haines, Jr.; "Pennsylvania and New Jersey, U.S., Church and Town Records, 1669-2013," digital images, *Ancestry.com* (https://www.ancestry.com/).

[872] Pennsylvania death certificate no. 8259 (1944), Russell R. Haines; Vital Statistics, Harrisburg. "Russell R. Haines [death notice]," *The Philadelphia Inquirer*, 13 Apr. 1944, p. 12, col. 1. "…husband of the late Evelyn H. Haines…."

[873] *Find A Grave*, database and images (http://findagrave.com), Robert [sic] R. Haines, memorial no. 207,774,772.

Figure 1. Montgomery County, Pennsylvania

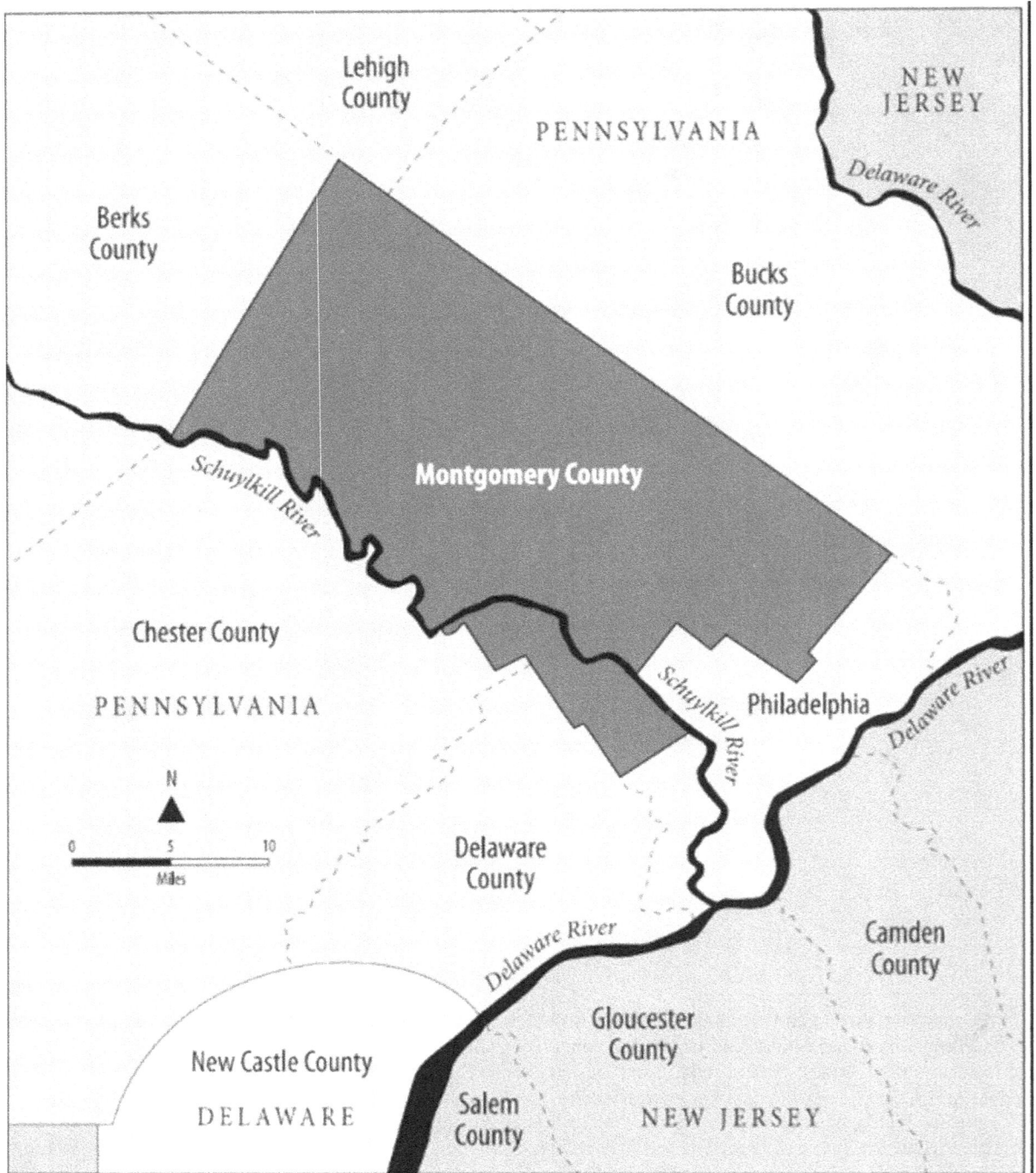

Lehigh County

PENNSYLVANIA

NEW JERSEY

Delaware River

Berks County

Bucks County

Schuylkill River

Montgomery County

Chester County

PENNSYLVANIA

Schuylkill River

Philadelphia

Delaware River

N

0   5   10
Miles

Delaware County

Camden County

Delaware River

New Castle County

DELAWARE

Salem County

Gloucester County

NEW JERSEY

Maps by MacNeill + Macintosh, Lambertville, NJ

Montgomery County is northwest of Philadelphia and is bounded in part by the Schuylkill River.

Figure 2. Terrain Near the Former Home of William Riley

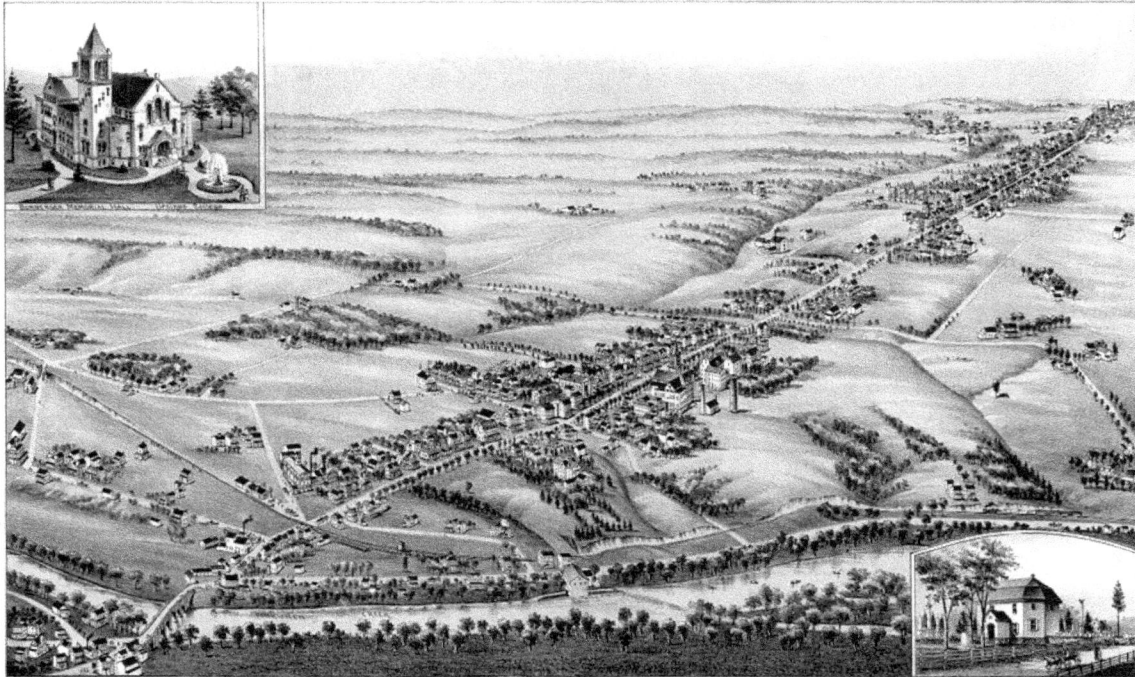

Drawing of Collegeville, Pennsylvania, and surrounding area. William Riley's former home was in nearby Oaks. Thaddeus Mortimer Fowler, "Panoramic View of Collegeville. Montgomery County, Pennsylvania, 1894"; digital image, *Pennsylvania Historical and Museum Commission Map Collection* (http://www.phmc.state.pa.us/).

Figure 3. Upper Providence and Lower Providence Townships

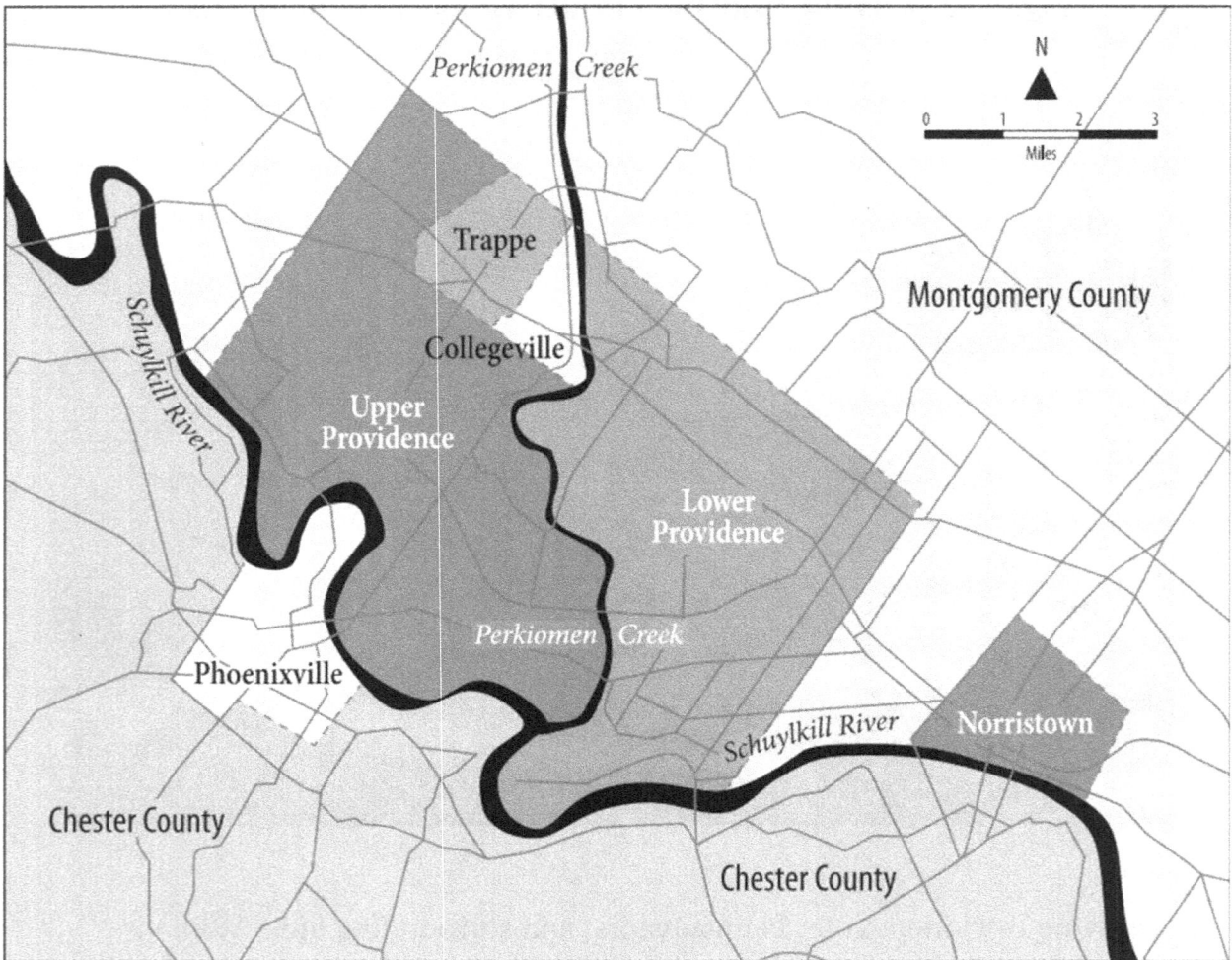

Upper Providence and Lower Providence Townships are separated by the Perkiomen Creek and bounded by the Schuylkill River.

Figure 4. Area of Oaks, Pennsylvania, about 1871

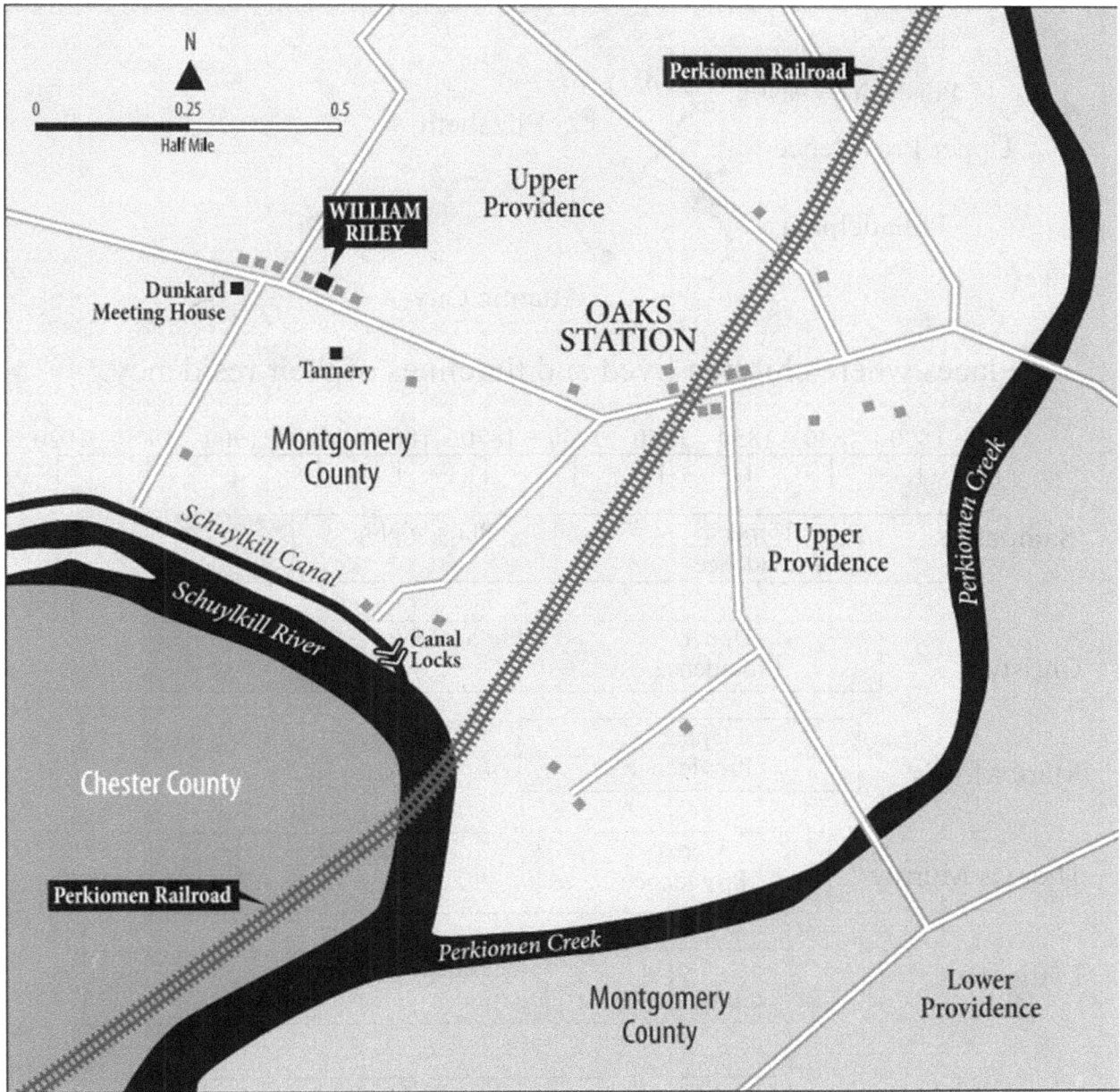

Map depicting features near Oaks, Upper Providence Township when William Riley resided there. Adapted from the 1871 map "Atlas of Montgomery County, Pennsylvania," *Pennsylvania Historical and Museum Commission* (http://www.phmc.state.pa.us/).

Figure 5. Migration of Children of William Riley

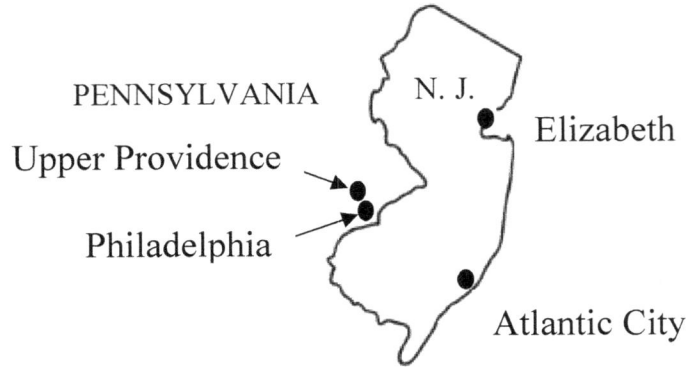

PENNSYLVANIA   N. J.

Upper Providence   →   Elizabeth

Philadelphia   →

Atlantic City

Places where children lived and timelines of their residency.

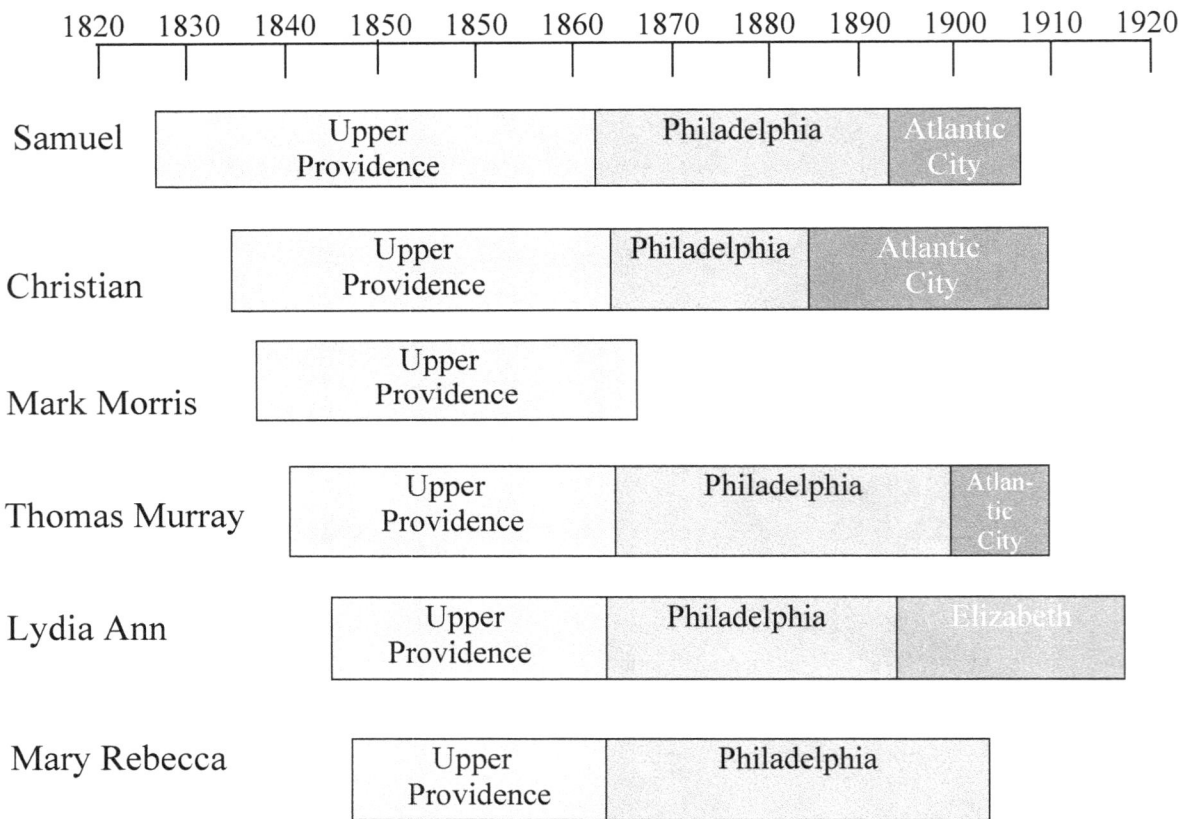

	1820	1830	1840	1850	1850	1860	1870	1880	1890	1900	1910	1920

Samuel — Upper Providence | Philadelphia | Atlantic City

Christian — Upper Providence | Philadelphia | Atlantic City

Mark Morris — Upper Providence

Thomas Murray — Upper Providence | Philadelphia | Atlantic City

Lydia Ann — Upper Providence | Philadelphia | Elizabeth

Mary Rebecca — Upper Providence | Philadelphia

Figure 6. Stagehands, Atlantic City Theater, 1917

Photograph, stage of unknown theater, 1917. Left, standing with hat, Charles Bradford Riley. Right, sitting in chair, Abraham Landis Riley, Sr. Left, first row on floor, Edwin Glover, brother-in-law of Abraham L. Riley, Sr.

Persons identified by Henrietta (Riley) Camp. Photograph given to author by Mrs. Camp about 1990 who inherited it from her father, Abraham L. Riley, Sr. For relationship of Edwin Glover to Abraham L. Riley, Sr., see David Joseph Riley, "Felix Kesler (1842–1910), St. Louis Photographer: His Swiss Origins and Descendants," *St. Louis Genealogical Society Quarterly* 53 (Fall 2019), 93-109.

Figure 7. Stagehands, Atlantic City Theater, 1919

Photograph, stage of an unknown theater, 1919. Left, second row, standing, with hand on man in front, Charles Bradford Riley. Sitting, front row, center, without a hat, Charles William Riley, son of Charles Bradford Riley. Right, front row, sitting, Abraham L. Riley, Sr. Seated to his right, Russell Fulmer Sackett.

Persons identified by Henrietta (Riley) Camp who gave the photograph to author about 1990. Mrs. Camp inherited it from her father, Abraham L. Riley, Sr. According to Mrs. Camp (interview with author ca. 1990), family members and in-laws pictured in Figures 6 and 7 belonged to the same stagehands' union.

Figure 8. Plats of Deeds of William Riley and Neighbors

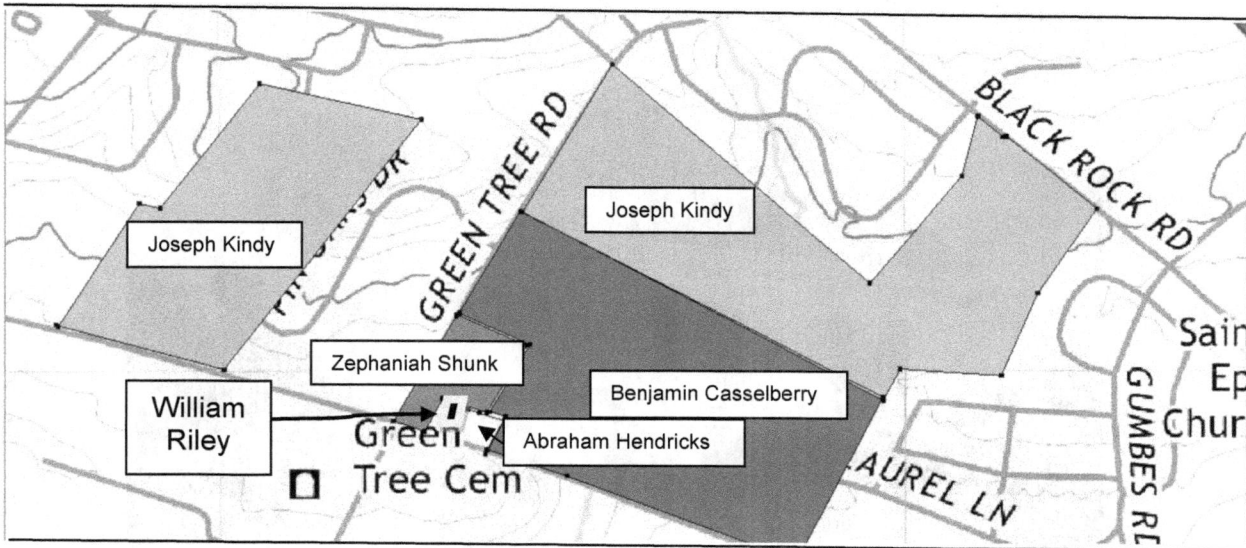

Scale: 3,000 ft. ━━━━━━━━━

Plats of deeds of William Riley and selected neighbors superimposed on a modern map. Neighbors were the abutting landowners named in William Riley's deed.

Grantor	Grantee	Execution date	Book and page
David Rittenhouse	William Riley	7 Mar. 1854	97: 55
David Rittenhouse	Benjamin Casselberry	27 Mar. 1854	95: 518
David Rittenhouse	Zephaniah Shunk	7 Mar. 1854	93: 89
Jacob Z. Gotwals	Joseph Kindy	3 Apr. 1858	109: 387
Samuel Suplee	Joseph Kindy	25 Mar. 1857	107: 347

The area of William's lot was 39.6 perches or 0.25 acres. William's deed was obtained from the Montgomery County Recorder of Deeds Office by Joel D. Alderfer, Mennonite Historians of Eastern Pennsylvania, Harleysville, Pa. The other deeds were viewed at *FamilySearch.org* (https://www.familysearch.org/) > Catalogue > United States, Pennsylvania, Montgomery > Land and property > Deeds, 1784-1866; index, 1784-1877 > Grantor Index, L-S. No deed was recorded for Abraham Hendricks; his land s inferred from William Riley's deed. Plats were created using DeedMapper 4.2.

Figure 9. House Formerly Owned by William Riley

The house is located at 1118 Egypt Road, Upper Providence Twp., Pennsylvania. Photographed by A. Landis Riley, Oxnard, Calif. in 1996. Evidence that William Riley owned the house is that a copy of a deed dated 7 Mar. 1854 was found in the attic by A. Landis Riley.

Figure 10. Properties of Christian Fulmer Riley and His Sons

Map of area of North Broad Street, Philadelphia, ca. 1880. Shown are locations of properties of Christian Fulmer Riley and his sons, Henry Landis Riley and William R. Riley.

Circle, blacksmith shop of Christian Fulmer Riley. His son, Henry Landis Riley, resided there. *Triangle*, residence of William R. Riley on French Street. *Star*, North Broad Street. *Arrow*, directional indicator. For sources, see text.

Library of Congress Geography and Map Division, digital images (https://blogs.loc.gov/maps/category/geography-and-map-division/). The distance between the blacksmith shop and William R. Riley's house is approximately 800 ft. Distance computed using *Google Maps.com* (https://www.google.com/maps/).

Figure 11. Map of Atlantic City, New Jersey

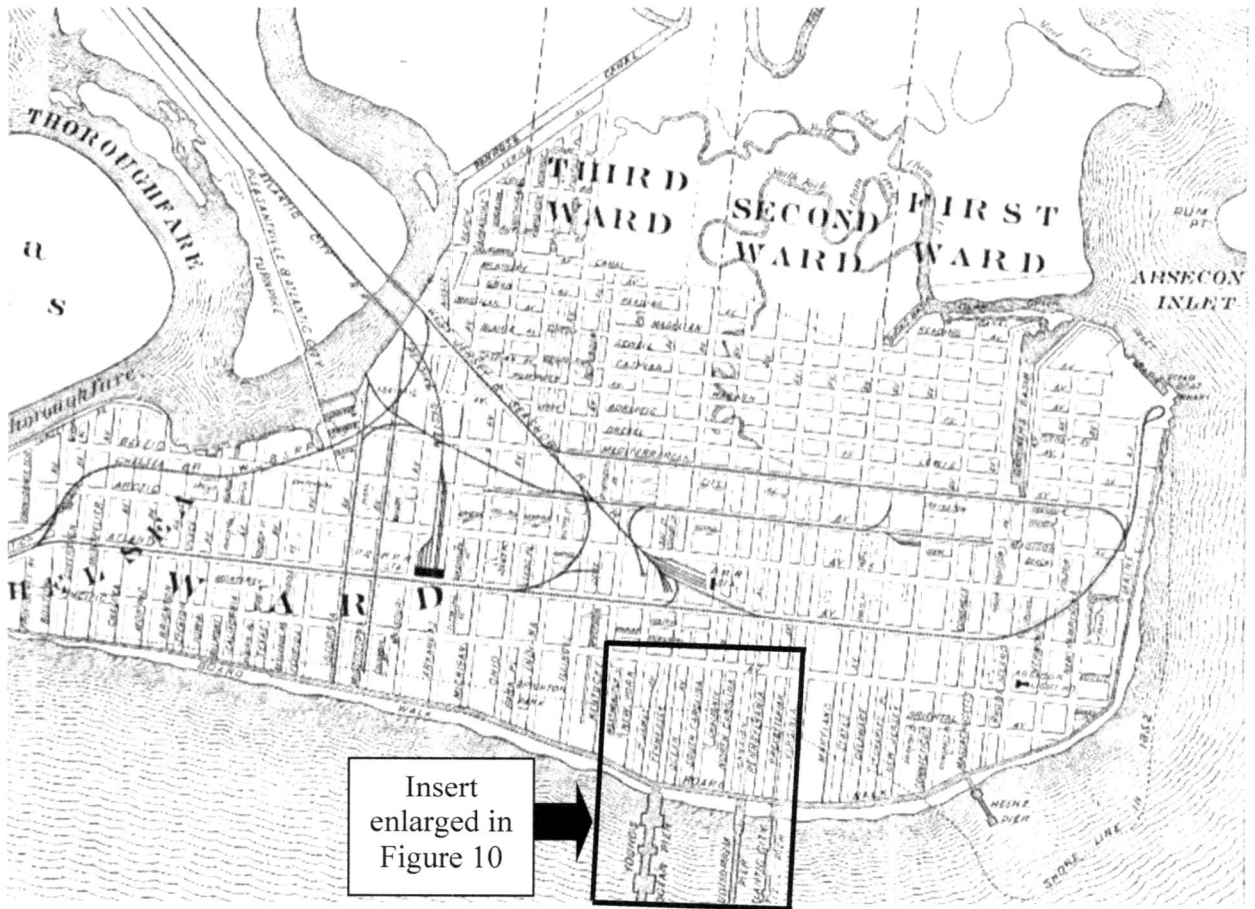

Map of Atlantic City, New Jersey, ca. 1906. *Atlantic City Directory for 1906* (Philadelphia: James Gopsill's Sons, 1906), sixth page.

Figure 12. Inset of Map of Atlantic City Showing St. James Place

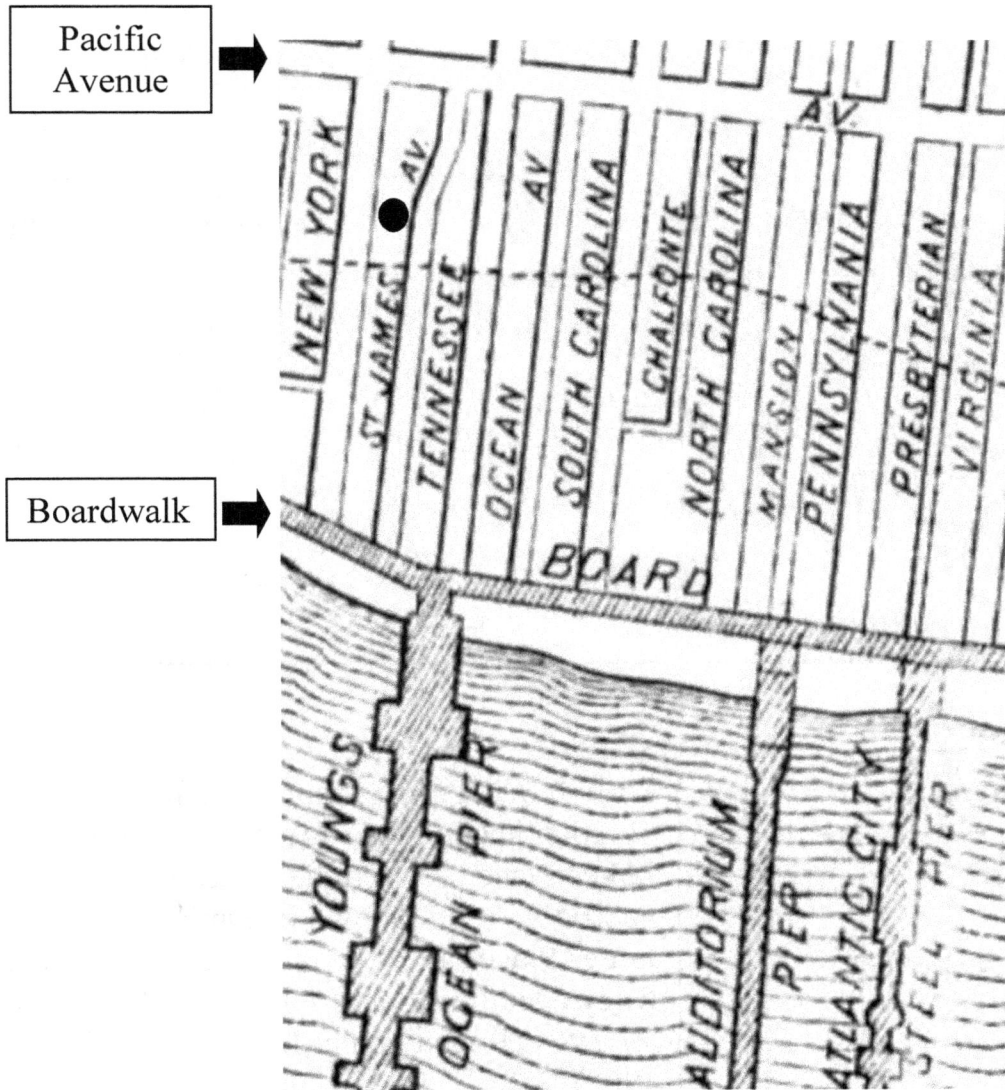

Inset of map in Figure 9 shown is a portion of St. James Place extending from Pacific Avenue to the Boardwalk. The black circle indicates the location of the former house of Christian F. Riley at 118 St. James Place. Several amusement piers extend into the Atlantic Ocean.

Figure 13. Fire Insurance Map of Atlantic City

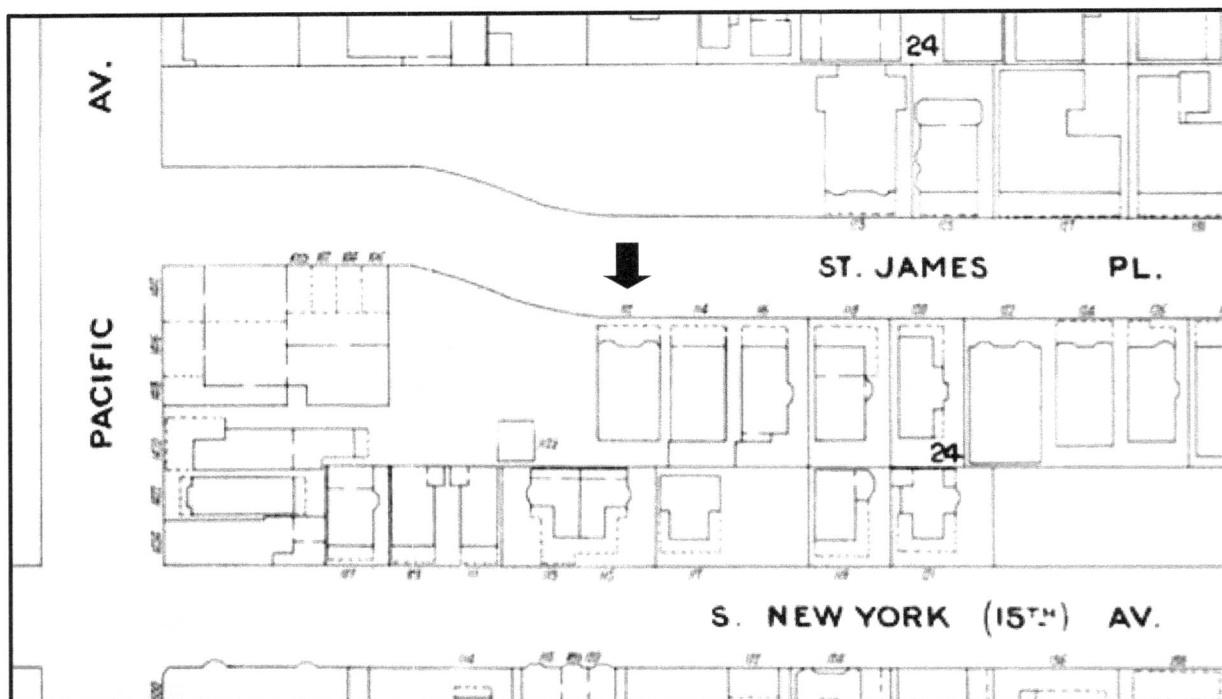

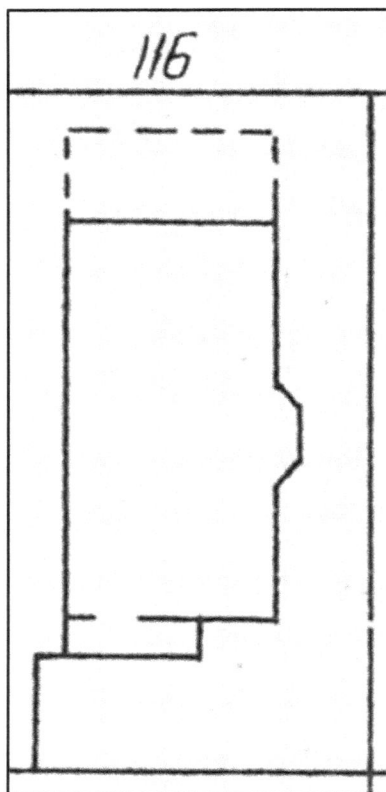

Portion of a 1906 Sanborn Fire Insurance Map of Atlantic City, New Jersey. *Above*, St. James Place between the Boardwalk and Pacific Avenue. Shown is number 116 St. James Place (arrow) which Christian Fulmer Riley occupied. See *Atlantic City Directory for 1905* (Philadelphia: James Gospill's Sons, 1905), 378.

Left, enlargement of the home lot. The three-story structure which was purchased in Nov. 1899 was on a 40 × 75 ft. lot. See Christian F. Riley, Sr., et ux. and Horace F. Nixon, mortgage deed, Christian F. Riley, Sr., pension application no. S.C. 1,069,104, Civil War, Record Group 15, National Archives-Washington.

Figure 14. Abraham Landis Riley, Sr. and Family

Undated photograph of family of Abraham Landis Riley, Sr. Left to right, Edwin Glover Riley (1911–1989), Lillie Carolinia/Caroline (Kesler) Riley (1880–1966), Abraham Landis Riley, Jr. (1904–1983), Abraham Landis Riley, Sr. (1874–1939), and Henrietta Kesler (Riley) Camp (1907–1999). The photograph was probably taken ca. 1930. It was passed down from Lillie Riley to her son Edwin Riley to his son A. Landis Riley. Image sent to author by A. Landis Riley.

Figure 15. Riley's Esso Station, Atlantic City

Lillie (Kesler) Riley operated the gas station in the 1940s. See text for sources. The identity of the structure was confirmed by Lillie's granddaughter who visited the gas station as a child. Marion (Riley) Mitchell [ADDRESS FOR PRIVATE USE], Northfield, N.J., interview by the author, 14 Mar. 2022. Photograph was passed from Lillie Riley to her son, Edwin Riley, to his son, A. Landis Riley, who provided the image to the author. Photograph was probably taken in the 1940s based on the make and year of the nearest automobile. *HubcapCafe.com* (http://www.hubcapcafe.com/ocs/pages01/ford4004.htm).

Females are referred to under both their birth and married names.
Localities—including cemeteries and churches—are indexed under the name of the state.
Index terms grouped under headings include battles, companies, diseases, geographic names, and occupations.
Index terms may be in footnotes and are designated by page and footnote number (n).

Cook (*continued*)

George, 8
Laura Elizabeth, 6, 8-10
William, 29n405

Cope

Anna Elizabeth (Funk), 35
Amandamus/Amandus B. F.,
    35
B. Frank, 35n499
Clinton B., 35n499
Daniel, 35n499, 36n506
Edwardene/Edith/Eda Mcgill,
    14, 35, 36
Samuel Ellsworth, 35n499

Coventry

Agnes Robertson (Brown), 22
Harlan Hough, 22

Christian

Harry Clayton, 55n765
Margaret, 21, 54, 55
Margaret (Potts), 55
Joseph, 55

Cramer

Margaret Goldie, 56

crime/criminal, 47

–D–

Day

Katherine Mae, 54

Delaware

Wilmington, 38

Denmark

Nørresundby Sogn Parish
    (Aalborg Municipality),
    41n575

Dettra

Catharine, 17
(unspecified), 52

denominations, religious. *See*
religions

Devendorf

Laura E. or H., 39

diseases

accidents/injuries
    automobile, 49, 53, 57
    burn, 40
    fall, 21
    fracture, skull, 53
    wound, 19
cancer/carcinoma
    bladder, 60, 63
    breast, 38
    lung, 34
    prostate, 28
    stomach, 26, 62
cardiovascular
    angina, 11
    atherosclerosis, 25, 52, 53
    endocarditis, 20, 22, 59
    failure, heart, 22, 24, 27, 28,
        49, 59
    myocarditis, 59, 61
    pericarditis, 10
gastrointestinal
    cirrhosis, liver, 24, 61
    gastroenteritis, 24
infectious
    cholera, 33
    diarrhea, 16
    diphtheria, 46
    measles, 33
    meningitis, 46
    scarlet fever, 35
    septicemia, 50
    poliomyelitis, 19
    pneumonia, 18, 22, 27, 34,
        60
    tuberculosis/consumption, 8,
        18, 24, 44
    typhoid fever, 5
neurologic
    edema, brain, 23
    encephalomalacia, 43
    epilepsy, 14, 26
    hydrocephalus, 14
    stroke/cerebral hemorrhage,
        embolus, or thrombosis
        50, 55, 56, 58, 59
other
    arthritis, 18
    diabetes mellitus, 25
    miscarriage, 50
    placenta, retention of, 34
    surgery, complications of,
        26
pulmonary
    edema, 11, 15, 39
    emphysema, 7

diseases (*continued*)

    thrombosis, pulmonary
        artery, 34
    renal
        nephritis, 59

disability, 4, 9, 19

divorce/separation, 31n431, 38,
    39n551, 43n601, 47, 56n782

Dixon

Doris, 31

–E–

Emantvout

John S., 11

Emmitt

Mary Anne (Getty), 23, 57, 58
Mary/Fannie Rebecca, 59
Sylvania B. (Wall), 59
William, 57
William Getty, 59
William Henry, 23, 57, 58
Rebecca (Clark), 57

–F–

Fedigan

Mary L., 34n485

First Purchasers (of Provence of
    Pennsylvania), 2

Fitzwater

Joseph, 49, 52

Florida

Atlantis, 42
Greenwood Cemetery (St.
    Petersburg), 21
Jacksonville, 50
Lake Co., 54n757
Port Charlotte, 54
Seminole Co., 43n601
Southeastern Crematory (Punta
    Gorda), 54
St. Petersburg, 8, 10, 21

Fort

Cornelius/Corneline Ernest, 44,
    45

Fort (*continued*)

Emma Martha (−?−), 45n627

Freeman

Albert Allen (father of Harry
  Grant Freeman, Sr.), 40
Albert Allen, 40
Annie/Anna/Ane Albertine
  Esther (Neilsen)
  Anderson/Andersen, 41
Charles Edward, 42
Esther (Bowers), 41
Gertrude May (Jones) Hawkes,
  40
Hannah Jane (Poist), 40
Hazel Noll, 42
Helen W. (Jachen) Meak, 41
Harry Grant, Jr., 41
Harry Grant, Sr., 15, 39, 40
Lillian May/Mae, 41
Lillian E. (Hall), 41
May Sloan, 40
Servetus Carlile, 41
Virginia Gertrude, 41
Virginia Gertrude (Riley), 15,
  39, 50

Funk

Anna Elizabeth, 35

−G−

Galinger/Gilinger

Elizabeth, 8

Germanic countries. *See* Baden,
Grand Duchy of. *See*
Württemberg, Kingdom of

Getty

Ann (Selfridge), 22
Ellen Jane, 24, 59, 60
Emma Bradley, 24, 61, 62
Joseph, 22
Mary Anne, 23, 57, 58
Mary Rebecca (Riley), 7, 22,
  23, 57, 59, 61
Robert H., Jr., 24
Robert S., 7, 22, 23
Samuel, 23

Gibson

Alexander, (father of
  Alexander Quigley), 41n578
Alexander Quigley, Jr., 41
Clara (−?−), 41n578

Gibson (*continued*)

John Tom, 31n431
Lillian May/Mae (Freeman),
  41

Gilmour

Emily/Emma Gertrude (Riley),
  43
Gertrude Emily. *See*, Gilmour,
  Emily/Emma Gertrude
  (Riley)
Marion Elizabeth, 60
Thomas Chiles, 43

Gorman

Mary A., 59

Green

Earl H., 60n836
Helen R., 60
John W., 60n836
Lillian (Brinton), 60n836

Griffith

Beryl Myers, 62

Grimes

Eliza (−?−), 44n615
Josiah, 44n615
Margaret, 44

−H−

Haines

Benjamin Ayres, Jr., 24, 61, 62
Benjamin Ayres, Sr., 61
Beryl Myers (Griffith), 62
Emma Bradley (Getty), 24, 61,
  62
Evelyn/Evelynn Bancroft
  (Holland), 63
Herbert Ayres, 62
Julia Mary (Stroup), 62
Mary (McLean), 62
Robert Benjamin, 62
Russell Roy, Sr., 63

Hall

Lillian E., 41

Hallman/Hollman

Abraham H., 17, 50n696
Ann/Anna Rebecca, 6, 7, 10

Hallman/Hollman (*continued*)

Ann/Anna Maria, 3n29, 4n45,
  6, 7, 18
Catharine (Weber), 7, 18
Jacob, 6n72, 7, 18

Harris

Dorothy Barbara, 51
Florence M. (Whitworth), 51
Helen Elizabeth (Schofstall),
  51
James Robertson, Jr., 51
Jessie B., 50
Lemuel George, 51
Mary (McAdams), 18, 49-51
Minnie Lee, 28
Mildred Naomi. *See* Harris,
  Naomi M.
Naomi M., 51

Harding

John William Richard, Jr., 61
Miriam Drusilla (Bowker), 61

Hawkins

Elizabeth Ann, 44

Hawkes

George L., 40n565
Gertrude May (Jones), 40

highways/streets

Broad Street (Philadelphia),
  12, 13, 32, 36
Lincoln Highway (U.S. Route
  30, Pennsylvania), 49
St. James Place (Atlantic City),
  13
White Horse Pike (New
  Jersey), 48

Hines

Emma, 34n480

Holland

Evelyn/Evelynn Bancroft, 63

Holmes

Sarah C. (Ryan), 28

Houck/Hauck

(−?−) (Small), wife of Peter, 31

Houck/Hauck (*continued*)

Elizabeth/Lizzie/Eliza H., 14,
31-33
Margaret, 34
Peter, 31

hotel, 12

Illinois

Beardstown, 47
Carrolton, 30
Rose Lawn Memorial Gardens
(Bethalto), 30

incarceration, 4

Indigenous people, 1

industries

factory
carpet, 4
(unspecified), 3
glue and fertilizer, 3
shirt, 10
iron works, 50, 53
mill
steel, 25
textile, 4, 25, 58, 60
(unspecified), 3

institutions, public

Allentown State Hospital
(Allentown, Pa.), 26n354
Philadelphia Home for the
Incurables (Philadelphia,
Pa.), 18
Rittersville Asylum (Hanover,
Lehigh Co., Pa.), 26
Western State Penitentiary
(Pittsburgh, Pa,), 4n47,
47n656

invalid. *See* disability

Jachen/Jochen

Edward E., 40n572
Helen W., 40
Maude (Wainwright), 40n572

Jones

Albert P., 40n565
Gertrude May, 40

Kansas

Mission Twp., 27n381

Kelley

Albert James, Jr., 38n533
Albert James, Sr., 38
Ora Louise May (Tyson), 15,
37
Lillian Dorothy (Smith),
38n533

Kesler

Felix John, 47
Henrietta (Kuhl), 47
Lillie Carolinia/Caroline, 16,
47, 48

Kuhl

Henrietta, 47

labor

blue-collar workers, 4
child, 4

Landes

Jacob, 12n158

Landis

Anna T. or F., 6, 12, 13, 32
Henry George, 12
Magdalena Showalter
(Alderfer), 12

Latimer

Dorothy (Broome), 56
Joan, 56n783

Le Van

Barbara Anne (Martin),
17n224, 53n753, 54n753,
54n754
Deborah, 17n224, 53n735,
53n741, 54n754

Lincoln

Abraham (U.S. President), 8

Maryland

Baltimore City, 42

Martin

Barbara Anne, 17n224,
53n753, 54n753, 54n754
Benjamin Yost, 54
Helen Bechtel (Riley), 53n735,
54

Maurer

Emma (Hines), 34n480
Franklin Linford/Lynford, 34
Franklin P., 34n480
Katherine/Kathryn Hauck
(Riley), 34n481, 34

Mathis

Alice H., 39

McAdams

John Robertson, 49
Mary E., 18, 49-50
Mary (Patterson), 49

McCarraher

Emma Bechtel (Riley), 53
John Dewey, 53

McGettigan

Dorothy Marie, 27
James F., 26

McGinley

Estella A. (Riley), 25, 26
James F., 26

McKittrick

Harriet Riley (Brown), 21
William Buchanan, 21

McLean

Mary, 62

Meak

Helen W. (Jachen), 40

Merkel

June Ann, 31

Michael

Mary E., 26

Michigan

Christian Memorial Cemetery
(Avon), 28
Pontiac, 28

Mickle

Craig Bispham, 36n508
Florence Virginia (Riley), 37
Harry Sherats/Sherdts, 37

Miller

Esther Lansdowne, 53
Hannah Detwiller, 53

military units

213th Regiment, Pennsylvania
Inf., 3n23
73rd Regiment, Pennsylvania
Inf., 10n255
Pennsylvania Light Artillery,
22
Thirty-First Regiment–Second
Reserve, Pennsylvania
Vols., 12

Mitchell

Marion (Riley), 48n668

Moses

Dorothy B. (Harris), 51
Silas Lee, 51

musician 8, 12. *See also* band

–N–

Nappell

Edward Royer, 39
Mabel Elizabeth (Riley), 39

native Americans, *See* Indigenous
people

Neal

Mary Eleanor, 34

Neilsen

Annie/Anna/Ane Albertine
Esther, 41

Neville

Emily/Emma Gertrude (Riley)
Gilmour, 43
Gertrude Emily. *See*, Neville,
Emily/Emma Gertrude
(Riley) Gilmour
Tilford Davis, 43

New Jersey

Absecon Presbyterian Church
Cemetery (Absecon), 42
Atlantic City Cemetery
(Pleasantville), 11, 16, 30,
37, 39-41, 44, 46-49
Atlantic City, 3, 4, 6, 7, 9, 11-
16, 18, 19, 21, 29, 30, 35-48,
54-57
Beverly National Cemetery
(Beverly), 47
Bridgeton, 57
Brigantine, 39n552
Camden, 48
Central Methodist Church
(Atlantic City), 57
Cherry Hill, 55n765
Cinnaminson, 37
Elizabeth, 7, 20, 21
Evergreen Cemetery (Hillside),
20
First Methodist Episcopal
Church (Atlantic City),
16n210, 39n552, 44n606
First Presbyterian Church
(Atlantic City), 14n192,
16n215, 35n497, 46n635
Galloway, 48
Laurel Memorial Park
(Pomona, Galloway Twp.),
37, 41, 45
Laurel Memorial Park (Egg
Harbor), 14, 21, 30, 35, 54
Linden, 18, 52
Marlton, Evesham Twp., 55
Mount Holly, 53
Northfield, 15, 42, 47
Perth Amboy, 20
Phillipsburg, 9, 29
Pleasantville Cemetery. *See*
Atlantic City Cemetery
Pleasantville, 16, 29, 41
Rio Grande (Middle and Lower
Twps.), 34n475
Roselle Park, 22
Somers Point, 30, 36, 46

New Jersey (*continued*)

St. Andrew's Lutheran Church
(Atlantic City), 29
St. Paul's Methodist Church
(Atlantic City), 16n211, 37,
44n612, 46n638
Ventnor, 43, 46
Wesley United Methodist
Church (Pleasantville),
40n559, 41n569, 41n578
Westminster Presbyterian
Church (Atlantic City),
56n783
Winslow, 47

New York

Mount Vernon Trinity Church
(Mount Vernon), 44n611
Mount Vernon, 44
New York City, 44
Otego, 30
Richmond Hill, 21
Tottenville, 20

Nicholson

Bertha Miriam, 43

North Carolina

Roxboro, 61
St. Marks's Episcopal Church
Columbarium (Roxboro), 61

–O–

occupations

architecture and engineering
engineer, 4
arts and entertainment
agent, theatrical, 4, 38
caddy, golf, 4
entertainer, 4
manager, conventions, 4
property man, theater, 38
superintendent, theater 4
construction and extraction
laborer, 3, 22
education and training
teacher, 4, 12
farming
laborer, farm, 17
food services
butcher, 3, 20
confectioner, 20
healthcare support
matron, old age home, 4, 33
homemaker, 3

About the Author

An award-winning author, David Joseph Riley holds a certificate from the Boston University's Genealogical Research certificate program and attended the Institute of Genealogy and Historical Research. He is Professor Emeritus, Rutgers Robert Wood Johnson Medical School, New Brunswick, New Jersey and a retired pulmonary disease physician. Dr. Riley is a descendant of William Riley. His address is 88 Woodside Drive, Lumberton, NJ 08048-5274, and his email is drdavidjriley@gmail.com.

www.ingramcontent.com/pod-product-compliance
Lightning Source LLC
Chambersburg PA
CBHW081159270326
41930CB00014B/3218